11th International Workshop on Finite State Methods and Natural Language Processing

(FSMNLP 2013)

AA005821

St. Andrews, Scotland
15-17 July 2013

ISBN: 978-1-62993-003-9

Printed from e-media with permission by:

Curran Associates, Inc.
57 Morehouse Lane
Red Hook, NY 12571

CURRAN ASSOCIATES INC. proceedings.com

Some format issues inherent in the e-media version may also appear in this print version.

Printed by Curran Associates, Inc. (2013)

For permission requests, please contact the Association for Computational Linguistics at the address below.

Association for Computational Linguistics
209 N. Eighth Street
Stroudsburg, Pennsylvania 18360

Phone: 1-570-476-8006
Fax: 1-570-476-0860

acl@aclweb.org

Additional copies of this publication are available from:

Curran Associates, Inc.
57 Morehouse Lane
Red Hook, NY 12571 USA
Phone: 845-758-0400
Fax: 845-758-2634
Email: curran@proceedings.com
Web: www.proceedings.com

Introduction

These proceedings contain the papers presented at the 11th International Conference on Finite-State Methods and Natural Language Processing (FSMNLP 2013), held in St Andrews, Scotland (UK), July 15–17, 2013.

This series of conferences is the premier forum of the ACL Special Interest Group on Finite-State Methods (SIGFSM). It serves researchers and practitioners working on:

- natural language processing (NLP) applications or language resources,
- theoretical and implementational aspects, or
- their combinations

that have obvious relevance or an explicit relation to finite-state methods.

This volume contains the 8 long and 9 short papers presented at the conference. In total, 26 papers (11 long and 15 short papers) were submitted and double-blind refereed. The overall acceptance rate was 69%, noting one paper was withdrawn after acceptance. Each long paper was reviewed by at least 3 programme committee members and each short paper by at least 2. The programme committee was composed of internationally leading researchers and practitioners selected from academia, research labs, and companies.

I would like to thank the programme committee for their hard work, the referees for their valuable feedback, the invited speakers and the presenters of tutorials for their contributions and the many local staff and students for their tireless efforts. We are particularly indebted to the Scottish Informatics & Computer Science Alliance for their financial support. Most generous support was received from VisitScotland.

MARK-JAN NEDERHOF

Sponsors:

University of
St Andrews

600
YEARS

sicsa*
The Scottish Informatics &
Computer Science Alliance

VisitScotland™
Scotland's National Tourism Organisation
Buidheann Turasachd Nàiseanta na h-Alba

Chair:

Mark-Jan Nederhof (University of St Andrews)

Local Organizing Committee:

Per Ola Kristensson (University of St Andrews)
Martin McCAffery (University of St Andrews)
Shyam Reyal (University of St Andrews)
Vinodh Rajan (University of St Andrews)

Invited Speakers:

Alexander Clark (King's College London)
Bill Byrne (University of Cambridge)

Tutorials by:

Ruth Hoffmann (University of St Andrews)
Bevan Jones (University of Edinburgh)
Kousha Etessami (University of Edinburgh)

Program Committee:

Iñaki Alegria (University of the Basque Country)
Francisco Casacuberta (Instituto Tecnológico de Informática, Spain)
Jan Daciuk (Gdańsk University of Technology, Poland)
Frank Drewes (Umeå University, Sweden)
Dale Gerdemann (University of Tübingen, Germany)
Mike Hammond (University of Arizona, USA)
Colin de la Higuera (University of Nantes, France)
Mans Hulden (Ikerbasque, Basque Country)
André Kempe (Nuance Communications, Germany)
Marco Kuhlmann (Uppsala University, Sweden)
Andreas Maletti (Universität Stuttgart, Germany)
Kemal Oflazer (Sabanci University, Turkey)
Maite Oronoz Anchordoqui (University of the Basque Country)
Laurette Pretorius (University of South Africa)
Strahil Ristov (Rudjer Boskovic institute, Croatia)
Frederique Segond (Viseo Innovation, France)
Max Silberztein (Université de Franche-Comté, France)
Richard Sproat (Google, USA)
Heiko Vogler (Technical University Dresden, Germany)
Anssi Yli-Jyrä (University of Helsinki, Finland)
Menno Van Zaanen (Tilburg University, Netherlands)
Lynette Van Zijl (Stellenbosch University, South Africa)

Additional reviewers:

Fabienne Braune (Universität Stuttgart, Germany)
Matthias Büchse (Technical University Dresden, Germany)
Jean-Christophe Janodet (University of Evry, France)
Johannes Osterholzer (Technical University Dresden, Germany)
Nina Seemann (Universität Stuttgart, Germany)

Table of Contents

Conference Program

Sunday, July 14, 2013

18:00–19:00 Wine Reception

Monday, July 15, 2013

8:30–9:20 Registration

9:20–9:30 Opening

9:30–10:30 Keynote Lecture: Alexander Clark: Towards a theory of context-free languages

10:30–11:00 Break

11:00–11:30 *Computing the Most Probable String with a Probabilistic Finite State Machine*
Colin de la Higuera and Jose Oncina

11:30–12:00 *Stochastic Bi-Languages to model Dialogs*
M. Inés Torres

12:00–12:30 *ZeuScansion: a tool for scansion of English poetry*
Manex Agirrezabal, Bertol Arrieta, Aitzol Astigarraga and Mans Hulden

12:30–13:15 Lunch

13:15–14:00 Business Meeting

14:00–14:20 *A Convexity-based Generalization of Viterbi for Non-Deterministic Weighted Automata*
Marc Dymetman

14:20–14:40 *Processing Structured Input with Skipping Nested Automata*
Dominika Pawlik, Aleksander Zabłocki and Bartosz Zaborowski

14:40–15:00 *Synchronous Regular Relations and Morphological Analysis*
Christian Wurm and Younes Samih

Monday, July 15, 2013 (continued)

15:00–15:30 Break/Posters/Demos

15:30–16:30 Tutorial: Ruth Hoffmann: Experimenting with finite state automate in GAP

Tuesday, 16th July 2013

09:00–10:00 Keynote Lecture: Bill Byrne: Pushdown Automata in Statistical Machine Translation

11:00–11:30 Break/Posters/Demos

13:00–14:00 Lunch

14:15–16:30 Guided Walk and Visit of MUSA

18:15–21:00 Conference Dinner and Concert

Wednesday, 16th July 2013

9:00-11:00 Tutorial: Bevan Jones: Variational inference for tree automata and tree transducers

11:00-11:30 Break

11:30–12:00 *Multi-threaded composition of finite-state-automata*
Bryan Jurish and Kay-Michael Würzner

12:00–12:30 *On Finite-State Tonology with Autosegmental Representations*
Anssi Yli-Jyrä

12:30–13:30 Lunch

13:30–13:50 *A Finite-State Approach to Translate SNOMED CT Terms into Basque Using Medical Prefixes and Suffixes*
Olatz Perez-de-Vinaspre, Maite Oronoz, Manex Agirrezabal and Mikel Lersundi

13:50–14:10 *Syncretism and How to Deal with it in a Morphological Analyzer: a German Example*
Katina Bontcheva

14:10–14:30 *Finite State Approach to the Kazakh Nominal Paradigm*
Bakyt M Kairakbay and David L Zaurbekov

14:30–15:00 Break/Posters/Demos

15:00–17:00 Tutorial: Kousha Etessami: Algorithms and complexity of analyzing unrestricted stochastic context-free grammars

17:00–17:10 Closing

Computing the Most Probable String with a Probabilistic Finite State Machine

Colin de la Higuera
Université de Nantes,
CNRS, LINA, UMR6241,
F-44000, France
cdlh@univ-nantes.fr

Jose Oncina
Dep. de Lenguajes y Sistemas Informáticos,
Universidad de Alicante,
Alicante, Spain
oncina@ua.es

Abstract

The problem of finding the consensus / most probable string for a distribution generated by a probabilistic finite automaton or a hidden Markov model arises in a number of natural language processing tasks: it has to be solved in several transducer related tasks like optimal decoding in speech, or finding the most probable translation of an input sentence. We provide an algorithm which solves these problems in time polynomial in the inverse of the probability of the most probable string, which in practise makes the computation tractable in many cases. We also show that this exact computation compares favourably with the traditional Viterbi computation.

1 Introduction

Probabilistic finite state machines are used to define distributions over sets of strings, to model languages, help with decoding or for translation tasks. These machines come under various names, with different characteristics: probabilistic (generating) finite state automata, weighted machines, hidden Markov models (HMMs) or finite state transducers...

An important and common problem in all the settings is that of computing the most probable event generated by the machine, possibly under a constraint over the input string or the length. The typical way of handling this question is by using the Viterbi algorithm, which extracts the most probable path/parse given the requirements.

If in certain cases finding the most probable parse is what is seeked, in others this is computed under the generally accepted belief that the computation of the most probable string, also called the consensus string, is untractable and that the Viterbi score is an acceptable approximation. But the probability of the string is obtained by summing over the different parses, so there is no strong reason that the string with the most probable parse is also the most probable one.

The problem of finding the most probable string was addressed by a number of authors, in computational linguistics, pattern recognition and bio-informatics [Sima'an, 2002, Goodman, 1998, Casacuberta and de la Higuera, 1999, 2000, Lyngsø and Pedersen, 2002]: the problem was proved to be $\mathcal{NP}$-hard; the associated decision problem is $\mathcal{NP}$-complete in limited cases only, because the most probable string can be exponentially long in the number of states of the finite state machine (a construction can be found in [de la Higuera and Oncina, 2013]). As a corollary, finding the most probable translation (or decoding) of some input string, when given a finite state transducer, is intractable: the set of possible transductions, with their conditional probabilities can be represented as a PFA.

Manning and Schütze [1999] argue that the Viterbi algorithm does not allow to solve the decoding problem in cases where there is not a one-to-one relationship between derivations and parses. In automatic translation Koehn [2010] proposes to compute the top n translations from word graphs, which is possible when these are deterministic. But when they are not, an alternative in statistical machine translation is to approximate these thanks to the Viterbi algorithm [Casacuberta and Vidal, 2004]. In speech recognition, the optimal decoding problem consists in finding the most probable sequence of utterances. Again, if the model is non-deterministic, this will usually be achieved by computing the most probable path instead.

In the before mentioned results the weight of each individual transition is between 0 and 1 and the score can be interpreted as a probability. An interesting variant, in the framework of multiplicity automata or of *accepting* probabilistic finite automata (also called Rabin automata), is the question, known as the *cut-point emptiness* problem, of the existence of a string whose weight is above a specific threshold; this problem is known to be undecidable [Blondel and Canterini, 2003].

In a recent analysis, de la Higuera and Oncina [2013] solved an associated decision problem: is there a string whose probability is above a given threshold? The condition required is that we are given an upper bound to the length of the most probable string and a lower bound to its probability. These encouraging results do not provide the means to actually compute the consensus string.

In this paper we provide three main results. The first (Section 3) relates the probability of a string with its length; as a corollary, given any fraction p, either all strings have probability less than p, or there is a string whose probability is at least p and is of length at most $\frac{(n+1)^2}{p}$ where n is the number of states of the corresponding PFA. The second result (Section 4) is an algorithm that can effectively compute the consensus string in time polynomial in the inverse of the probability of this string. Our third result (Section 5) is experimental: we show that our algorithm works well, and also that in highly ambiguous settings, the traditional approach, in which the Viterbi score is used to return the string with the most probable parse, will return sub-optimal results.

2 Definitions and notations

2.1 Languages and distributions

Let $[n]$ denote the set $\{1,\ldots,n\}$ for each $n \in \mathbb{N}$. An *alphabet* Σ is a finite non-empty set of symbols called *letters*. A *string* w over Σ is a finite sequence $w = a_1 \ldots a_n$ of letters. Letters will be indicated by $a, b, c, \ldots$, and strings by $u, v, \ldots, z$. Let $|w|$ denote the length of w. In this case we have $|w| = |a_1 \ldots a_n| = n$. The *empty string* is denoted by λ.

We denote by $\Sigma^\star$ the set of all strings and by $\Sigma^{\leq n}$ the set of those of length at most n. When decomposing a string into sub-strings, we will write $w = w_1 \ldots w_n$ where $\forall i \in [n]\ w_i \in \Sigma^\star$.

A *probabilistic language* $\mathcal{D}$ is a probability distribution over $\Sigma^\star$. The probability of a string $x \in \Sigma^\star$ under the distribution $\mathcal{D}$ is denoted as $Pr_{\mathcal{D}}(x)$ and must verify $\sum_{x\in\Sigma^\star} Pr_{\mathcal{D}}(x) = 1$. If L is a language (thus a set of strings, included in $\Sigma^\star$), and $\mathcal{D}$ a distribution over $\Sigma^\star$, $Pr_{\mathcal{D}}(L) = \sum_{x\in L} Pr_{\mathcal{D}}(x)$.

If the distribution is modelled by some syntactic machine $\mathcal{M}$, the probability of x according to the probability distribution defined by $\mathcal{M}$ is denoted by $Pr_{\mathcal{M}}(x)$. The distribution modelled by a machine $\mathcal{M}$ will be denoted by $\mathcal{D}_{\mathcal{M}}$ and simplified to $\mathcal{D}$ if the context is not ambiguous.

2.2 Probabilistic finite automata

Probabilistic finite automata (PFA) are generative devices for which there are a number of possible definitions [Paz, 1971, Vidal et al., 2005]. In the sequel we will use λ-free PFA: these do not have empty (λ) transitions: this restriction is without loss of generality, as algorithms [Mohri, 2002, de la Higuera, 2010] exist allowing to transform, in polynomial time, more general PFA into PFA respecting the following definition:

Definition 1. *A λ-free* Probabilistic Finite Automaton (PFA) *is a tuple $\mathcal{A} = \langle \Sigma, Q, S, F, \delta \rangle$, where:*

- *Σ is the alphabet;*
- *$Q = \{q_1, \ldots, q_{|Q|}\}$ is a finite set of* states;
- *$S : Q \to \mathbb{R} \cap [0, 1]$ (initial probabilities);*
- *$F : Q \to \mathbb{R} \cap [0, 1]$ (final probabilities);*
- *$\delta : Q \times \Sigma \times Q \to \mathbb{R} \cap [0, 1]$ is the complete transition function; $\delta(q, a, q') = 0$ can be interpreted as "no transition from q to q' labelled with a".*

S, δ and F are functions such that:

$$\sum_{q\in Q} S(q) = 1, \tag{1}$$

and $\forall q \in Q$,

$$F(q) + \sum_{a\in\Sigma,\ q'\in Q} \delta(q, a, q') = 1. \tag{2}$$

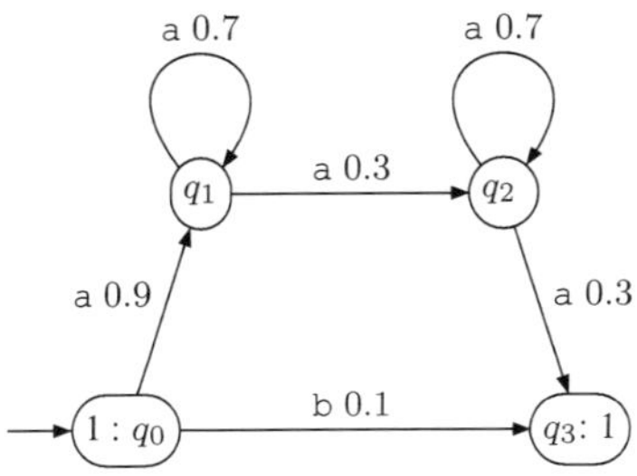

Figure 1: Graphical representation of a PFA.

An example of a PFA is shown in Fig. 1.

Given $x \in \Sigma^\star$, $\Pi_\mathcal{A}(x)$ is the set of all paths accepting x: an *accepting* x-path is a sequence $\pi = q_{i_0} a_1 q_{i_1} a_2 \ldots a_n q_{i_n}$ where $x = a_1 \cdots a_n$, $a_i \in \Sigma$, and $\forall j \in [n]$ such that $\delta(q_{i_{j-1}}, a_j, q_{i_j}) \neq 0$.

The probability of the path π is defined as $Pr_\mathcal{M}(\pi) = S(q_{i_0}) \cdot \prod_{j\in[n]} \delta(q_{i_{j-1}}, a_j, q_{i_j}) \cdot F(q_{i_n})$ and the probability of the string x is obtained by summing over the probabilities of all the paths in $\Pi_\mathcal{A}(x)$. An effective computation can be done by means of the Forward (or Backward) algorithm [Vidal et al., 2005].

We denote by $|\mathcal{A}|$ the size of $\mathcal{A}$ as one more than the number of its states. Therefore, for $\mathcal{A}$ as represented in Figure 1, we have $|\mathcal{A}| = 5$.

We do not recall here the definitions for hidden Markov models. It is known that one can transform an HMM into a PFA and vice-versa in polynomial time [Vidal et al., 2005].

2.3 The problem

The goal is to find the *most probable string* in a probabilistic language. This string is also named the *consensus* string.

Name: Consensus string (CS)
Instance: A probabilistic machine $\mathcal{M}$
Question: Find $x \in \Sigma^\star$ such that $\forall y \in \Sigma^\star$ $Pr_\mathcal{M}(x) \geq Pr_\mathcal{M}(y)$.

For example, for the PFA from Figure 1, the consensus string is `aaaaa`. Note that the string having the most probable single parse is `b`.

2.4 Associated decision problem

In [de la Higuera and Oncina, 2013] the following decision problem is studied:

Name: Bounded most probable string (BMPS)
Instance: A λ-free PFA $\mathcal{A}$, an integer $p \geq 0$, an integer b
Question: Is there in $\Sigma^{\leq b}$ a string x such that $Pr_\mathcal{A}(x) > p$?

BMPS is known to be $\mathcal{NP}$-hard [Casacuberta and de la Higuera, 2000]. De la Higuera and Oncina [2013] present a construction proving that the most probable string can be of exponential length: this makes the bound issue crucial in order to hope to solve CS. The proposed algorithm takes p and b as arguments and solves BMPS in time complexity $O(\frac{b|\Sigma|\cdot|Q|^2}{p})$. It is assumed that all arithmetic operations are in constant time.

The construction relies on the following simple properties, which ensure that only a reasonable amount of incomparable prefixes have to be scrutinized.

Property 1. $\forall u \in \Sigma^\star$, $Pr_\mathcal{A}(u\,\Sigma^\star) \geq Pr_\mathcal{A}(u)$.

Property 2. *If X is a set of strings such that (1) $\forall u \in X, Pr_\mathcal{A}(u\,\Sigma^\star) > p$ and (2) no string in X is a prefix of another different string in X, then $|X| < \frac{1}{p}$.*

3 Probable strings are short

Is there a relation between the lengths of the strings and their probabilities? In other words, can we show that a string of probability at least p must be reasonably short? If so, the b parameter is not required: one can compute the consensus string without having to guess the bound b. Let us prove the following:

Proposition 1. *Let $\mathcal{A}$ be a λ-free* PFA *with n states and w a string.*
Then $|w| \leq \frac{(n+1)^2}{Pr_\mathcal{A}(w)}$.

As a corollary,

Corollary 1. *Let $\mathcal{A}$ be a λ-free* PFA *with n states. If there is a string with probability at least p, its length is at most $b = \frac{(n+1)^2}{p}$.*

Proof. Let w be a string of length `len` and $Pr_\mathcal{A}(w) = p$. A path is a sequence $\pi = q_{i_0} a_1 q_{i_1} a_2 \ldots a_{\texttt{len}} q_{i_{\texttt{len}}}$, with $a_i \in \Sigma$.

Let $\Pi^j_\mathcal{A}(w)$ be the subset of $\Pi_\mathcal{A}(w)$ of all paths π for which state q_j is the most used state in π.

If, for some path π, there are several values j such that q_j is the most used state in π, we arbitrarily add π to the $\Pi^j_\mathcal{A}(w)$ which has the smallest index j.

Then, because of a typical combinatorial argument, there exists at least one j such that

$Pr_{\mathcal{A}}(\Pi^j_{\mathcal{A}}(w)) \geq \frac{p}{n}$. Note that in any path in $\Pi^j_{\mathcal{A}}(w)$ state q_j appears at least $\frac{\texttt{len}+1}{n}$ times. Consider any of these paths π in $\Pi^j_{\mathcal{A}}(w)$. Let k be the smallest integer such that $q_{i_k} = q_j$ (ie the first time we visit state q_j in path π is after having read the first k characters of w). Then for each value k' such that $q_{i_{k'}} = q_j$, we can shorten the path π by removing the cycle between q_{i_k} and $q_{i_{k'}}$ and obtain in each case a path for a new string, and the probability of this path is at least that of π.

We have therefore at least $\frac{\texttt{len}+1}{n} - 1$ such alternative paths for π.

We call Alt(π, j) the set of alternative paths for π and q_j. Hence $|\text{Alt}(\pi, j)| \geq \frac{\texttt{len}+1}{n} - 1$.

And therefore

$$Pr_{\mathcal{A}}(\text{Alt}(\pi, j)) \geq \left(\frac{\texttt{len}+1}{n} - 1\right) Pr_{\mathcal{A}}(\pi).$$

We now want to sum this quantity over the different π in $\Pi^j_{\mathcal{A}}(w)$. Note that there could be a difficulty with the fact that two different paths may share an identical alternative that would be counted twice. The following lemma (proved later) tells us that this is not a problem.

Lemma 1. *Let π and π' be two different paths in $\Pi^j_{\mathcal{A}}(w)$, and π'' be a path belonging both to* Alt(π, j) *and to* Alt(π', j). *Then $Pr_{\mathcal{A}}(\pi'') \geq Pr_{\mathcal{A}}(\pi) + Pr_{\mathcal{A}}(\pi')$.*

Therefore, we can sum and

$$\sum_{\pi \in \Pi^j_{\mathcal{A}}(w)} Pr_{\mathcal{A}}(\text{Alt}(\pi, j)) \geq \left(\frac{\texttt{len}+1}{n} - 1\right) \frac{p}{n}.$$

The left hand side represents a mass of probabilities distributed by $\mathcal{A}$ to other strings than w. Summing with the probability of w, we obtain:

$$\begin{aligned}
\left(\frac{\texttt{len}+1}{n} - 1\right) \cdot \frac{p}{n} + p &\leq 1 \\
(\texttt{len}+1-n) \cdot p + pn^2 &\leq n^2 \\
(\texttt{len}+1-n) &\leq \frac{n^2(1-p)}{p} \\
\texttt{len} &\leq \frac{n^2(1-p)}{p} + n - 1
\end{aligned}$$

It follows that $\texttt{len} \leq \frac{(n+1)^2}{p}$.

□

Proof of the lemma. $\pi'' = \pi_j$ and $\pi'' = \pi'_{j'}$. Necessarily we have $j = j'$.

Now $q_{i^1_k} w_k q_{i^1_{k+1}} w_{k+1} \cdots w_{k+t} q_{i^1_{k+t}}$ and $q_{i^2_k} w_k q_{i^2_{k+1}} w_{k+1} \cdots w_{k+t} q_{i^2_{k+t}}$ are the two fragments of the paths that have been removed from π and π'. These are necessarily different, but might coincide in part. Let h be the first index for which they are different, ie $\forall z < h, q_{i^1_z} = q_{i^2_z}$ and $q_{i^1_h} \neq q_{i^2_h}$.

We have:

$P(q_{i^1_{h-1}}, w_h, q_{i^1_h}) + P(q_{i^2_{h-1}}, w_h, q_{i^2_h}) \leq 1$ and the result follows.

□

We use Proposition 1 to associate with a given string w an upper bound over the probability of any string having w as a prefix:

Definition 2. *The* Potential Probability $\mathcal{PP}$ *of a prefix string w is*

$$\mathcal{PP}(w) = \min(Pr_{\mathcal{A}}(w\,\Sigma^\star), \frac{|\mathcal{A}|^2}{|w|})$$

$\mathcal{PP}(w)$ is also an upper bound on the probability of any string having w as a prefix:

Property 3. $\forall u \in \Sigma^\star \; Pr_{\mathcal{A}}(wu) \leq \mathcal{PP}(w)$

Indeed, $Pr_{\mathcal{A}}(wu) \leq Pr_{\mathcal{A}}(w\,\Sigma^\star)$ and, because of Proposition 1, $Pr_{\mathcal{A}}(wu) \leq \frac{|\mathcal{A}|^2}{|wu|} \leq \frac{|\mathcal{A}|^2}{|w|}$.

This means that we can decide, for a given prefix w, and a probability to be improved, if w is *viable*, ie if the best string having w as a prefix can be better than the proposed probability. Furtermore, given a PFA $\mathcal{A}$ and a prefix w, computing $\mathcal{PP}(w)$ is simple.

4 Solving the consensus string problem

Algorithm 1 is given a PFA $\mathcal{A}$ and returns the most probable string. The bounds obtained in the previous section allow us to explore the viable prefixes, check if the corresponding string improves our current candidate, add an extra letter to the viable prefix and add this new prefix to a priority queue.

The priority queue (**Q**) is a structure in which the time complexity for insertion is $O(\log |\mathbf{Q}|)$ and the extraction (**Pop**) of the first element can take place in constant time. In this case the order for the queue will depend on the value $\mathcal{PP}(w)$ of the prefix w.

Data: a PFA $\mathcal{A}$
Result: w, the most probable string

```
Current_Prob = 0;
Q = [λ];
Continue = true;
while not(Empty(Q)) and Continue do
    w = Pop(Q);
    if PP(w) > Current_Prob then
        p = Pr_A(w);
        if p > Current_Prob then
            Current_Prob = p;
            Current_Best = w;
        foreach a ∈ Σ do
            if PP(wa) > Current_Prob then
                Insert(wa, PP(wa), Q)
    else
        Continue = false;
return Current_Best
```

Algorithm 1: Finding the Consensus String

Analysis: Let p_{opt} be the probability of the consensus string. Let **Viable** be the set of all strings w such that $\mathcal{PP}(w) \geq p_{\text{opt}}$.

- **Fact 1.** Let w be the first element of **Q** at some iteration. If $\mathcal{PP}(w) < p_{\text{opt}}$, every other element of **Q** will also have smaller $\mathcal{PP}$ and the algorithm will halt. It follows that until the consensus string is found, the first element w is in **Viable**.

- **Fact 2.** If $w \in$**Viable**, $\mathcal{PP}(w) \geq p_{\text{opt}}$, therefore $\frac{|\mathcal{A}|^2}{|w|} \geq p_{\text{opt}}$ so $|w| \leq \frac{|\mathcal{A}|^2}{p_{\text{opt}}}$.

- **Fact 3.** There are at most $\frac{1}{p_{\text{opt}}}$ pairwise incomparable prefixes in **Viable**. Indeed, all elements of **Viable** have $\mathcal{PP}(w) = \min(Pr_{\mathcal{A}}(w\,\Sigma^\star), \frac{|\mathcal{A}|^2}{|w|}) \geq p_{\text{opt}}$ so also have $Pr_{\mathcal{A}}(w\,\Sigma^\star) \geq p_{\text{opt}}$ and by Property 2 we are done.

- **Fact 4.** There are at most $\frac{1}{p_{\text{opt}}} \cdot \frac{|\mathcal{A}|^2}{p_{\text{opt}}}$ different prefixes in **Viable**, as a consequence of facts 2 and 3.

- **Fact 5.** At every iteration of the main loop at most $|\Sigma|$ new elements are added to the priority queue.

- **Fact 6.** Therefore, since only the first elements of the priority queue will cause (at most $|\Sigma|$) insertions, and these (fact 1) are necesarily viable, the total number of insertions is bounded by $|\Sigma| \cdot \frac{|\mathcal{A}|^2}{p_{\text{opt}}} \cdot \frac{1}{p_{\text{opt}}}$.

The time complexity of the algorithm is proportional to the number of insertions in the queue and is computed as follows:

- $|\mathbf{Q}\,|$ is at most $\frac{|\Sigma|\cdot|\mathcal{A}|^2}{p_{\text{opt}}^2}$;

- Insertion of an element into **Q** is in $O\left(\log\left(\frac{|\Sigma|\cdot|\mathcal{A}|^2}{p_{\text{opt}}^2}\right)\right)$.

5 Experiments

From the theoretical analysis it appears that the new algorithm will be able to compute the consensus string. The goal of the experiments is therefore to show how the algorithm scales up: there are domains in natural language processing where the probabilities are very small, and the alphabets very large. In others this is not the case. How well does the algorithm adapt to small probabilities? A second line of experiments consists in measuring the quality of the most probable parse for the consensus string. This could obviously not be measured up to now (because of the lack of an algorithm for the most probable string). Finding out how far (both in value and in rank) the string returned by the Viterbi algorithm is from the consensus string is of interest.

5.1 Further experiments

A more extensive experimentation may consist in building a collection of random PFA, in the line of what has been done in HMM/PFA learning competitions, for instance [Verwer et al., 2012]. A connected graph is built, the arcs are transformed into transitions by adding labels and weights. A normalisation phase takes place so as to end up with a distribution of probabilities.

The main drawback of this procedure is that, most often, the consensus string will end up by being the empty string (or a very short string) and any algorithm will find it easily.

Actually, the same will happen when testing on more realistic data: a language model built from n-grams will often have as most probable string the empty string.

An extensive experimentation should also compare this algorithm with alternative techniques which have been introduced:

A first extension of the Viterbi approximation is called *crunching* [May and Knight, 2006]: instead of just computing for a string the probability of the best path, with a bit more effort, the value associated to a string is the sum of the probabilities of the n best paths.

Another approach is *variational decoding* [Li et al., 2009]: in this method and alternatives like Minimum Risk Decoding, a best approximation by n-grams of the distribution is used, and the most probable string is taken as the one which maximizes the probability with respect to this approximation. These techniques are shown to give better results than the Viterbi decoding, but are not able to cope with long distance dependencies.

Coarse-to-fine parsing [Charniak et al., 2006] is a strategy that reduces the complexity of the search involved in finding the best parse. It defines a sequence of increasingly more complex Probabilistic Context-Free grammars (PCFG), and uses the parse forest produced by one PCFG to prune the search of the next more complex PCFG.

5.2 A tighter bound on the complexity

The complexity of the algorithm can be measured by counting the number of insertions into the priority queue. This number has been upper-bounded by $|\Sigma| \cdot \frac{|\mathcal{A}|^2}{p_{\text{opt}}^2}$. But it is of interest to get a better and tighter bound. In order to have a difficult set of test PFAs we built a family of models for which the consensus string has a parametrized length and where an exponentially large set of strings has the same length and slightly lower probabilities than the consensus string.

In order to achieve that, the states are organised in levels, and at each level there is a fixed number of states (multiplicity). One of the states of the first level is chosen as initial state. All the states have an ending probability of zero except for one unique state of the last level; there is a transition from each state of level n to all states of level $n+1$ but also to all the states of level $k \leq n$.

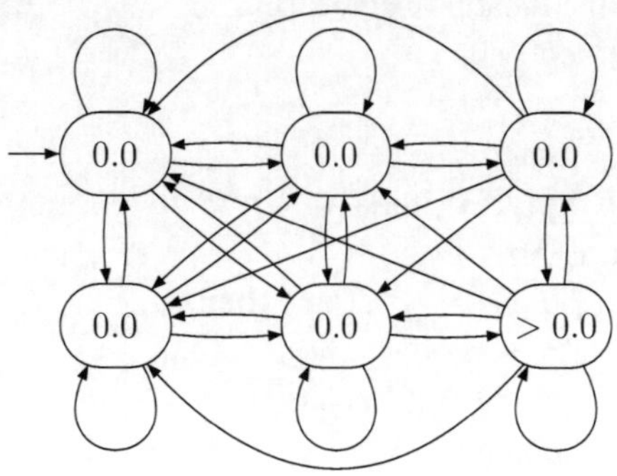

Figure 2: The topology of an automaton with 3 levels and multiplicity 2

An example of this structure, with 3 levels and multiplicity 2 is represented in Fig. 2. The shortest string with non-null probability will be of length $n-1$ where n is the number of levels.

A collection of random PFA was built with vocabulary size varying from 2 to 6, number of levels from 3 to 5, and the multiplicity from 2 to 3. 16 different PFA were generated for each vocabulary size, number of levels and multiplicity. Therefore, a total of 480 automata were built. From those 16 were discarded because the low probability of the consensus string made it impossible to deal with the size of the priority queue. 464 automata were therefore considered for the experiments.

In the first set of experiments the goal was to test how strong is the theoretical bound on the number of insertions in the priority queue.

Fig. 3 plots the inverse of the probability of the consensus string versus the number of insertions in the priority queue. The bound from Section 4 is

$$|\mathbf{Q}| \leq \frac{|\Sigma| \cdot |\mathcal{A}|^2}{p_{\text{opt}}^2}$$

Our data indicates that

$$|\mathbf{Q}| \leq \frac{1}{p_{\text{opt}}^2} \leq \frac{|\Sigma| \cdot |\mathcal{A}|^2}{p_{\text{opt}}^2}$$

Furthermore, $\frac{2}{p_{\text{opt}}}$ seems empirically to be a better bound: a more detailed mathematical analysis could lead to prove this.

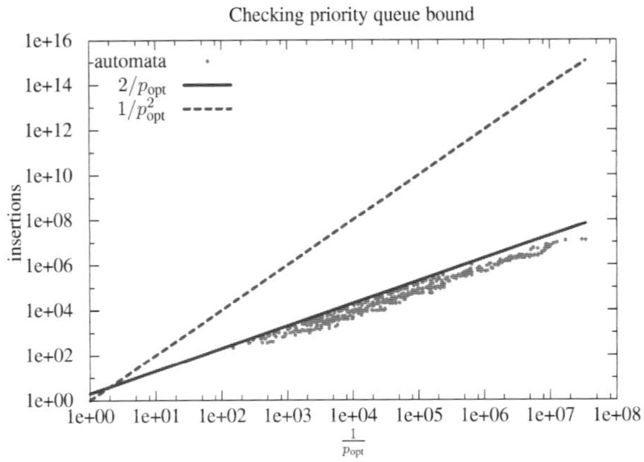

Figure 3: Number of insertions made in the priority queue

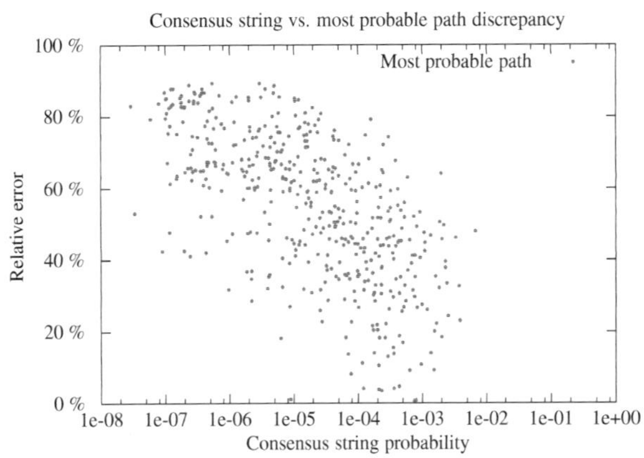

Figure 4: Most probable path accuracy

5.3 How good is the Viterbi approximation?

In the literature the string with the most probable path is often used as an approximation to the consensus string. Using the same automata, we attempted to measure the distance between the probability of the string returned by the Viterbi algorithm, which computes the most probable parse, and the probability of the consensus string.

For each automaton, we have measured the probability of the most probable string (p_{opt}) and the probability of the most probable path (p_p).

In 63% of the 464 PFA the consensus string and the string with the most probable path were different, and in no case does the probability of the consensus string coincide with the probability of the most probable path.

Figure 4 shows the relative error when using the probability of the most probable path instead of the probability of the consensus string. In other words we measure and plot $\frac{p_{\text{opt}}-p_p}{p_{\text{opt}}}$. It can be observed that the relative error can be very large and increases as the probability of the consensus string decreases. Furthermore, we ran an experiment to compute the rank of the string with most probable path, when ordered by the actual probability. Over the proposed benchmark, the average rank is 9.2 and the maximum is 277.

6 Conclusion

The algorithm provided in this work allows to compute the most probable string with its exact probability. Experimentally it works well in settings where the number of paths involved in the sums leading to the computation of the probability is large: in artificial experiments, it allowed to show that the best string for the Viterbi score could be outranked by more that 10 alternative strings.

Further experiments in natural language processing tasks are still required in order to understand in which particular settings the algorithm can be of use. In preliminary language modelling tasks two difficulties arose: the most probable string is going to be extremely short and of little interest. Furthermore, language models use very large alphabets, so the most probable string of length 10 will typically have a probability of the order of 10^{-30}. In our experiments the algorithm was capable of dealing with figures of the order of 10^{-6}. But the difference is clearly impossible to deal with.

The proposed algorithm can be used in cases where the number of possible translations and paths may be very large, but where at least one string (or translation) has a reasonable probability. Other future research directions concern in lifting the λ-freeness condition by taking into acount λ-transitions on the fly: in many cases, the transformation is cumbersome. Extending this work to probabilistic context-free grammars is also an issue.

Acknowledgement

Discussions with Khalil Sima'an proved important in a previous part of this work, as well as later help from Thomas Hanneforth. We also wish to thank the anonymous reviewer who pointed out a certain number of alternative heuristics that should be compared more extensively.

The first author acknowledges partial support by the Région des Pays de la Loire. The second author thanks the Spanish CICyT for partial support of this work through projects TIN2009-14205-C04-C1, and the program CONSOLIDER INGENIO 2010 (CSD2007-00018).

References

V. D. Blondel and V. Canterini. Undecidable problems for probabilistic automata of fixed dimension. *Theory of Computer Systems*, 36(3):231–245, 2003.

F. Casacuberta and C. de la Higuera. Optimal linguistic decoding is a difficult computational problem. *Pattern Recognition Letters*, 20(8):813–821, 1999.

F. Casacuberta and C. de la Higuera. Computational complexity of problems on probabilistic grammars and transducers. In A. L. de Oliveira, editor, *Grammatical Inference: Algorithms and Applications, Proceedings of* ICGI *'00*, volume 1891 of LNAI, pages 15–24. Springer-Verlag, 2000.

F. Casacuberta and E. Vidal. Machine translation with inferred stochastic finite-state transducers. *Computational Linguistics*, 30(2):205–225, 2004.

E. Charniak, M. Johnson, M. Elsner, J. L. Austerweil, D. Ellis, I. Haxton, C. Hill, R. Shrivaths, J. Moore, M. Pozar, and T. Vu. Multilevel coarse-to-fine PCFG parsing. In *Proceedings of* HLT-NAACL *2006*. The Association for Computer Linguistics, 2006.

C. de la Higuera. *Grammatical inference: learning automata and grammars*. Cambridge University Press, 2010.

C. de la Higuera and J. Oncina. The most probable string: an algorithmic study. *Journal of Logic and Computation, doi: 10.1093/logcom/exs049*, 2013.

J. T. Goodman. *Parsing Inside–Out*. PhD thesis, Harvard University, 1998.

P. Koehn. *Statistical Machine Translation*. Cambridge University Press, 2010.

Z. Li, J. Eisner, and S. Khudanpur. Variational decoding for statistical machine translation. In *Proceedings of* ACL/IJCNLP *2009*, pages 593–601. The Association for Computer Linguistics, 2009.

R. B. Lyngsø and C. N. S. Pedersen. The consensus string problem and the complexity of comparing hidden Markov models. *Journal of Computing and System Science*, 65(3):545–569, 2002.

C. Manning and H. Schütze. *Foundations of Statistical Natural Language Processing*. MIT Press, 1999.

J. May and K. Knight. A better n-best list: Practical determinization of weighted finite tree automata. In *Proceedings of* HLT-NAACL *2006*. The Association for Computer Linguistics, 2006.

M. Mohri. Generic e-removal and input e-normalization algorithms for weighted transducers. *International Journal on Foundations of Computer Science*, 13(1):129–143, 2002.

A. Paz. *Introduction to probabilistic automata*. Academic Press, New York, 1971.

K. Sima'an. Computational complexity of probabilistic disambiguation: NP-completeness results for language and speech processing. *Grammars*, 5(2):125–151, 2002.

S. Verwer, R. Eyraud, and C. de la Higuera. Results of the pautomac probabilistic automaton learning competition. In *Journal of Machine Learning Research - Proceedings Track*, volume 21, pages 243–248, 2012.

E. Vidal, F. Thollard, C. de la Higuera, F. Casacuberta, and R. C. Carrasco. Probabilistic finite state automata – part I and II. *Pattern Analysis and Machine Intelligence*, 27(7):1013–1039, 2005.

Stochastic Bi-Languages to model Dialogs

M. Inés Torres
Dpto. Electricidad y Electrónica
Universidad del País Vasco. Bilbao, Spain
manes.torres@ehu.es

Abstract

Partially observable Markov decision Processes provide an excellent statistical framework to deal with spoken dialog systems that admits global optimization and deal with uncertainty of user goals. However its put in practice entails intractable problems that need efficient and suboptimal approaches. Alternatively some pattern recognition techniques have also been proposed. In this framework the joint probability distribution over some semantic language provided by the speech understanding system and the language of actions provided by the dialog manager need to be estimated. In this work we propose to model this joint probability distribution by stochastic regular *bi-languages* that have also been successfully proposed for machine translation purposes. To this end a Probabilistic Finite State Bi-Automaton is defined in the paper. As an extension to this model we also propose an attributed model that allows to deal with the task attribute values. Valued attributed are attached to the states in such a way that usual learning and smoothing techniques can be applied as shown in the paper. As far as we know it is the first approach based on stochastic bi-languages formally defined to deal with dialog tasks.

1 Introduction

Spoken Dialogue Systems (SDS) aim to enable people to interact with computers, using the spoken language in a natural way (Young, 2000; Raux et al., 2006). However, the management of an SDS is a very complex task that involves many other problems to be solved like the Automatic Speech Recognition (ASR), semantic representation and understanding, answer generation, etc. According to the information provided by the user and the history of previous dialogues the dialogue manager must decide the next action to be taken. Due to its complexity the design of dialogue managers has been traditionally related to rules based methodologies (Lee et al., 2006), sometimes combined with some statistical knowledge (Varges et al., 2009). These methodologies have been successfully used for specific tasks. But they are hard to be developed and they lack sensitivity to changes present in real tasks. Then plan-based and task-independent dialogue managers have been also proposed (Raux et al., 2006; Bohus and Rudnicky, 2009). In addition, statistical models based on Markov Decision Processes can be found for dialogue managers (Levin et al., 2000; Young, 2000).

Partially Observable Markov Decision Processes (POMDP) provided an excellent statistical framework that admits global optimization and deal with uncertainty of user goals (Williams and Young, 2007). This formulation is now considered as the state of the art of statistical SDSs. However, its put in practice entails intractable problems that need efficient and suboptimal approaches such as factorization of the state space and partition of the dialogue state distributions (Williams and Young, 2007; Williams, 2010; Lee and Eskenazi, 2012a; S. Young and Williams, 2013).

On the other hand new and challenging natural language processing tasks involving dialog are also arising in the last years. Some examples include the analysis, or generation, of online debates (Walker et al., 2012) and the story generation for games using film dialog corpora as training sample (Lin and Walker, 2011).

In the pattern recognition framework statistical models have also been proposed to represent SDS (Georgila et al., 2006; Griol et al., 2008). Specifically in the interactive pattern recognition framework (Toselli et al., 2011; Torres et al., 2012) the joint probability distribution over some semantic language provided by the speech understanding system and the hypotheses provided by the dialog manager need to be estimated.

In this work we propose to model this joint probability distribution by stochastic regular *bi-languages*. These languages have also been successfully proposed to deal with machine translation (Torres and Casacuberta, 2011). To this end a Probabilistic Finite State Bi-Automaton is defined (PFSBA) in the paper. As an extension to this model we also propose an attributed model that allows to deal with the task attribute values. Valued attributed are attached to the states in such a way that usual learning and smoothing techniques can be applied as shown in the paper. As far as we know it is the first approach based on stochastic languages formally defined to deal with dialog tasks. Section 2 presents spoken dialog systems as a statistical, and interactive, pattern recognition problem.

Section 3 summarizes basic concepts related to stochastic regular *bi-languages* and then proposes a probabilistic finite-state *bi-automata* to model dialogs. We then extend this proposal to define an attributed model in Section 4. In Section 5 we deal with learning and smoothing procedures as well as with dialog generation and human-machine interaction tasks. Finally some concluding remarks are presented in Section 6

2 Spoken Dialog Systems

A classical pattern recognition system derives an hypothesis from some input stimulus, according to some previously obtained model. Let us now consider an SDS as an interactive pattern recognition system (Toselli et al., 2011). Let h be the an hypothesis or output that the dialog manager of an SDS proposes. Then the user provides some feedback sig-

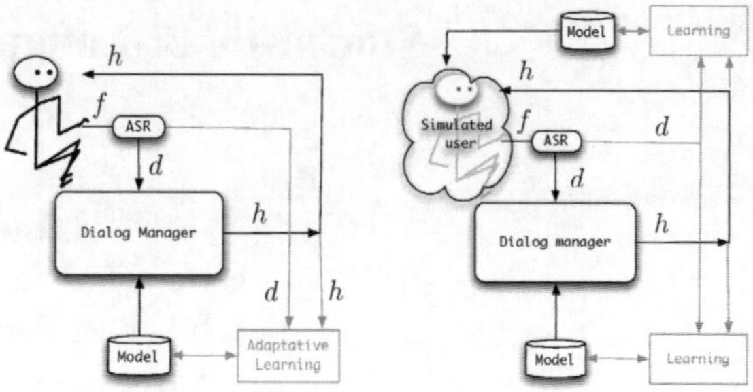

Figure 1: a) Diagram of an SDS where a Dialog Manager provides an hypothesis h given the previous hypothesis and a decoding d of a user feedback f. b) In the next interaction step a *Simulated User* provides the feedback f given its previous feedback and the system hypothesis h.

nals, f, which iteratively help the dialog manager to refine or to improve its hypothesis until it is finally accepted by the user, as the diagram in Figure 1 a) shows. The hypotheses of the dialog manager are usually called *actions* in SDS literature. These actions typically consist in machine turns that include queries to a database to get the information required by the user, questions to the user to complete the data the system needs to fulfill user goals, strategies to recover recognition or understanding errors, turns providing information to the user as well as greeting turns.

A basic simplification is to ignore the user feedback except for the last interaction or hypothesis h'. Assuming the classical *minimum-error criterion* the Baye's decision rule is simplified to maximize the posterior $P(h|h', f)$, and a *best* hypothesis $\hat{h}$ is obtained as follows:

$$\hat{h} = \arg\max_{h \in \mathcal{H}} P(h|h', f) \quad (1)$$

This maximization procedure defines the way the dialog manager of an SDS chooses the best hypothesis in the space of hypotheses $\mathcal{H}$, i.e. the best action at each interaction step, given the previous hypothesis h' and the user feedback f. However, alternative criteria could also be considered to make this decision. In fact, the strategy of dialog managers is usually based on maximizing the probability of achieving the unknown user goals at the end of the interaction procedure while minimizing the cost of getting them (Williams and Young, 2007).

In an SDS, the interpretation of the user feedback f can not be considered a deterministic process. In fact the space of decoded feedbacks $\mathcal{D}$ is the output of an ASR system. Thus a *best* hypothesis can be obtained as follows (Toselli et al., 2011; Torres et al., 2012):

$$\begin{aligned} \hat{h} &= \arg\max_{h\in\mathcal{H}} \sum_{d\in\mathcal{D}} P(h,d|h',f) \\ &\approx \arg\max_{h\in\mathcal{H}} \max_{d\in\mathcal{D}} P(h|d,h')P(f|d)P(d|h') \end{aligned}$$

where f is the user turn, d is the decoding of the user turn, h is the hypothesis or the output produced by the system and h' is the *history of the dialog*.

A suboptimal approach can be considered through a two step decoding: find first an optimal user feedback $\hat{d}$ and then, use $\hat{d}$ to decode system hypothesis $\hat{h}$ as follows:

$$\hat{d} = \arg\max_{d\in\mathcal{D}} P(f|d)P(d|h') \quad (2)$$

$$\hat{h} \approx \arg\max_{h\in\mathcal{H}} P(h|\hat{d},h') \quad (3)$$

Simulated User

The development of a complete SDS requires an online learning to train the dialog manager strategy. Therefore, a large amount of dialogues is needed together with real users with different goals, expectations and behaviors. Thus, statical dialog managers are usually trained by *simulated users* (Levin et al., 2000). A *simulated user* must provide the feedback f to the system at each interaction step. The user feedback f depends on its previous feedback f' according to some unknown distribution $P(f|f',h)$, which represents the user response to the history of system hypotheses and user feedbacks. This distribution considers the user behavior and stands for the user model $\mathcal{M}_\mathcal{U}$ and can also be defined considering now the user point of view. However, feedback f' produced by the user in the previous interaction is not corrupted by any noisy channel, such as an ASR system, before arriving to the user again. Thus, a deterministic decoding $d : \mathcal{F} \rightarrow \mathcal{D}$ maps each user turn signal into its corresponding unique decoding $d' = d(f')$ before arriving to the *user model*. Consequently the *best* decoded user feedback $\hat{d}$ is the one that maximizes the posterior $P_{\mathcal{M}_\mathcal{U}}(d|d',h)$

$$\hat{d} = \arg\max_{d\in\mathcal{D}} P(d|d',h) \approx \arg\max_{d\in\mathcal{D}} P_{\mathcal{M}_\mathcal{U}}(d|d',h) \quad (4)$$

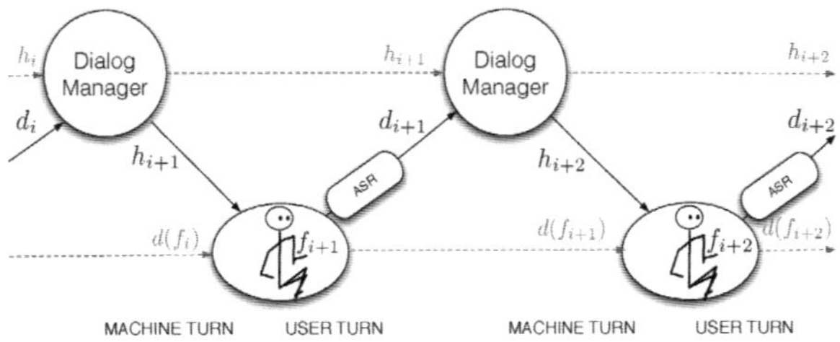

Figure 2: User-Manager interaction steps

where $\hat{d}$ is estimated using only the hypothesis produced by the system and the feedback produced by the user in the previous interaction step according to its *user model*. Figure 1 b) shows a *simulated user* interacting with a dialog manager according with a model of the *user behavior*. Equation (4) represents the way the user model decides the feedback to be produced at each interaction step. As in the case of the dialog manager, alternative criteria could be also considered to simulate the user behavior. In fact, many simulated user models can be found in the bibliography related to SDSs (Levin et al., 2000; Georgila et al., 2006; Lee and Eskenazi, 2012b). Figure 2 shows some user-manager interaction steps.

3 Probabilistic Finite State Bi-Automata to model Dialogs

In this section we are defining a probabilistic finite-state model to deal with both the dialog manager hypothesis probability distribution $P(h|d,h')$ and the user feedback probability distribution $P(d|h,d')$. The model will be able to generate dialogs as alternative sequences of dialog manager hypothesis $\tilde{h}_i$ and decoding of user feedbacks $\tilde{d}_i$ as in Figure 2.

Some basic definitions

We first summarize the basic definitions of bi-string and stochastic regular bi-language provided by Torres and Casacuberta (2011). Let Σ and Δ be two finite alphabets and $\Sigma^{\leq m}$ and $\Delta^{\leq n}$, the finite sets of sequences of symbols in Σ and Δ of length up to m and n respectively. Let $\Gamma \subseteq (\Sigma^{\leq m} \times \Delta^{\leq n})$ be a finite alphabet (*extended alphabet*) consisting of pairs of strings, that we call *extended symbols*, $(s_1 \ldots s_i : t_1 \ldots t_j) \in \Gamma$ such that $s_1 \ldots s_i \in \Sigma^{\leq m}$ and $t_1 \ldots t_j \in \Delta^{\leq n}$ with $0 \leq i \leq m$ and $0 \leq j \leq n$.

Definition 3.1. *A bi-language is a set of strings over an extended alphabet Γ, i.e., a set of strings of the form $\mathbf{b} = b_1 \dots b_k$ such that $b_i \in \Gamma$ for $0 \leq i \leq k$. A string over an extended alphabet Γ will be called bi-string.*

Torres and Casacuberta (2011) defined a stochastic *bi-language* as follows:

Definition 3.2. *Given two finite alphabets Σ and Δ, a stochastic bi-language $\mathcal{B}$ is a probability distribution over Γ^* where $\Gamma \subseteq (\Sigma^{\leq m} \times \Delta^{\leq n})$, $m, n \geq 0$. Let $\mathbf{z} = z_1 \dots z_{|\mathbf{z}|}$ be a bi-string such that $z_i \in \Gamma$ for $1 \leq i \leq |\mathbf{z}|$. If $Pr_{\mathcal{B}}(\mathbf{z})$ denotes the probability of the bi-string $\mathbf{z}$ under the distribution $\mathcal{B}$ then $\sum_{\mathbf{z} \in \Gamma^*} Pr_{\mathcal{B}}(\mathbf{z}) = 1$.*

Model definition

Let Σ be the finite alphabet of semantic symbols provided by some speech understanding system. Thus, $\tilde{d}_i = d_1 \dots d_{|\tilde{d}_i|} \in \Sigma^{\leq m}$ represents the decoding of a user feedback f. Let now Δ be the finite alphabet of dialog acts that compose each of the hypotheses $\tilde{h}_i = h_1 \dots h_{|\tilde{h}_i|} \in \Delta^{\leq n}$ provided by the dialog manager. Let $\mathbf{z}$ be a *bi-string* over the extended alphabet $\Gamma \subseteq \Sigma^{\leq m} \times \Delta^{\leq n}$ such as $\mathbf{z} : \mathbf{z} = z_1 \dots z_{|\mathbf{z}|}$, $z_i = (\tilde{d}_i : \tilde{h}_i)$ where $\tilde{d}_i = d_1 \dots d_{|\tilde{d}_i|} \in \Sigma^{\leq m}$ and $\tilde{h}_i = h_1 \dots h_{|\tilde{h}_i|} \in \Delta^{\leq n}$. Extended symbols $(\tilde{d}_i : \tilde{h}_i) \in \Gamma$ have been obtained through some alignment between $\Sigma^{\leq m}$ and $\Delta^{\leq n}$, i.e. between pairs of user feedbacks decoding provided at a user turn and dialog manager hypotheses provided at the next machine turn.

Let us now define a Dialog Model $\mathcal{DM}$ as a Deterministic and Probabilistic Finite-State *Bi-Automaton* (Torres and Casacuberta, 2011) $\mathcal{DM} = (\Sigma, \Delta, \Gamma, Q, \delta, q_0, P_f, P)$ where

- Σ and Δ are two finite alphabets representing semantic symbols provided by the user and dialog acts provided by the dialog manager respectively, Γ is an extended alphabet such that $\Gamma \subseteq (\Sigma^{\leq m} \times \Delta^{\leq n})$, $m, n \geq 0$. ϵ represents the empty symbol for both alphabets, i.e., $\epsilon \in \Sigma$, $\epsilon \in \Delta$ and $(\tilde{\epsilon} : \tilde{\epsilon}) \in \Gamma$. To simplify let $\tilde{\epsilon}$ be ϵ.

- $Q = Q_{\mathcal{M}} \bigcup Q_{\mathcal{U}}$ is a finite set of states labelled by bi-strings $(\tilde{d}_i : \tilde{h}_i) \in \Gamma$. The set $Q_{\mathcal{M}}$ includes machine states before a machine turn providing an hypothesis and the set $Q_{\mathcal{U}}$ includes user states before providing a feedback.

- $\delta \subseteq Q \times \Gamma \times Q$ is the union of two sets of transitions $\delta = \delta_{\mathcal{M}} \bigcup \delta_{\mathcal{U}}$ as follows:
  - $\delta_{\mathcal{M}} \subseteq Q_{\mathcal{M}} \times \Gamma \times Q_{\mathcal{U}}$ is a set of transitions of the form $(q, (\epsilon : \tilde{h}_i), q')$ where $q \in Q_{\mathcal{M}}$, $q' \in Q_{\mathcal{U}}$ and $(\epsilon : \tilde{h}_i) \in \Gamma$
  - $\delta_{\mathcal{U}} \subseteq Q_{\mathcal{U}} \times \Gamma \times Q_{\mathcal{M}}$ is a set of transitions of the form $(q, (\tilde{d}_i : \epsilon), q')$ where $q \in Q_{\mathcal{U}}$, $q' \in Q_{\mathcal{M}}$ and $(\tilde{d}_i : \epsilon) \in \Gamma$

- $q_0 \in Q_{\mathcal{M}}$ is the unique initial state and it is labelled as $(\epsilon : \epsilon)$.

- $P_f : Q \rightarrow [0, 1]$ is the final-state probability distribution

- $P : \delta \rightarrow [0, 1]$ defines transition probability distributions ($P(q, b, q') \equiv Pr(q', b|q)$ for $b \in \Gamma$ and $q, q' \in Q$) such that:

$$P_f(q) + \sum_{b \in \Gamma, q' \in Q} P(q, b, q') = 1 \quad \forall q \in Q \quad (5)$$

where a transition (q, b, q') is completely defined by q and b. Thus, $\forall q \in Q$, $\forall b \in \Gamma$ $|\{q' : (q, b, q')\}| \leq 1$

Let $\mathbf{z}$ be a *bi-string* over the extended alphabet $\Gamma \subseteq \Sigma^{\leq m} \times \Delta^{\leq n}$ such as $\mathbf{z} : \mathbf{z} = z_1 \dots z_{|\mathbf{z}|}$, $z_i = (\tilde{d}_i : \tilde{h}_i)$. $\mathbf{z}$ represents a dialog when z_i is of the form $z_i = (\epsilon : \tilde{h}_i)$ for machine turns m_i and $z_i = (\tilde{d}_i : \epsilon)$ for user turns u_i. Both, user and machine turns can also be null *bi-strings* of the form $(\epsilon : \epsilon)$. Let now $\theta = (q_0, z_1, q'_1, z_2, q_2, \dots, q'_{|\mathbf{z}|-1}, z_{|\mathbf{z}|}, q_{|\mathbf{z}|})$, $q_i \in Q_{\mathcal{M}}$, $q'_i \in Q_{\mathcal{U}}$, be a path for $\mathbf{z}$ in $\mathcal{DM}$. The probability of generating θ is:

$$Pr_{\mathcal{DM}}(\theta) = \left(\prod_{j=1}^{|\mathbf{z}|} P(q_{j-1}, z_j, q'_j) \right) \cdot P_f(q_{|\mathbf{z}|}) \quad (6)$$

$\mathcal{DM}$ is unambiguous. Then, a given *bi-string* $\mathbf{z}$ can only be generated by $\mathcal{DM}$ through a unique valid path $\theta(\mathbf{z})$. Thus, the probability of generating $\mathbf{z}$ with $\mathcal{DM}$ is $Pr_{\mathcal{DM}}(\mathbf{z}) = Pr_{\mathcal{DM}}(\theta(\mathbf{z}))$.

Figure 3 shows a $\mathcal{DM}$ where bold lines define path θ matching some *bi-string*.

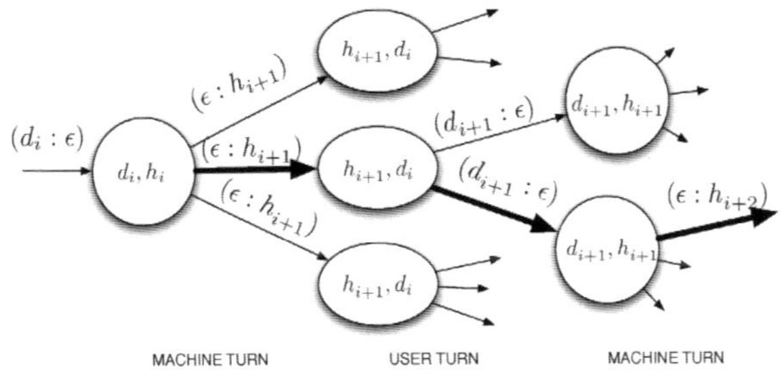

Figure 3: Probabilistic bi-automata $\mathcal{DM}$ defined in Section 3. Bold lines show a path θ matching some *bi-string*

Example Consider a simple railway information system where the alphabet of semantic units provided by the speech understanding system is defined as $\Sigma = \{Question, Sched, dest, orig, confirm\_y, confirm\_n, want, \ldots\}$ and the alphabet of dialog acts provided by the dialog manager is defined as $\Delta = \{Open, Close, Consult, Inf\_dest, Ask\_confirm, Ask\_day, \ldots\}$. Figure 4 shows a piece of a dialog labelled by sequences of symbols of Σ and Δ. This *dialog* is represented by the *bi-string* $\mathbf{z} = \{([\epsilon] : [Open])\ ([Question][Sched][dest] : [\epsilon])\ ([\epsilon] : [Consult\_sched][Inf\_dest][Ask\_confirm])\ ([Confirm\_y][want][orig] : [\epsilon])\ ([\epsilon] : [Ask\_day])\ ([Confirm\_y][day] : [\epsilon])\}$.

Machine: Welcome to the railway information system. Can I help you? *M:[Open]*
User: I would like some information on train schedules to Edinburgh. *U:[Question][Sched][dest]*
Machine: OK. I am looking for train schedules to Edinburgh. Is that ok? *M: [Consult_sched][Inf_dest] [Ask_confirm]*
User: Yes. I would like to travel from London. *U:[Confirm_y][want][orig]*
Machine: Are you traveling today? *M: [Ask_day]*
User: Yes, today *U: [Confirm_y][day]*
......

Figure 4: An example of a dialog in a railway information task. Machine turns are labelled as sequences $\tilde{h}_i \in \Delta^{\leq n}$ and User turns are labelled as sequences of decoding units $\tilde{d}_i \in \Sigma^{\leq m}$

Let us now consider a dialog model $\mathcal{DM}$ inferred from a training corpus consisting of dialogs of the railway information task such as the one shown in Figure 4. The sequence of states that correspond to the generation of the *bi-string* $\mathbf{z}$ is shown in the first column of Table 1. The second column shows the corresponding state labels as well as the next machine or user turn. The probability of *bi-string* $\mathbf{z}$ being generated by $\mathcal{DM}$ is calculated as $Pr_{\mathcal{DM}}(\mathbf{z}) = Pr_{\mathcal{DM}}(\theta(\mathbf{z}))$ according to Equation 6 where θ is the path for $\mathbf{z}$ in $\mathcal{DM}$, i.e. $\theta = (q_0, z_1, q_1, z_2, q_2, z_3, q_3, z_4, q_4, z_5, q_5, z_6, q_6, \ldots)$, $q_0, q_2, q_4, q_6 \in Q_{\mathcal{M}}$, $q_1, q_3, q_5 \in Q_{\mathcal{U}}$ as shown in Table 1, z_1, z_3, z_5 represent dialog manager hypotheses of the form $z_i = (\epsilon : \tilde{h}_i)$ and z_2, z_4, z_6 represent user feedback decodings of the form $z_i = (\tilde{d}_i : \epsilon)$.

4 Attributed model

The Dialog Model $\mathcal{DM}$ defined in Section 3 considers actions proposed by the dialog manager, i.e. sequences of dialog acts $\tilde{h}_i$ and sequences of decoding of user feedbacks $\tilde{d}_i$. Additionally, each machine and/or user state need to be labelled with the values of all relevant internal variables, which can be updated after each user turn. Thus, an additional alphabet appears to represent valued attributes of these internal variables, thus leading to an *attributed* model.

Attributed finite automata were proposed for syntactic pattern recognition in the nineties (Koski et al., 1995). The concept of attributed automata is a generalization of a finite automaton with attributes attached to states and contextual conditions as well as computational relations attached to transitions (Meriste, 1994). A transition is labelled with an input symbol, a context condition and an attribute evaluation function. Attributed automata specify context-sensitive languages. However in cases of finite domains of attributes an attributed automaton can be transformed to a finite automaton which simulates its external behavior, i.e. the attributed recognizer. This simulation is based on homomorphisms (Meriste, 1994). Stochastic versions of attributed grammar were then developed (Abney, 1997). However Abney (1997) showed that attribute-value grammars cannot be modeled adequately using statistical techniques which assume that statistical dependencies are accidental. More-

Table 1: The sequence of states along with their state labels that correspond to the generation of the *bi-string* $\mathbf{z} = \{([\epsilon] : [Open])\ ([Question][Sched][dest] : [\epsilon])\ ([\epsilon] : [Consult\_sched][Inf\_dest][Ask\_confirm])\ ([Confirm\_y][want][orig] : [\epsilon])\ ([\epsilon] : [Ask\_day])\ ([Confirm\_y][day] : [\epsilon])\}$. This *bi-string* represents the dialog in the Example

state	state label ($\tilde{d}_i : \tilde{h}_i$) and turn	state attributes
$q_0 \in Q_{\mathcal{M}}$	$([\epsilon] : [\epsilon])$ *M:[Open]*	none
$q_1 \in Q_{\mathcal{U}}$	$([\epsilon] : [Open])$ *U:[Question][Sched][dest]*	none
$q_2 \in Q_{\mathcal{M}}$	$([Question][Sched][dest] : [Open])$ *M: [Consult_sched][Inf_dest] [Ask_confirm]*	$Sched\_0.75\ dest\_0.25$
$q_3 \in Q_{\mathcal{U}}$	$([Question][Sched][dest] : [Consult\_sched][Inf\_dest][Ask\_confirm])$ *U:[Confirm_y][want][orig]*	$Sched\_0.75\ dest\_0.25$
$q_4 \in Q_{\mathcal{M}}$	$([Confirm\_y][want][orig] : [Consult\_sched][Inf\_dest][Ask\_confirm])$ *M: [Ask_day]*	$Sched\_c\ dest\_c\ orig\_0.75$
$q_5 \in Q_{\mathcal{U}}$	$([Confirm\_y][want][orig] : [Ask\_day])$ *U: [Confirm_y][day]*	$Sched\_c\ dest\_c\ orig\_0.75$
$q_6 \in Q_{\mathcal{M}}$	$([Confirm\_y][day] : [Ask\_day])$	$Sched\_c\ dest\_c\ orig\_c\ day\_0.50$

over, hard computational problems arise that need specific parser methods (Osborne, 2000; Malouf and van Noord, 2004).

In this section we propose an extension of the Dialog Model previously defined by adding a new alphabet of attributes. Assuming only discrete domains for the attributes they can be easily represented by a third string to be added to the state labels. Let us consider a dialog task characterized by a discrete set of internal variables such as *date, hour, time, dest, ...* These internal variables are a subset of the semantic decoding set, i.e. the subset of Σ set that consists of task dependent symbols. These internal variables can lead to simple $known, unknown$ attributes that can just be represented by the presence or absence of the attribute at each state. Thus, the new alphabet represents just the knowledge of the value as $\Omega = \{day, hour, time, dest, ...\}$. But we may desire a more detailed description of these values, such as *confirmed, known_to_some_extend, unknown,...* where *known_to_some_extend* can be quantified by a short set of confidence scores. Thus, the new alphabet is now $\Omega = \{day\_c, day\_0.75, day\_0.5, day\_0.25, hour\_c, hour\_0.75, hour\_0.5, hour\_0.25, ...\}$ where day_c means that the value of attribute day is confirmed and $day\_0.75$, $day\_0.5$ and $day\_0.25$ represent different confidence scores for the attribute value.

The model $\mathcal{DM}$ previously defined in Section 3 can now be extended to get an *attributed* model $\mathcal{A\_DM}$ by just adding another finite alphabet as follows $\mathcal{A\_DM} = (\Sigma, \Delta, \Gamma, \Omega, Q, \delta, q_0, P_f, P)$ where

- Σ and Δ are two finite alphabets representing semantic symbols provided by user and dialog acts provided by the dialog manager respectively, as defined in Section 3. Ω is a new finite set of symbols representing discrete valued attributes related with the dialog task.
- $Q = Q_{\mathcal{M}} \bigcup Q_{\mathcal{U}}$ is a finite set of states labelled by bi-strings $(\tilde{d}_i : \tilde{h}_i) \in \Gamma$ where now the valued attributes are also included $\tilde{w}_i \in \Omega^*$ as follows: $[(\tilde{d}_i : \tilde{h}_i), \tilde{w}_i]$
- $\delta \subseteq Q \times \Gamma \times Q$ is the union of two sets of transitions $\delta = \delta_{\mathcal{M}} \bigcup \delta_{\mathcal{U}}$, as defined in Section 3.
- $q_0 \in Q_{\mathcal{M}}$ is the unique initial state and it is labelled as $[(\epsilon : \epsilon), \epsilon]$
- $P_f : Q \rightarrow [0, 1]$ and $P : \delta \rightarrow [0, 1]$ define the final and transition probability distributions as before in Section 3.

The knowledge of the attributes leads to different strategies for the dialog manager. A score of 0.25 would lead to a *ask_confirm* dialog act whereas a confirmed value wouldn't need such a confirmation. Thus, the transition function $\delta \subseteq Q \times \Gamma \times Q$ and the transition probability distribution $P : \delta \rightarrow [0, 1]$ have a strong dependency of internal attributed attached to the states.

Example Let $\mathcal{A\_DM}$ be an attributed model inferred from a training corpus consisting of dialogs of the railway information task such as the one shown in Figure 4 where the attribute alphabet has been defined as $\Omega = \{Sched\_c, ..., Sched\_0.25, dest\_c, ..., orig\_c, orig\_0.25, \dots\}$. Third column in Table 1 shows the attributes attached to each state of the path θ for the *bi-tring* $\mathbf{z}$ when generated by the $\mathcal{A\_DM}$. The attributes first appear after the first user turn, which ask for schedules and inform about destination. But the ASR provides low confidence about the recognized values. Thus, the next machine hypothesis is an $Ask\_confirm$ dialog act. Finally machine state q_6 has attached two confirmed attributes and one more with some confidence score.

5 Putting models to work

In this section we deal with practical issues related to the use of the proposed models. We first deal with the learning and smoothing procedures. We then show two different application tasks: dialog generation and human-machine interaction.

Learning and smoothing models

Get a dialog corpus consisting of pairs of user and system turns. Then get the model topology as well as an initial maximum likelihood estimation of the parameters of both dialog manager and simulated user probability distributions. This model needs to deal also with unseen events, i.e. unknown situations at training corpus. The dialog manager can provide an hypothesis $(\epsilon : \tilde{h}_i)$ that does not lead to any of the existing states created when trained form the dialog corpus. In the same way simulated user can provide a user feedback $(\tilde{d}_i : \epsilon)$ not appearing in the training corpus, so not in the model. The model needs to be generalized in order to deal with any hypothesis or user feedback. Thus a back-off smoothing strategy needs to be carried out. This strategy creates new edges to existing nodes, when possible. Alternatively it searches for similar nodes to create the new edges (Torres et al., 2012). Thus the similarity between pairs of states needs to be estimated. States of the proposed models are labelled by $[(\tilde{d}_i : \tilde{h}_i), \tilde{w}_i]$, $(\tilde{d}_i : \tilde{h}_i) \in \Gamma \subseteq \Sigma^{\leq m} \times \Delta^{\leq n}$ and $\tilde{w}_i \in \Omega^*$. In practice, a string consisting of the concatenation of $\tilde{d}_i$, $\tilde{h}_i$ and $\tilde{w}_i$ is used. As a consequence string metrics like Levenshtein distance can be easily used to measure similarity between pairs of states (Georgila et al., 2006).

Generating dialogs: cooperative models

Figure 3 shows the way to generate dialogs with the proposed model. Let us train two models, one acts as a dialog manager and provides hypotheses according to Equation 3 and the other one acts as a simulated user according to Equation 4. However, different strategies can be defined in order to get a higher variability of dialogs. As an example Torres et al. (2012) proposes a random user feedback choice of decoded signals among the one defined in each state. Preliminary experiments were carried to generate a set of dialogs by training a model from dialog corpus representing real man machine dialogs aimed to get bus information systems. These experiments showed manageable model sizes, good task completion rates and good model behaviors.

On the other hand this formulation also suggests the joint decoding of user and machine turns. Find first a suboptimal best path $\hat{\theta}$ with a maximization approach and then estimate the best *bi-string* as follows:

$$\hat{\theta} \approx \arg\max_{\theta \in g(\mathbf{z})} Pr_{\mathcal{A\_DM}}(\theta) \quad (7)$$

$$\hat{\mathbf{z}} = \arg\max_{\mathbf{z}} Pr_{\mathcal{A\_DM}}(\hat{\theta}(\mathbf{z})) \quad (8)$$

where $g(\mathbf{z})$ denotes the set of possible paths in $\mathcal{A\_DM}$ matching $\mathbf{z}$ and $\hat{\mathbf{z}} = z_1 \dots z_{|\mathbf{z}|}$, $z_i = (\tilde{d} : \tilde{h}_i)$ represents the best estimated dialog consisting of *bi-strings* z_i of the form $z_i = (\epsilon : \tilde{h}_i)$ for machine turns and on the form $z_i = (\tilde{d}_i : \epsilon)$ for user turns.

Human machine interaction

The proposed models can also be used to model SDS. The first model obtained from a dialog corpus would need to be improved by defining different dialog manager strategies and simulated user behaviors. Error recovery strategies need also be defined to deal with ASR errors. Then run the system until desired dialog goals are successfully achieved for different simulated user behaviors. Finally run the SDS with real users and use adaptive learning to obtain a dialog manager adapted to real interaction feedbacks.

6 Concluding remarks and future work

Some statistical pattern recognition techniques have been proposed to deal with spoken dialog systems. Specifically in the interactive pattern recognition framework the joint probability distribution over some semantic language provided by the speech understanding system and the language of actions provided by the dialog manager need to be estimated. In this work we have proposed to model this joint probability distribution by stochastic regular *bi-languages* that have also been successfully used for machine translation purposes. To this end a Probabilistic Finite State Bi-Automaton has been defined in the paper. As an extension to this model we have also proposed an attributed model that allows to deal with the task attribute values. Valued attributed are attached to the states in such a way that usual learning and smoothing techniques can be applied. As far as we know it is the first approach based on stochastic bi-languages formally defined to deal with dialog tasks.

Acknowledgments

This work has been partially supported by the Spanish Ministry of Science under grant TIN2011-28169-C05-04 and by the Basque Government under grant IT685-13.

References

Steven P. Abney. 1997. Stochastic attribute-value grammars. *Computational Linguistics*, 23:597–618.

Dan Bohus and Alexander I. Rudnicky. 2009. The ravenclaw dialog management framework: Architecture and systems. *Computer Speech and Language*, 23:332–361.

Kallirroi Georgila, James Henderson, and Oliver Lemon. 2006. User simulation for spoken dialogue systems: Learning and evaluation. In *Proc. of Interspeech*.

David Griol, Lluís F. Hurtado, Encarna Segarra, and Emilio Sanchis. 2008. A statistical approach to spoken dialog systems design and evaluation. *Speech Communication*, 50:666–682.

Antti Koski, Martti Juhola, and Merik Meriste. 1995. Syntactic recognition of ecg signals by attributed finite automata. *Pattern Recognition*, 28:1927–1940.

Sungjin Lee and M. Eskenazi. 2012a. Pomdp-based let's go system for spoken dialog challenge. In *IEEE SLT Workshop*, pages 61–66.

Sungjin Lee and Maxine Eskenazi. 2012b. An unsupervised approach to user simulation: toward self-improving dialog systems. In *Proc. of SIGDIAL*, pages 50–59, Korea.

Cheongjae Lee, Sangkeun Jung, Jihyun Eun, Minwoo Jeong, and Gary Geunbae Lee. 2006. A situation-based dialogue management using dialogue examples. In *Proceedings of ICASSP*, pages 69–72.

Esther Levin, Roberto Pieraccini, and Wieland Eckert. 2000. A stochastic model of human-machine interaction for learning dialog strategies. *IEEE Transaction on Speech and Audio Processing*, 8(1):11–23.

Grace I. Lin and Marilyn A. Walker. 2011. All the world's a stage: Learning character models from film. In *Proceedings of the Conference on Artificial Intelligence and Digital Entertainment*.

Robert Malouf and Gertjan van Noord. 2004. Wide coverage parsing with stochastic attribute value grammars. In *Proceedings of the first International Conference on Natural Language Processing*, Hainan, China.

Merik Meriste. 1994. Attributed automata. some results and open problems. Technical report, Computer Science Department. Institute of Cybernetics, Estonian Academy of Sciences, December.

Miles Osborne. 2000. Estimation of stochastic attribute-value grammars using an informative sample. In *Proc. 18th International Conference on Computational Linguistics*, pages 586–592.

Antoine Raux, Dan Bohus, Brian Langner, Alan W Black, and Maxine Eskenazi. 2006. Doing research on a deployed spoken dialogue system: One year of lets go! experience. In *Interspeech*, pages 65–68.

B. Thomson S. Young, M. Gasic and J. Williams. 2013. Pomdp-based statistical spoken dialogue systems: a review. *Proc IEEE*, to appear.

M. Inés Torres and F. Casacuberta. 2011. Stochastic k-tss bi-languages for machine translation. In *Proceedings of the 9th International Workshop on Finite State Models for Natural Language Processing (FSMNLP)*, pages 98–106, Blois (France). Association for Computational Linguistics.

M. Inés Torres, Jose Miguel Benedí, Raquel Justo, and Fabrizio Ghigi. 2012. Modeling spoken dialog systems under the interactive pattern recognition framework. In *SSPR&SPR. Lecture Notes on Computer Science*, pages 519–528.

Alejandro H. Toselli, Enrique Vidal, and Francisco Casacuberta, editors. 2011. *Multimodal Interactive Pattern Recognition and Applications*. Springer.

Sebastian Varges, Silvia Quarteroni, Giuseppe Riccardi, Alexei V. Ivanov, and Pierluigi Roberti. 2009. Combining pomdps trained with user simulations and rule-based dialogue management in a spoken dialogue system. In *Proc. of the ACL-IJCNLP*, pages 41–44.

Marilyn A. Walker, Pranav Anand, Rob Abbott, Jean E. Fox Tree, Craig Martell, and Joseph King. 2012. That's your evidence?: Classifying stance in online political debate. *Decision Support Systems*, 53:719–729.

Jason D. Williams and Steve Young. 2007. Partially observable markov decision processes for spoken dialog systems. *Computer Speech and Language*, 21:393–422.

J.D. Williams. 2010. Incremental partiten recombination for efficient tracking of multiple dialog states. In *Proceedings of International Conference on Acoustics, Speech and Signal Processing (ICASSP)*, Dallas, USA.

Steve Young. 2000. Probabilistic methods in spoken dialogue systems. *Philosophical Trans of the Royal Society*, 1769(358):1389–1402.

ZeuScansion: a tool for scansion of English poetry

Manex Agirrezabal, Bertol Arrieta, Aitzol Astigarraga
University of the Basque Country (UPV/EHU)
Dept. of Computer Science
20018 Donostia
manex.aguirrezabal@ehu.es
bertol@ehu.es
aitzol.astigarraga@ehu.es

Mans Hulden
University of Helsinki
Department of modern languages
Helsinki, Finland
mhulden@email.arizona.edu

Abstract

We present a finite state technology based system capable of performing metrical scansion of verse written in English. Scansion is the traditional task of analyzing the lines of a poem, marking the stressed and non-stressed elements, and dividing the line into metrical feet. The system's workflow is composed of several subtasks designed around finite state machines that analyze verse by performing tokenization, part of speech tagging, stress placement, and unknown word stress pattern guessing. The scanner also classifies its input according to the predominant type of metrical foot found. We also present a brief evaluation of the system using a gold standard corpus of human-scanned verse, on which a per-syllable accuracy of 86.78% is reached. The program uses open-source components and is released under the GNU GPL license.

1 Introduction

Scansion is a well-established form of poetry analysis which involves marking the prosodic meter of lines of verse and possibly also dividing the lines into feet. The specific technique and scansion notation may differ from language to language because of phonological differences. Scansion is traditionally done manually by students and scholars of poetry. In the following, we present a finite-state based software tool—ZeuScansion— for performing this task with English poetry, and provide a brief evaluation of its performance on a gold standard corpus of poetry in various meters.

1.1 Scansion

Conventionally, scanning a line of poetry should yield a representation where every syllable is marked with a level of stress—typically two or more levels are used—and groups of syllables are divided into units of feet. Consider, for example, the following line from John Keats' poem *To autumn*.

```
To swell the gourd, and plump the hazel shells
```

Here, a natural analysis is as follows:

```
-    '      -    '     -    '     -   '  -   '
To swell |the gourd |and plump |the haz|el shells
```

We use the symbol ' to denote marked (ictic) syllables, and - to denote unmarked ones (non-ictic). That is, we have analyzed the line in question to follow a stress pattern

DE-DUM DE-DUM DE-DUM DE-DUM DE-DUM

and also to consist of five feet of two syllables each in the order unstressed-stressed. Indeed, this is the most common meter in English poetry: *iambic pentameter*.

The above example is rather clear-cut. How a particular line of verse *should* be scanned, however, is often a matter of contention. Consider a line from the poem *Le Monocle de Mon Oncle* by Wallace Stevens:

```
I wish that I might be a thinking stone
```

Here, matters are much more murky. Regarding the ambiguity in this line, the poet Alfred Corn notes that

> ...there is in fact room for disagreement about the scansion of this line. But Stevens is among the most regular of the metrists, and he probably heard it as five iambic feet.[1] Still, an alternative scansion is: one iamb, followed by a pyrrhic foot,[2] followed by two strong stresses, followed by two iambs.

In line with the above commentary, the following represents several alternative analyses of the line in question:

```
Examp.: I wish that I might be a thinking stone

1st:    - '   -  '  -  '  -  '  -    '

2nd:    - '   -  -  '  '  -  '  -    '

3rd:    - '   -  '  '  '  -  '  -    '

4th:    - '   -  -  -  '  -  '  -    '
```

The first variant is the meter (probably) intended by the author. The second line is Corn's alternative scansion. The third and fourth lines show the output of the software tools Scandroid and ZeuScansion, respectively.

In short, evaluating the output of automatic scansion is somewhat complicated by the possibility of various good interpretations. As we shall see below, when evaluating the scansion task, we use a gold standard that addresses this and accepts several possible outputs as valid.

2 The output of ZeuScansion

As there exist many different established systems of scansion, especially as regards minor details, we have chosen a rather conservative approach, which also lends itself to a fairly mechanical, linguistic rule based implementation. In the system, we distinguish three levels of stress, and mark each line with a stress pattern, as well as make an attempt to analyze the

[1]Iambic foot: A weak-stressed syllable followed by a strong-stressed syllable.

[2]Pyrrhic foot: Two syllables with weak stress.

Disyllabic feet	
- -	pyrrhus
- '	iamb
' -	trochee
' '	spondee

Trisyllabic feet	
- - -	tribrach
' - -	dactyl
- ' -	amphibrach
- - '	anapest
- ' '	bacchius
' ' -	antibacchius
' - '	cretic
' ' '	molossus

Table 1: Metrical feet used in English poetry

predominant format used in a poem. The following illustrates the analysis produced by our tool of a stanza from Lewis Carroll's poem *Jabberwocky*:

```
1 He took his vorpal sword in hand:
2 Long time the manxome foe he sought-
3 So rested he by the Tumtum tree,
4 And stood awhile in thought.

1 - ' - `- ' - '
2 ' ' - `' ' - '
3 ' `- - - - `- '
4 - ' -' - '
```

In addition to this, the system also analyzes the different types of feet that make up the line (discussed in more detail below). ZeuScansion supports most of the common types of foot found in English poetry, including *iambs*, *trochees*, *dactyls*, and *anapests*. Table 1 shows a more complete listing of the type of feet supported.

2.1 Metrical patterns

Once we have identified the feet used in a line, we can analyze for each line the most likely meter used. This includes common meters such as:

- Iambic pentameter: Lines composed of 5 iambs, used by *Shakespeare* in his *Sonnets*.
- Dactylic hexameter:[3] Lines composed of 6

[3]Also known as *heroic hexameter*

dactyls, used by *Homer* in the *Iliad*.

- Iambic tetrameter: Lines composed of 4 iambs, used by *Robert Frost* in *Stopping by Woods on a Snowy Evening*.

For example, if we provide Shakespeare's *Sonnets* as input, ZeuScansion classifies the work as *iambic pentameter* in its global analysis (line-by-line output omitted here):

```
Syllable stress _'_'_'_'_'
Meter: Iambic pentameter
```

3 Related work

There exist a number of projects that attempt to automate the scansion of English verse. In this section, we present some of them.

Scandroid (2005) is a program that scans English verse in iambic and anapestic meter, written by Charles O. Hartman (Hartman, 1996). The source code is available.[4] The program can analyze poems and check if their stress pattern is iambic or anapestic. But, if the input poem's meter differs from those two, the system forces each line into iambic or anapestic feet, i.e. it is specifically designed to only scan such poems.

AnalysePoems is another tool for automatic scansion and identification of metrical patterns written by Marc Plamondon (Plamondon, 2006). In contrast to *Scandroid*, *AnalysePoems* only identifies patterns; it does not impose them. The program also checks rhymes found in the input poem. It is reportedly developed in *Visual Basic* and the .NET framwork; however, neither the program nor the code appear to be available.

Calliope is another similar tool, built on top of *Scandroid* by Garrett McAleese (McAleese, 2007). It is an attempt to use linguistic theories of stress assignment in scansion. The program seems to be unavailable.

Of the current efforts, (Greene et al., 2010) appears to be the only one that uses statistical methods in the analysis of poetry. For the learning process, they used sonnets by Shakespeare, as well as a number of others works downloaded from the Internet.[5] Weighted finite-state transducers were used for stress assignment. As with the other documented projects, we have not found an implementation to review.

[4]http://oak.conncoll.edu/cohar/Programs.htm

[5]http://www.sonnets.org

4 Method

Our tool is largely built around a number of rules regarding scansion developed by Peter L. Groves (Groves, 1998). It consists of two main components:

(a) An implementation of Groves' rules of scansion—mainly a collection of POS-based stress-assignment rules.

(b) A pronunciation lexicon together with an out-of-vocabulary word guesser.

(a) Groves' rules

Groves' rules assign stress as follows:

1. Primary step: Mark the stress of the primarily stressed syllable in content words.[6]

2. Secondary step: Mark the stress of (1) the secondarily stressed syllables of polysyllabic content words and (2) the most strongly stressed syllable in polysyllabic function words.[7]

In section 5 we present a more elaborate example to illustrate how Groves' rules are implemented.

(b) Pronunciation lexicon

To calculate the basic stress pattern of words necessary for step 1, we primarily use two pronunciation dictionaries: The CMU Pronouncing Dictionary (Weide, 1998) and NETtalk (Sejnowski and Rosenberg, 1987). Each employs a slightly different notation, but they are similar in content: they both mark three levels of stress, and contain pronunciations and stress assignments:

```
NETTALK format:
abdication     @bdIkeS-xn     2<>0>1>0<<0

CMU format:
INSPIRATION    IH2 N S P ER0 EY1 SH AH0 N
```

The system uses primarily the smaller NETtalk dictionary (20,000 words) and falls back to use CMU (125,000 words) in case a word is not found

[6]Content words are nouns, verbs, adjectives, and adverbs.

[7]Function words are auxiliaries, conjunctions, pronouns, and prepositions.

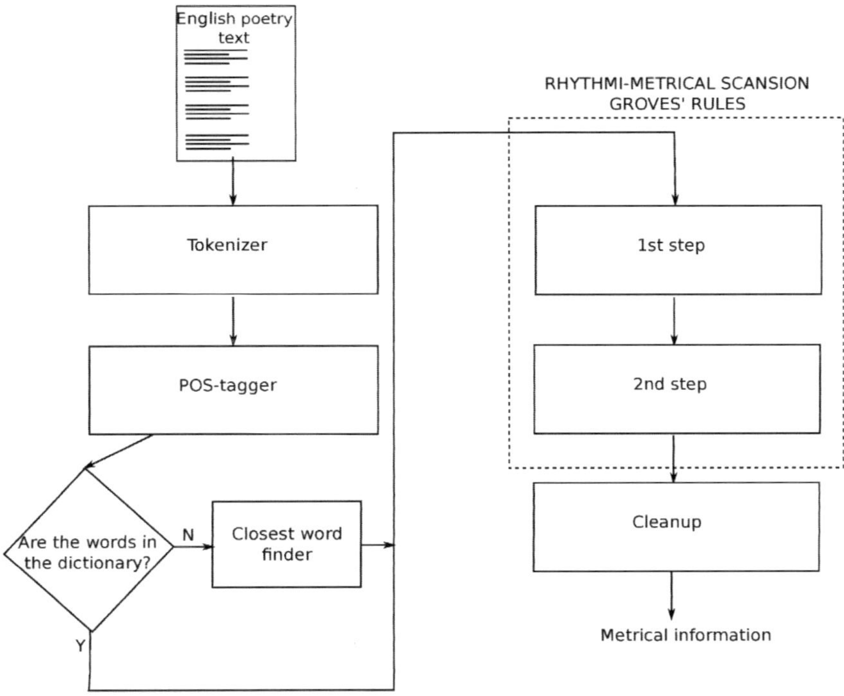

Figure 1: Structure of ZeuScansion

in NETtalk. The merged lexicon, where NETtalk pronunciations are given priority, contains some 133,000 words.

5 *ZeuScansion*: Technical details

The structure of the system is divided into the subtasks shown in figure 1. We begin with preprocessing and tokenization, after which words are part-of-speech tagged. Following that, we find the default stresses for each word, guessing the stress patterns if words are not found in the dictionary. After these preliminaries, we apply the steps of Groves' scansion rules and perform some cleanup of the result.

The toolchain itself is implented as a chain of finite-state transducers using the *foma*[8] toolkit (Hulden, 2009), save for the part-of-speech tagger which is a Hidden Markov Model (HMM) implementation (Halácsy et al., 2007). We use *Perl* as a glue language to communicate between the components.

[8]http://foma.googlecode.com

Preparation of the corpus

After tokenization,[9] we obtain the part of speech tags of the words of the poem. For the POS-tagger, we trained Hunpos[10] (Halácsy et al., 2007) with the Wall Street Journal English corpus (Marcus et al., 1993). While other more general corpora might be more suitable for this task, we only need to distinguish between function and non-function words, and thus performance differences would most likely be slight.

Once the first process is completed, the system starts applying Groves' rules, which we have encoded as finite-state transducers. To apply the rules, however, we must know the stress pattern of each word. The main problem when assigning patterns is that the pronunciation of some words will be unknown, even though the dictionaries used are quite large. This often occurs because a word is either misspelled, or because the poem is old and uses archaic vocabulary or spellings.

The strategy we used to analyze such words was to find a 'close' neighboring word in the dictionary, relying on an intuition that words that differ very lit-

[9]https://code.google.com/p/foma/wiki/FAQ
[10]https://code.google.com/p/hunpos

tle in spelling from the sought-after word are also likely pronounced the same way.

Finding the closest word

In order to find what we call the 'closest word' in the dictionary, we construct a finite-state transducer from the existing dictionaries in such a way that it will output the most similar word, according to spelling, using a metric of word distances that we have devised for the purpose. Among other things, the metric assigns a higher cost to character changes toward the end of the word than to those in the beginning (which reflect the onset of the first syllable), and also a higher cost to vowel changes. Naturally, fewer changes overall also result in a lower cost. For example, in the following line from Shakespeare's *Romeo and Juliet*:

And ***usest*** *none in that true use indeed*

we find the word **usest**, which does not appear in our lexicon.[11] Indeed, for this word, we need to make quite a few changes in order to find a good 'close' match: **wisest**.

Groves' rules

Once we have obtained the stress pattern for each word, we begin to apply Groves' rules: to stress the primarily stressed syllable in content words. This is implemented with a finite state transducer built from replacement rules (Beesley and Karttunen, 2003) that encode the steps in the rules. In our *Hamlet* example, for instance, our input to this stage looks like this:

```
to+-+TO be+′+VB or+-+CC not+′+RB to+-+TO ...
that+-+IN is+-+VBZ the+-+DT question+′-+NN

the+-+DT uncertain+-′-+JJ sickly+`-+JJ
appetite+′--+NN to+-+TO please+′+VB
```

Next, we apply the second rule—that is, we mark the secondarily stressed syllables of polysyllabic content words and the most strongly stressed syllable in polysyllabic function words:

```
to+-+TO be+′+VB or+-+CC not+′+RB to+-+TO ...
that+-+IN is+-+VBZ the+-+DT question+′-+NN

the+-+DT uncertain+`′-+JJ sickly+`-+JJ
appetite+′-`+NN to+-+TO please+′+VB
```

[11] The archaic second-person singular simple present form of the verb **use**.

The last step is to remove all the material not needed to work with stress patterns. In this part, we get as input a sequence of tokens with a specified structure:

```
inspiration+`-′-+NN
```

For the cleanup process, we use a transducer that removes everything before the first + character and everything after the second + character. It next removes all the + characters, so that the only result we get is the stress structure of the input word.

Global analysis

After the stress rules are applied, we attempt to divide lines into feet in order to produce a global analysis of the poem. Since foot-division can be ambiguous, this is somewhat non-trivial. Consider, for instance, the meter:

```
_′ __′ __′ __′ _
```

which could be analyzed as consisting mainly of (1) amphibrachs [-'-], (2) trochees ['-] and (3) iambs [-']. All three patterns appear four times in the line. For such cases, we have elaborated a scoring system for selecting the appropriate pattern: we give a weight of 1.0 for hypothetical disyllabic patterns, and a weight of 1.5 for trisyllabic ones. In this example, this would produce the judgement that the structure is amphibrachic tetrameter (1.5×4 matches = 6).

Foot	Pattern	N° matches	Score
Amphibrach	–′ –	4	6
Iamb	–′	4	4
Trochee	′ –	4	4
Anapest	’–	3	4.5
Dactyl	’–	3	4.5
Pyrrhus	- -	3	3

6 Evaluation

As the gold standard material for evaluation, we used a corpus of scanned poetry, *For Better For Verse*, from the University of Virginia.[12] We extracted the reference analyses from this website, which originally was built as an interactive on-line tutorial to train people in the scansion of English poetry in traditional meter. Sometimes several analyses

[12] http://prosody.lib.virginia.edu

	Scanned lines	Correctly scanned
No CWF	759	173
With CWF	759	199
No CWF	Accuracy: 22.79%	
With CWF	Accuracy: 26.21%	

	Scanned sylls.	Correctly scanned
No CWF	7076	5802
With CWF	7076	5999
No CWF	Accuracy: 81.995%	
With CWF	Accuracy: 86.78%	

Table 2: ZeuScansion evaluation results against the *For better or Verse* corpus. The CWF label indicates whether the closest word finder was used for assigning stress to unknown words.

are given as correct. The results of the evaluation are given in table 2. As seen, 86.78% of syllables are scanned correctly in the best configuration. We include scores produced without the word guesser component to show its significance in the process.

For checking the number of correctly scanned syllables on each line, we use *Levenshtein* distance in comparing against the gold standard. We do this in order not to penalize a missing or superfluous syllable—which are sometimes present—with more than 1 count. For example, the two readings of Stevens' poem mentioned in the introduction would be encoded in the corpus as

−+−+−+−+−+ | −+−−++−+−+

while our tool marks the line in question as

−+−−−+−+−+

after conversion to using only two levels of stress from the original three-level marking. Here, the minimum *Levenshtein* distance between the analysis and the reference is one, since changing one − to a + in the analysis would equal the first 'correct' possibility in the gold standard.

Closest word finder

Since the closest word finder has some impact on the overall quality of the system, we have evaluated that component separately. Figure 2 shows a graph illustrating the increasing coverage of words depending on distance to the neighboring word used as a pronunciation guide for out-of-vocabulary items. The first column of the graph (NC) represents the percentage of the corpus that could be read using only the dictionaries, while in the following ones, we show the improvements we get in terms of coverage using various substitutions. The codes that appear in the lower part of figure 2 refer to the allowed changes. The first letter can be either `B` or `E`. If it is `B`, the changes will be made in the beginning of the word. The character following the hyphen describes the changes we allow subsequently: for example, `VC` corresponds to the change of one vowel and one consonant.

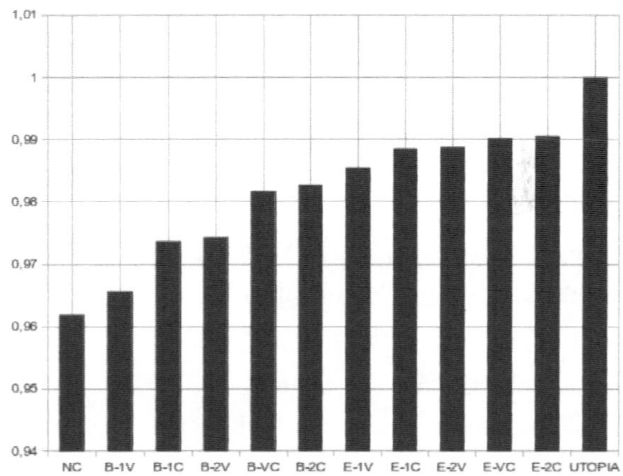

Figure 2: Evaluation of the closest word finder

7 Discussion and future work

In this work, we have presented a basic system for scansion of English poetry. The evaluation results are promising: a qualitative analysis of the remaining errors reveals that the system, while still containing errors vis-à-vis human expert judgements, makes very few egregious errors. The assignment of global meter to entire poems is also very robust. We expect to develop the system in several respects. Of primary concern is to add statistical information about the global properties of poems to resolve uncertain cases in a manner consistent with the overall structure of a given poem. Such additions could resolve ambiguous lines and try to make them fit the global pattern of a poem. Secondly, there is still room for improvement in unknown word performance. Also, the part-of-speech tagging process may be profitably replaced by a deterministic FST-based tagger such as Brill's tagger, as presented in Roche and Schabes (1995). This would allow the representation of the entire tool as a single FST.

We believe that the availability of a gold-standard corpus of expert scansion offers a valuable improvement in the quantitative assessment of the performance of future systems and modifications.

Acknowledgments

We must refer to Herbert Tucker, author of the "For Better for Verse" project, which has been fundamental to evaluate our system. We also must mention the Scholar's Lab, an arm of the University of Virginia Library, without whose aid in development and ongoing maintenance support the cited project would be impossible. Joseph Gilbert and Bethany Nowviskie have been most steadily helpful there.

References

Beesley, K. R. and Karttunen, L. (2003). Finite-state morphology: Xerox tools and techniques. *CSLI, Stanford.*

Carroll, L. (2003). *Alice's adventures in wonderland and through the looking glass.* Penguin.

Fussell, P. (1965). *Poetic Meter and Poetic Form.* McGraw Hill.

Greene, E., Bodrumlu, T., and Knight, K. (2010). Automatic analysis of rhythmic poetry with applications to generation and translation. In *Proceedings of the 2010 Conference on Empirical Methods in Natural Language Processing*, pages 524–533. Association for Computational Linguistics.

Groves, P. L. (1998). *Strange music: the metre of the English heroic line*, volume 74. English Literary Studies.

Halácsy, P., Kornai, A., and Oravecz, C. (2007). Hunpos: an open source trigram tagger. In *Proceedings of the 45th Annual Meeting of the ACL on Interactive Poster and Demonstration Sessions*, pages 209–212. Association for Computational Linguistics.

Hartman, C. O. (1996). *Virtual muse: experiments in computer poetry.* Wesleyan University Press.

Hulden, M. (2009). Foma: a finite-state compiler and library. In *Proceedings of the 12th Conference of the European Chapter of the Association for Computational Linguistics: Demonstrations Session*, pages 29–32. Association for Computational Linguistics.

Keats, J. (2007). *Poems published in 1820.* Project Gutenberg.

Marcus, M. P., Marcinkiewicz, M. A., and Santorini, B. (1993). Building a large annotated corpus of english: The penn treebank. *Computational linguistics*, 19(2):313–330.

McAleese, G. (2007). Improving scansion with syntax: an investigation into the effectiveness of a syntactic analysis of poetry by computer using phonological scansion theory. -.

Plamondon, M. R. (2006). Virtual verse analysis: Analysing patterns in poetry. *Literary and Linguistic Computing*, 21(suppl 1):127–141.

Roche, E. and Schabes, Y. (1995). Deterministic part-of-speech tagging with finite-state transducers. *Computational linguistics*, 21(2):227–253.

Sejnowski, T. J. and Rosenberg, C. R. (1987). Parallel networks that learn to pronounce English text. *Complex systems*, 1(1):145–168.

Shakespeare, W. (1609). *Shakespeare's sonnets.* Thomas Thorpe.

Shakespeare, W. (1997). *Romeo and Juliet.* Project Gutenberg.

Shakespeare, W. (2000). *The tragedy of Hamlet*, volume 1122. Project Gutenberg.

Stevens, W. (1923). *Harmonium.* Academy of American Poets.

Weide, R. (1998). The CMU pronunciation dictionary, release 0.6.

A Convexity-based Generalization of Viterbi for Non-Deterministic Weighted Automata

Marc Dymetman
Xerox Research Centre Europe
Grenoble, France
marc.dymetman@xrce.xerox.com

Abstract

We propose a novel approach for the max-string problem in acyclic nondeterministic weighted FSA's, which is based on a convexity-related notion of domination among intermediary results, and which can be seen as a generalization of the usual dynamic programming technique for finding the max-path (a.k.a. Viterbi approximation) in such automata.

1 Introduction

Let A be an acyclic weighted finite-state automaton (WFSA) on a vocabulary V with weights in the (extended) set of non-negative reals $\mathbb{R}_+^\infty = [0, \infty]$, which we assume to be combined multiplicatively.

We can consider two problems. The first one, *max-path*, is to find the *path* π of maximum weight in the automaton, that is, the path that maximizes the product of the weights associated with its transitions; the second one, *max-string*, is to find the *string* x in V^* that maximizes the sum of the weights of all the paths that yield x. While the max-string problem is often the most important in principle, it is much more difficult to solve than the max-path problem; in fact (Casacuberta and de la Higuera, 2000) show that the problem is NP-hard: they describe a class of acyclic weighted automata that encode the Satisfiability problem (SAT) in such a way that identifying the max-string in such automata in polynomial time would imply a polynomial solution to SAT. In practice, one tends to use the max-path solution as a proxy to the max-string solution; this approximation employs the *Viterbi* algorithm (Viterbi, 1967), and is widely used in speech recognition, machine translation and other NLP tasks. The contribution of this paper is to propose a novel approach for the max-string problem over the "sum-times" semiring $K_s \equiv (\mathbb{R}_+^\infty, +, \cdot, 0, 1)$, involving a generalization of the Viterbi procedure.

A naive approach to the max-string problem would consist in enumerating all the paths, summing the weights of paths corresponding to the same string, and outputting the maximum string.

Another, more appealing, approach consists in noting that in the case of a *deterministic* weighted automaton A', the max-string and max-path problems coincide, and therefore in trying to determinize A, and then apply the standard Viterbi algorithm. However, while existing techniques for determinizing a weighted automaton (Mohri, 1997; Mohri, 2009) work reasonably well in some practical cases over the "max-times" semiring $(\mathbb{R}_+^\infty, \max, \cdot, 0, 1)$,[1] they often — rather counter-intuitively — lead to combinatorial explosion when working in the sum-times semiring, even in cases where the automaton is acyclic and where the classical (unweighted) determinization of A does not explode (Buchsbaum et al., 1998).[2] While the applications of determinization cited in (Mohri, 2009) to such domains as speech recognition tend to focus on the max-times semiring, we are aware of one application where determinization is based on the sum-times semiring, but in a slightly different formal situation (May and Knight, 2006). In this paper, the authors generalize the determinization technique of (Mohri, 1997) from string to tree automata, and then address the question of determinizing a weighted tree

[1] This semiring is isomorphic to the more common "tropical" semiring, through a logarithmic mapping.

[2] A simple example of a cyclic automaton over the sum-times semiring which is not determinizable at all is given in (Aminof et al., 2011).

automaton generating a set of trees, where each tree represents a possible translation of a fixed source sentence, in the context of a syntax-based SMT system (they also present an application to data-oriented parsing). In this way they are often able, at least for short sentences, to find the translation tree of maximum total weight in reasonable time. A similar technique, directly based on (Mohri, 1997), but using the sum-times semiring over a string automaton, could presumably be tempted for the weighted lattices produced by a phrase-based translation system such as Moses (Koehn et al., 2007), but we are not aware of any such attempt.

The novelty of our approach to the max-string problem is that it bypasses the need for a preliminary determinization of the automaton before applying Viterbi, but instead proposes to apply a generalization of Viterbi directly to the original non-deterministic automaton. Let us now describe this approach.

Elements of V are called symbols, elements of V^* strings. It will be convenient to assume that the automaton A has a special form: (i) it has exactly one initial state q_0 and one final state q_f, (ii) there is a special "end-of-string" symbol $ in V, (iii) $ only appears on transitions to q_f, and no other symbol can appear on such a transition, (iv) transitions labeled with $ have weight 1 or 0.[3]

In a nutshell and informally, the main idea is then the following. Consider a string $x = a_1 a_2 \ldots a_k$. If A were deterministic, then, starting from q_0, this string would end in a single state q and would assign to this state a certain weight w equal to the product of the weights associated with the transitions of x; then, if some other string x' also ended in q, but with a higher weight w', then we would know that x could not be a prefix of the max-string for A; this observation contains the essence of the Viterbi procedure: for each state q, it is sufficient to only "remember" the prefix string producing the highest weight at q. Now, when A is non-deterministic, the string x can end in *several* states $q_1, ..., q_m$ simultaneously, with weights $w_1, ..., w_m$; in this case, if it happens that some other string x' ends in the same states, but with weights $w'_1, ..., w'_m$ s.t. $w'_1 > w_1, ..., w'_m > w_m$, then it can be shown that x cannot be a prefix of the max-string for A, and we can then discard x; as we will see, we can also discard x under weaker "domination" conditions, namely when the weight vector $w = (w_1, ..., w_m)$ associated with x belongs to a certain kind of convex hull of "dominating" vectors associated with a set S of prefix strings. Using this observation, we only need to explicitely store the set S of dominating prefix strings; whatever the suffix used to go to the final state, at least one of these dominating prefixes will lead to a better result with this suffix than using a dominated prefix x with the same suffix.

[3]These conditions are not restrictive, as it is easy to transform any A into this form, by adding to each final state of the original automaton an outgoing edge of weight 1 with label $ and target q_f. It can be verified that the weight of a string of symbols $a_1 a_2 \ldots a_k$ relative to the original automaton is equal to that of the string $a_1 a_2 \ldots a_k\$$ relative to the transformed automaton.

2 Preliminaries

Automata and transition matrices Let us define $U = V \setminus \{\$\}$. The weighted automaton A can be viewed as associating, with each symbol $a \in U$ a transition matrix, that we will also call a, of dimension $D \times D$ over the non-negative reals $\mathbb{R}_+^\infty$, where D is the number of non-final states in A; the coordinate a_{ij} of that matrix is equal to the weight of the transition of label a between q_i and q_j, this weight being null if there is no such transition. The initial state q_0 of the automaton can be identified with the D-dimensional line vector $(1, 0, ..., 0)$, and the distribution of weights over the (non-final) states of A after having consumed the string $a_1 a_2 \ldots a_k$ is then given by the D-dimensional line vector $(1, 0, ..., 0) \cdot a_1 \cdot a_2 \ldots \cdot a_k$, where the $a_1, \ldots, a_k$'s are identified with their matrices.

Due to our assumptions on the symbol $, we can identify $ with a D-dimensional *column* vector $(w_0, w_1, ..., w_{D-1})^\top$, where w_i is equal to 1 or to 0. The weight relative to the automaton of a string of the form $a_1 a_2 \ldots a_p\$$ is then obtained by computing the scalar value $(1, 0, ..., 0) \cdot a_1 \cdot a_2 \cdots \cdot a_p \cdot \$$, which can also be viewed as a scalar product of a line vector with the column vector $.

Convex, ortho and ortho-convex hulls We now need to introduce the notions of convex, ortho, and ortho-convex hulls. Let d be a positive integer, and let S be a set (finite or not) of d-dimensional vectors over the non-negative reals. We say that:

- The vector u is in the *convex-hull* (or *c-hull*) of S iff we can write u as a finite sum $u = \sum_j \alpha_j s_j$, with $s_j \in S$, $j \in [1, m]$, $\sum_j \alpha_j =$

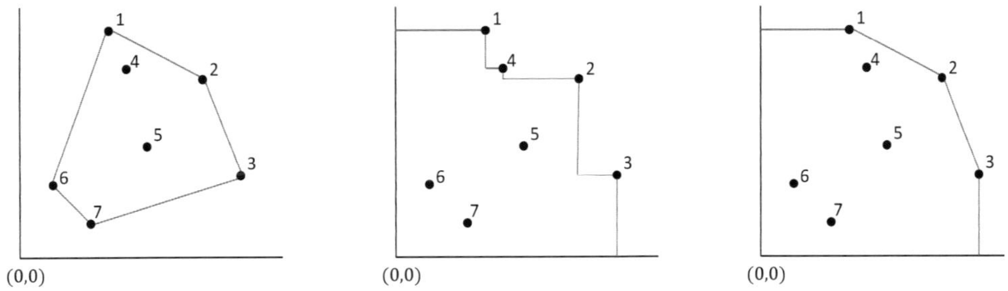

Figure 1: The sets $\{1, 2, 3, 6, 7\}$ [left pane], $\{1, 2, 3, 4\}$ [middle pane], and $\{1, 2, 3\}$ [right pane] are subsets of dominators of the set $W = \{1, 2, 3, 4, 5, 6, 7\}$, respectively relative to the notions of convex-hull, ortho-hull, and ortho-convex hull.

$1, \alpha_j \geq 0$. This is the standard notion.

- The vector u is in the *ortho-hull* (or *o-hull*) of S iff there exists a $v \in S$ s.t. $u \leq v$, where the inequality is interpreted to hold for each coordinate. The ortho-hull is in general not convex.
- The vector u is in the *ortho-convex-hull* (or *oc-hull*) of S iff u is in the ortho-hull of the convex-hull of S. It is easy to check that the ortho-convex-hull is convex.[4]

When a set W of d-vectors is contained in the hull of some subset $S \subset W$, then we will say that S is a set of "dominators" of W, relative to the specific notion of hull used. Figure 1 illustrates these notions for dimension $d = 2$.

Lemma *If x is in the convex-hull (resp. ortho-hull, ortho-convex-hull) of S, and if z is a non-negative d-vector, then there exists $s \in S$ such that $x.z \leq s.z$, where . denotes scalar product.*[5]

3 Algorithm

Algorithm 1 is our main algorithm. The integer k corresponds to a stage of the algorithm. W is a set of pairs of the form (*prefix, vector*), where *prefix* is a string not ending in \$, and *vector* is the D-dimensional vector associated with this prefix; for each stage k of the algorithm, $W = W_k$ contains only prefixes of length k, and $S = S_k$ is a subset of dominators of W_k; $F = F_k$ is either the empty set or is a singleton set containing a pair of the form (*string, number*), where *string* is a string ending in \$ and *number* is a scalar.

Algorithm 1 MAIN

1: $k \leftarrow 0, F \leftarrow \emptyset, W \leftarrow \{(\epsilon, (1, 0, \ldots, 0))\}$
2: **while** $W \neq \emptyset$ **do**
3: $\quad S \leftarrow$ DOMINATORS(W)
4: $\quad k \leftarrow k + 1$
5: $\quad (W, F) \leftarrow$ FORWARD(S, F)
6: **return** F

On line 1, we initialize F to the empty set, and W to the empty string prefix ϵ together with a vector carrying weight 1 on q_0 and weight 0 on the other states. On line 2, we loop until W is empty. On line 3, we extract a subset S of dominators from W, according to one of the three hull variants we have described. We then increment k, and on line 5, we compute through the FORWARD procedure the next version of W and F corresponding to strings of length $k + 1$. Lastly, on line 6, we return the final result F, which is either empty (when A does not recognize any string), or contains a pair (*string, number*) where *string* is a[6] max-string for A and *number* its total weight. The loop in line 2 terminates because the automaton is acyclic: all prefixes above a certain length will eventually be mapped to the null D-vector which will result in producing at a certain point an empty W_k.

[4] Our notion of oc-hull is related to that of *anti-blocking polyhedra* in the LP literature (Schrijver, 1998).

[5] *Proof sketch.* Suppose by contradiction that for all $s \in S$, we have $s.z < x.z$. But now (i) if x is in the convex-hull of S, then x can be written as the convex combination $x = \sum_i \alpha_i s_i$ of elements s_i in S; therefore $x.z = \sum_i \alpha_i s_i.z < x.z$, a contradiction; (ii) if x is in the ortho-hull of S, then there exists $s \in S$ s.t. $x \leq s$ coordinate-wise, hence $x.z \leq s.z$ by the non-negativity of z, again a contradiction; (iii) if x is in the ortho-convex-hull of S, then there exists x' s.t. $x \leq x'$ and x' can be written as $x' = \sum_i \alpha_i s_i$, and we can combine the two previous arguments to again reach a contradiction.

[6] The max-string is not always unique: several strings may reach the same maximum.

Algorithm 2 FORWARD(S, F)

1: $W \leftarrow \emptyset$
2: **for** $(\textit{prefix}, \textit{vector}) \in S$ **do**
3: $\quad F \leftarrow \text{MAX}(F, (\textit{prefix}.\$, \textit{vector}.\$))$
4: $\quad$ **for** $a \in U$ **and** $\textit{vector}.a \neq 0$ **do**
5: $\quad\quad W \leftarrow W \cup \{(\textit{prefix}.a, \textit{vector}.a)\}$
6: **return** (W, F)

Algorithm 2 defines the FORWARD procedure. We start by initializing W to the empty set, then for each pair $(\textit{prefix}, \textit{vector})$ in S we do the following. On line 3, we compute the concatenated string *prefix*.\$ along with its weight, given by the scalar product *vector*.\$; If *vector*.\$ is equal to 0, then MAX does not modify F, if F is empty MAX returns the singleton set $(\textit{prefix}.\$, \textit{vector}.\$)$, and finally if $F = \{(\textit{string}, \textit{number})\}$ it returns either $\{(\textit{string}, \textit{number})\}$ or $\{(\textit{prefix}.\$, \textit{vector}.\$)\}$ according to which of *number* or *vector*.\$ is the largest. On line 4, for each symbol a in U such that $\textit{vector}.a$ is not null, we add to W the pair consisting of the prefix string $\textit{prefix}.a$ and of the vector $\textit{vector}.a$. Finally we return the pair (W, F).

Theorem *Whatever the notion of hull used for defining* DOMINATORS *in Algorithm 1, if the result F is empty, then the language of the automaton is empty; otherwise $F = \{(\textit{string}, \textit{number})\}$, where 'number' is the maximum weight of a string relative to the automaton A, and where 'string' ends in \$ and is of weight 'number'.*[7]

We still need to explain how we define the DOMINATORS procedure in Algorithm 1, depending on which notion of hull is chosen. Line 3 of the algorithm consists in pruning the set of prefixes W to get the subset S, and the efficiency of the algorithm as a whole depends on pruning as much as possible at each level k, thus it is in our interest to extract a small set of dominators from W. To simplify the description here, we will pretend that an element $(\textit{prefix}, \textit{vector})$ of W is identified with its second component *vector*, and will identify W to a set of vectors; we can easily recover the prefix associated with each vector at the end of the process. Let us start with the simplest case, that of the ortho-hull. In that case, the minimal set of dominators for W is easily shown to be simply the set of all vectors that survive after eliminating any $w \in W$ s.t. there exists another $w' \in W$ with $w \leq w'$; a straightforward quadratic algorithm in the size of W can be designed for that purpose. If the hull is the convex-hull, the minimal set of dominators is the set of so-called *extreme points* from W, for which there exist several algorithms (Helbling, 2010). Overall, the ortho-convex hull is more effective at pruning than both the ortho- and the convex-hull. Let us therefore give some indications on how to compute a minimal set of dominators relative to the oc-hull.

Similar to the o-hull case, we want to eliminate any w from W which is in the oc-hull of the remaining vectors $w_1, ..., w_n$ of W. Such a vector is determined by the condition that one can find a convex combination $\sum_i \alpha_i w_i$ such that $w \leq \sum_i \alpha_i w_i$. We can directly map this problem into a Linear Programming format, for which a large number of solvers are available: the solver is asked to decide whether the following LP, in the variables $\alpha_1, ..., \alpha_n$, is *feasible*:[8]

$$\sum_i \alpha_i = 1,$$
$$\sum_i \alpha_i w_i - w \geq 0,$$
$$\alpha_i \geq 0, \forall i.$$

The complexity of this oc-hull algorithm is on the order of $n+1$ times the complexity for solving one instance of the LP above, which cannot be characterized simply and depends on the type of solver used (simplex vs. interior-point based). However, the preliminary experiments we have conducted indicate that it is more efficient to first prune W relative to the o-hull notion, which already eliminates many points and only then prune this intermediary result using the LP formulation above (this can be shown to preserve the notion of oc-dominators).

[7] *Proof sketch.* Let T be the set of strings (often, this set is actually a singleton) ending in \$ which do reach the actual max-string weight relative to the automaton. Call "rank" of a string $t \in T$ the largest number k such that a prefix of t appears in S_k, and let us focus on a t which has maximal rank k relative to the other elements of T, and on its prefix x of length k. In case $t = x.\$$, then t "makes it" to F in line 5 of Algorithm 1, and we are done. Otherwise t can be written as $t = x.a.z$, with $a \in U$, and with $x.a \notin S_{k+1}$. But then, by the Lemma, there exists $s \in S_{k+1}$ s.t., in vectorial terms, $x.a.z \leq s.z$, and therefore, because of the definition of T, the string $s.z$ also belongs to T; but $s.z$ has rank $k+1$, a contradiction.

[8] This LP is our adaptation to the ortho-convex-hull case of a similar program described by (Helbling, 2010) for the convex-hull case, of which more sophisticated versions are also proposed.

4 Conclusion

The procedure that we have described can be seen as a generalization of the standard Viterbi technique. Viterbi (even in the case of an original non-deterministic automaton) can be formulated in terms of a max-string problem over a certain deterministic automaton. For such a deterministic automaton, our procedure only produces vectors that are each placed on a *single* axis of $\mathbb{R}^D$, corresponding to the single state reached by the corresponding prefix. In this case it can be checked that o-dominators and oc-dominators lead to the same result, namely to *keeping the maximum point on each axis separately*, which exactly corresponds to the Viterbi procedure, which keeps the maximum on each state independently of other states.

It should also be noted that pruning the space of prefixes using the oc-hull construction appears to be the best we can hope to achieve if we are not allowed to use heuristics that look forward in the automaton: it can be shown that by appropriately choosing the weights of transitions not yet seen at level k, the max-string can be made to "select" *any* of the oc-dominators from W_k — this is however not true for the c-dominators or the o-dominators.

We believe the method to have potential applications to such domains as speech recognition or phrase-based statistical machine translation; the latter in particular tends to produce large word lattices where many paths can correspond to the same string; there the main object of interest is the max-string, to which the Viterbi best-path is only an approximation. More generally, the method could be of interest for doing inference with Hidden Markov Models, when the objects of real interest are not the hidden paths in the HMM, but rather the projections of these paths onto sequences of directly interpretable labels.

Acknowledgments

Thanks to Salah Aït-Mokhtar, Nicola Cancedda and András Sebö for discussions on a preliminary version of this paper, and to the anonymous reviewers for pointing to some important references that I had not identified.

References

B. Aminof, O. Kupferman, and R. Lampert. 2011. Rigorous approximated determinization of weighted automata. In *Logic in Computer Science (LICS), 2011 26th Annual IEEE Symposium on*, pages 345 –354, june.

Adam L. Buchsbaum, Raffaele Giancarlo, and Jeffery Westbrook. 1998. On the determinization of weighted finite automata. In *ICALP'98*, pages 482–493.

Francisco Casacuberta and Colin de la Higuera. 2000. Computational complexity of problems on probabilistic grammars and transducers. In *ICGI*, pages 15–24.

Christian Helbling. 2010. Extreme Points in Medium and High Dimensions. Master's thesis, Dpt of Computer Science, ETH Zrich.

Philipp Koehn, Hieu Hoang, Alexandra Birch, Chris Callison-Burch, Marcello Federico, Nicola Bertoldi, Brooke Cowan, Wade Shen, Christine Moran, Richard Zens, Chris Dyer, Ondrej Bojar, Alexandra Constantin, and Evan Herbst. 2007. Moses: Open source toolkit for statistical machine translation. In *ACL*. The Association for Computer Linguistics.

Jonathan May and Kevin Knight. 2006. A better n-best list: Practical determinization of weighted finite tree automata. In *HLT-NAACL*.

Mehryar Mohri and Michael Riley. 2002. An efficient algorithm for the n-best-strings problem. In *In Proceedings of the International Conference on Spoken Language Processing 2002 (ICSLP 02*.

Mehryar Mohri. 1997. Finite-state transducers in language and speech processing. *Comput. Linguist.*, 23(2):269–311.

Mehryar Mohri. 2009. Weighted automata algorithms. In Manfred Droste, Werner Kuich, and Heiko Vogler, editors, *Handbook of Weighted Automata*, pages 213–254. Springer.

Alexander Schrijver. 1998. *Theory of Linear and Integer Programming*. Wiley.

Andrew J. Viterbi. 1967. Error bounds for convolutional codes and an asymptotically optimum decoding algorithm. *IEEE Transactions on Information Theory*, IT-13(2):260–269, April.

Processing Structured Input with Skipping Nested Automata

Dominika Pawlik
University of Warsaw
Institute of Mathematics

Aleksander Zabłocki
University of Warsaw
Institute of Informatics

Bartosz Zaborowski
Polish Academy of Sciences
Institute of Computer Science

{dominika, olekz}@mimuw.edu.pl, b.zaborowski@ipipan.waw.pl

Abstract

We propose a new kind of finite-state automata, suitable for structured input characters corresponding to unranked trees of small depth. As a motivating application, we regard executing morphosyntactic queries on a richly annotated text corpus.

1 Introduction

Efficient lookup in natural language corpora becomes increasingly important, correspondingly to the growth of their size. We focus on complex queries, involving regular expressions over segments and specifying their syntactic attributes (e.g. "find all sequences of five nouns or gerunds in a row"). For such queries, indexing the corpus is in general not sufficient; finite-state devices come then as the natural tool to use.

The linguistic annotation of the text seems to be getting still more complex. To illustrate that, German articles in the IMS Workbench are annotated with sets of *readings*, i.e. possible tuples of the grammatical case, number and gender (an example is shown in Fig. 1a). Several other big corpora are stored in XML files, making it easy to extend their annotation in the future if so desired.

Hence, we consider a general setting where the segments are tree-shaped feature structures of fixed type, with list-valued attributes allowed (see Fig. 1a). A corpus query in this model should be a regular expression over segment specifications, being in turn Boolean combinations of attribute specifications, with quantifiers used in the case of list-valued attributes. We may also wish to allow specifying string-valued attributes by regular expressions. For instance, *der Tisch* /the table$_{masculine}$/ is a match for the expression[1]

$$\big[(\text{POS} \mathrel{!=} \mathsf{N} \ \vee\ \text{WORD} = \text{".*}sch\text{"})$$
$$\wedge\ \exists_{i \in \text{READ}}\,(i.\text{GEND} = \mathsf{m}\ \wedge\ i.\text{NUMB} = \mathsf{sg})\big]^*$$

describing sequences of segments having a masculine-singular reading, in which all nouns end with *sch*.

In this paper, we propose an adjustment of existing finite-state solutions suited for queries in such model. Our crucial assumption is that the input, although unranked, has a reasonably *bounded depth*, e.g. by 10. This is the case in morphosyntactic analysis (but often not in syntactic parsing).

2 Related Work

There are two existing approaches which seem promising for regex matching over structured alphabets. As we will see, each has an advantage over the other.

FSAP model. The first model relies on finite-state automata with predicates assigned to their edges (FSAP, (van Noord and Gerdemann, 2001)). (A FSAP runs as follows: in a single step, it tests which of the edges leaving the current states are labeled with a predicate satisfied by the current input symbol, and non-deterministically follows these edges). In our case, pattern matching can be realized by a FSAP over the infinite alphabet of *segments*: one segment becomes one input symbol, and segment specifications become predicates.

As showed by van Noord and Gerdemann, FSAPs are potentially efficient as they admit determinization. However, this involves some Boolean operations on the predicates used; as a result, testing predicates for segments might become involved. For example, a non-optimized (purely syntax-driven) evaluation of

$$\exists_{x \in \text{READ}}\, x.\text{CASE} = \mathsf{N} \wedge \exists_{y \in \text{READ}}\, y.\text{CASE} = \mathsf{G} \quad (1)$$

would consist of two iterations over all the readings (one looking for N and another for G), although in fact one iteration is clearly sufficient. As

[1] This example query is rather useless by itself; however, it compactly demonstrates several features which (variously combined) have been found needed in NLP applications.

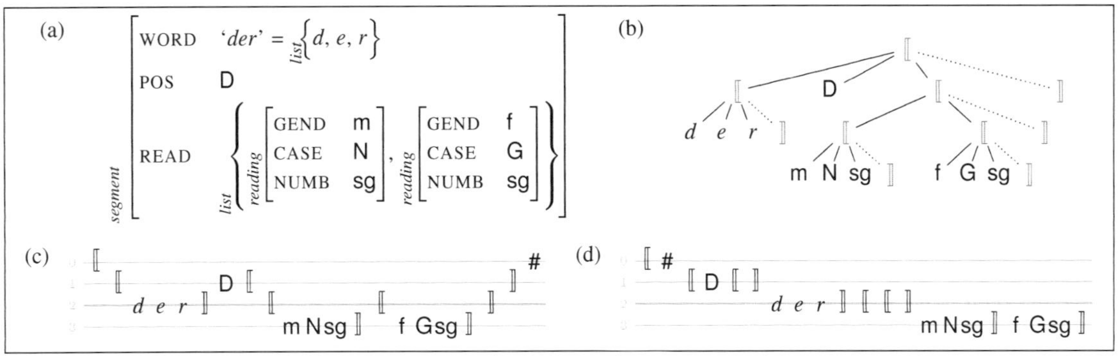

Figure 1: A sample segment for the German ambiguous article *der*, which can be masculine nominative as well as feminine genitive (for brevity, other its readings are ignored), presented as a typed feature structure (a) and as an unranked tree (b). Note that strings are treated as lists, which ensures finiteness of the alphabet. We adjust the tree representation by labeling every non-leaf with ⟦ and appending a new leaf labeled with ⟧ to its children. Parts (c) and (d) show respectively the prefix-order and breadth-first linearizations of the tree. For legibility, we display them stratified wrt. the original depth.

we will see, the other approach is free of this problem.

VPA model. Instead of treating segments as single symbols, we might treat our input as a bounded-depth ordered unranked tree over a finite alphabet (see Fig. 1b), which is a common perspective in the theory of XML processing and tree automata. Recently, several flavours of determinizable tree automata for unranked trees have been proposed, see (Comon et al., 2007), (Murata, 2001) and (Gauwin et al., 2008). Under our assumptions, all these models are practically covered by the elegant notion of *visibly pushdown automata* (VPA; see (Alur and Madhusudan, 2004)). As explained in (Alur and Madhusudan, 2009), executing a VPA on a given tree may be roughly understood as processing its prefix-order linearization (see Fig. 1b–c) with a suitably enhanced classical FSA. We omit the details as they are not important for the scope of this paper.

Discussion. FSAPs and VPAs both have potential advantages over each other. For the example rule (1), a naive FSAP will scan the input two times while a deterministic VPA will do it only once. On the other hand, the VPA will read all input symbols, including the irrelevant values of POS, GEND and NUMB, while a FSAP will simply *skip* over them.

We would like to combine these two advantages, that is, design a flavour of tree automata allowing both determinization and *skipping* in the above sense (see Fig. 2b for an example). Although this might be seen as a minor adjustment of the FSAP model (or one of the tree-theoretic models cited above), it looks to us that it has not been mentioned so far in the literature.[2]

Finally, we mention concepts which are only seemingly related. Some authors consider *jumping* or *skipping* for automata in different meanings, e.g. simply moving from a state to another, or compressing the input to the list of gap lengths between consecutive occurrences of a given symbol (Wang, 2012), which is somehow related but far less general. In some important finite-state frameworks, like XFST (Beesley and Karttunen, 2003) and NooJ, certain substrings (like +Verb) can be logically treated as single input symbols. However, what we need is nesting such clusters, combined with a choice for an automaton whether to inspect the contents of a cluster or to skip it over.

3 Skipping nested automata

Let Σ be a finite alphabet, augmented with additional symbols $\llbracket$, $\rrbracket$, $\#$ (see Fig. 1). We follow the definitions and notation for unranked Σ-trees from (Comon et al., 2007, Sec. 8), in particular, we identify a Σ-tree t with its labeling function $t : \mathbb{N}^* \supseteq Pos(t) \to \Sigma$. For $p \in Pos(t)$, we denote its depth (i.e. its length as a word) by $d(p)$.

Let $p \in Pos(t)$, $d \leq d(p) + 1$ and $s > 0$. We define the (d, s)-*successor* of p, denoted $p[d, s]$,

[2]A sort of skipping is allowed in tree walking automata (Aho and Ullman, 1971), which can be roughly described as Turing machines for trees. However, they do not allow skipping over several siblings at once. Also, as shown in (Bojańczyk and Colcombet, 2006), they may be not determinizable.

to be the s-th vertex at depth d following p in the prefix order[3], and leave it undefined if this vertex does not exist. We also set $p[d(p), 0] = p$.

A *skipping nested automaton* (SNA) over Σ is a tuple $A = (Q, Q_I, Q_F, \delta, d)$, where Q (resp. Q_I, Q_F) is the set of all (resp. initial, final) states, $d : Q \to \mathbb{N}$ is the *depth* function and $\delta \subseteq Q \times \Sigma \times Q \times \mathbb{N}_+$ is a finite set of transitions, such that

$$d(q) = 0 \quad \text{for } q \in Q_I,$$

$$d(q') \leq d(q) + 1 \quad \text{for } (q, \sigma, q', s) \in \delta.$$

(The intuitive meaning of $d(q)$ is the depth of the next symbol to be read when q is the current state, which leads to some kind of skipping. Introducing s will allow performing more general skips).

A *run* of A on a Σ-tree t is a sequence $\rho = \big((p_i, q_i)\big)_{i=0}^{n} \subseteq Pos(t) \times Q$ such that $p_0 = t(\varepsilon)$, $q_0 \in Q_I$ and for every $i < n$ there is $s \in \mathbb{N}$ such that $(q_i, t(p_i), q_{i+1}, s) \in \delta$ and $p_{i+1} = p_i[d(q_{i+1}), s]$. We say that ρ *reads* p_i and *skips over* all positions between p_i and p_{i+1} in the prefix order. We say that ρ is *accepting* if $q_n \in Q_F$. A tree is *accepted* by A if there is an accepting run on it. An example is shown in Fig. 2.

A run $\rho = \big((p_i, q_i)\big)_{i=0}^{n}$ is *crashing* if there is $(q_n, t(p_n), q_{n+1}, s) \in \delta$ such that $p_n[d(q_{n+1}), s]$ is undefined. (Intuitively, this means jumping to a non-existent node). We say that A *processes* t *safely* if *all* its runs on t are not crashing. This property turns out to be important for determinization (see Section 4). A tree t is *accepted safely* if it is processed safely and accepted.

In practice, safe processing of trees coming from *typed* feature structures (as in Fig. 1) can be ensured with the aid of analyzing the types. For example, the SNA shown in Fig. 2 can assume state q_2 only at (the start of) a *reading*, which must have four children; hence the skipping transition from q_2 to q_3 is safe. On the other hand, we cannot use e.g. a transition from q_1 to q_2 with $s = 3$ because a *list* (here, of readings) may turn out to have only one child. We omit a general formal treatment of this issue since it trivialises in our intended applications.

[3]This is the s-th child of p if $d = d(p) + 1$, and the s-th right sibling of the $\big(d(p) - d\big)$-fold parent of p otherwise. (Note that in the second case $d(p) - d$ must be non-negative; for $d(p) - d = 0$, the "0-fold parent" of p means simply p).

4 (Quasi-)determinization

A SNA $A = (Q, Q_I, Q_F, \delta, d)$ is *deterministic* if, for every q and σ, there is at most one $(q, \sigma, q', s) \in \delta$. By *quasi-determinization* we mean building a deterministic SNA $\overline{A} = (\overline{Q}, \overline{Q}_I, \overline{Q}_F, \overline{\delta}, \overline{d})$ which accepts *safely* the same trees which A does.

Let S denote the highest value of s appearing in A. We say that $(q, r) \in Q \times [0, S]$ is an *option for A at p wrt. p_0* if there is a run ρ of A on t which ends in $(p_0[d(q), r], q)$ such that p either is the final position of ρ or is skipped over by ρ in its last step. A state of $\overline{A}$ will be a set of possible options for A at a given position wrt. itself.

We define:

$$\overline{Q} = 2^{Q \times [0,S]}, \qquad \overline{Q}_I = \{\{(q, 0)\} \mid q \in Q_I\},$$

$$\overline{Q}_F = \{X \in \overline{Q} \mid X \cap (Q_F \times \{0\}) \neq \emptyset\}.$$

$$\overline{d}(X) = \max_{(q,r) \in X} d(q) \quad \text{for } X \in \overline{Q}.$$

It remains to define $\overline{\delta}$. For each $X \in \overline{Q}$, $\sigma \in \Sigma$, it shall contain a tuple $\big(X, \sigma, X'', s\big)$, where X'', s are computed by setting $d = \overline{d}(X)$, computing

$$X' = \big\{(q, r) \in X \,:\, d(q) < d \vee r > 0\big\} \cup$$
$$\{(q', r') \,:\, (q, \sigma, q', r') \in \delta, (q, 0) \in X,\, d(q) = d\},$$

(intuitively, this is the set of options for A at $p' = p[d(p), 1]$ wrt. p, provided that p' exists), then setting $d' = \overline{d}(X')$ and finally

$$s = \min\big\{r \,:\, (q, r) \in X',\, d(q) = d'\big\},$$

$$X'' = \big\{(q, r) \in X' \,:\, d(q) < d'\big\} \cup$$
$$\big\{(q, r - s) \,:\, (q, r) \in X',\, d(q) = d'\big\}.$$

(Explanation: $p'' = p[d', s]$ is the nearest (wrt. the prefix order) ending position of any of the runs corresponding to the options from X'; hence $\overline{A}$ may jump directly to p''; the options at p'' wrt. p are the same as at p', i.e. X'; hence, the target X'' is obtained from X' by "re-basing" from p to p''.)

While the trees *accepted safely* by A and $\overline{A}$ coincide, this is not true for simply *accepted* trees. For example, the tree t corresponding (in the prefix order) to $[\![a]\!]\#$ is accepted by A defined as

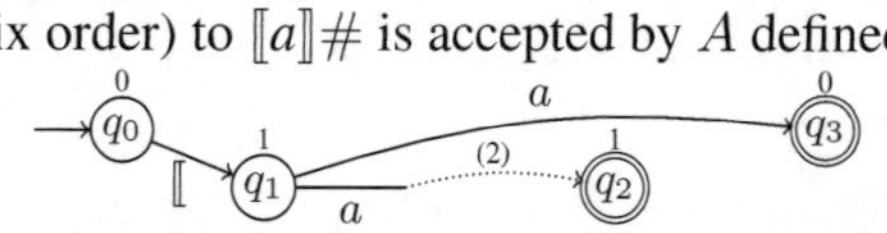

(there is a run ending in q_3) but not by $\overline{A}$ because for $X = \{(q_1, 0)\}$ and $\sigma = a$ we obtain $\overline{d}(X'') = \overline{d}(X') = 1$ and $s = 2$, leading to a crash in the only run of $\overline{A}$ on t.

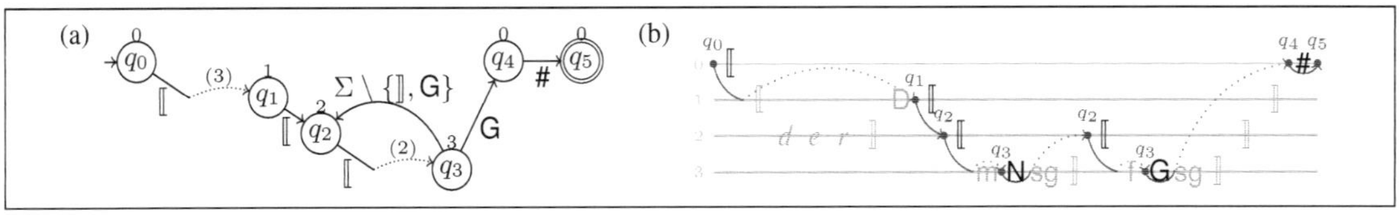

Figure 2: A SNA accepting a segment followed by # (end of input) and having a genitive reading (a), and its run on the segment from the previous figure (b). In part (a), numbers above states are their depths; numbers above dotted arcs are the values of s (not shown when $s = 1$). In part (b), the black symbols are read while the gray symbols are skipped over; this corresponds to the continuous and dotted arcs.

5 Practical use

In order to make SNA applicable, we should explain how to build SNAs corresponding to typical corpus queries, and also *how* skipping should be efficiently performed in practice.

It is straightforward to build a non-skipping SNA for a regular expression e over Σ provided that e does not contain ⟦ or ⟧ inside ?, * or $^+$, and all their occurrences are well-matched inside every branch of |. Under our assumption of bounded input depth, every regular expression can be transformed to an equivalent one of that form.

Skipping SNAs in our applications are defined by an additional regex construct _, matching any single sub-tree of the input. This is compiled into $\rightarrow\bigcirc \xrightarrow{\Sigma} \circledcirc$ (with $d \equiv 0$), which makes a skip if the input starts with ⟦. To enhance even longer skips, patterns of the form $\_\{n\}$ and ⟦e_*⟧ are suitably optimized. For example, the SNA of Fig. 2 recognizes ⟦__⟦_*⟦_G_*⟧_*⟧_*⟧#.

Proceeding to skipping in practice, we assume that, as a result of pre-processing, we are given the breadth-first linearization $\tilde{t} \in \Sigma^*$ of the input (see Fig. 1d), stored physically as an array (for a given i, accessing $\tilde{t}[i]$ takes a constant time), and that any occurrence of ⟦ at position i is equipped with the pointer $L(i)$ to its left-most child.[4] Moreover, we equip a deterministic SNA $\overline{A}$ with an array S such that, when $\overline{A}$ stays at p of depth d, $S[i]$ should point to the $(i, 1)$-successor of p for all $i < d$.[5] In this setting, the (d, s)-successor of the current position has index $S[d] + (s - 1)$, which is computable in constant time. Hence, we are able to run $\overline{A}$ efficiently (Fig. 3 shows an example). In particular, the running time is independent of the number of input symbols skipped over.

[4]Note that this is the way in which the original structure would be stored in memory by a standard C implementation.

[5]Upkeeping this requires only one memory access for every ⟦ processed; cf. (Alur and Madhusudan, 2004).

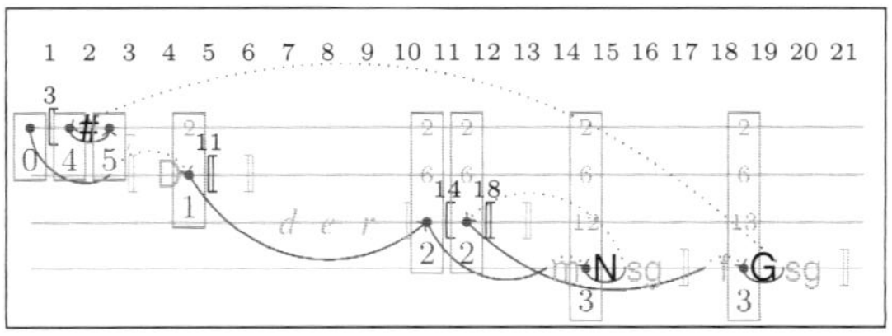

Figure 3: A run of the SNA from Fig. 2 on the input from Fig. 1d. The numbers above ⟦ are pointers to their left-most children. The bottom number in each frame indicates the current state; the remaining ones show the stack S ($S[i]$ appears at depth i).

6 Evaluation and conclusion

A preliminary version of our method has been used for finding the matches of relatively complex hand-written patterns aimed at shallow parsing and correcting errors in the IPI Corpus of Polish (Przepiórkowski, 2004). As a result, although the input size grew by about 30% due to introducing ⟦ and ⟧ nodes, over 75% of the obtained input was skipped, leading to an overall speed-up by about 50%. Clearly, empirical results may depend heavily on the particular input and queries. Hence, our solution may turn out to be narrowly scoped as well as to be useful in various aspects of XML processing. Note that, although the expressive power of SNAs as presented is rather weak, it seems to be easily extendable by integrating our main idea with the general VPA model.[6]

References

Alfred V. Aho and Jeffrey D. Ullman. 1971. Translations on a context-free grammar. *Information and*

[6]This would require some technical adjustments, incl. replacing absolute depths of states with relative jump heights of transitions, and bounding these by 1. We skip the details due to space limitations. For very shallow inputs (including the Spejd's case), these modifications would be rather disadvantageous.

Control, 19(5):439–475.

Rajeev Alur and P. Madhusudan. 2004. Visibly pushdown languages. In *Proceedings of the thirty-sixth annual ACM symposium on Theory of computing*, pages 202–211, New York, NY, USA. ACM.

Rajeev Alur and P. Madhusudan. 2009. Adding nesting structure to words. *J. ACM*, 56(3):16:1–16:43.

Kenneth R. Beesley and Lauri Karttunen. 2003. *Finite State Morphology*. CSLI Studies in Computational Linguistics. CSLI Publications.

Mikołaj Bojańczyk and Thomas Colcombet. 2006. Tree-walking automata cannot be determinized. *Theor. Comput. Sci.*, 350(2-3):164–173.

H. Comon, M. Dauchet, R. Gilleron, C. Löding, F. Jacquemard, D. Lugiez, S. Tison, and M. Tommasi. 2007. Tree automata techniques and applications. `http://www.grappa.univ-lille3.fr/tata`. release October, 12th 2007.

Olivier Gauwin, Joachim Niehren, and Yves Roos. 2008. Streaming tree automata. *Inf. Process. Lett.*, 109(1):13–17.

Makoto Murata. 2001. Extended path expressions for XML. In Peter Buneman, editor, *PODS*. ACM.

Gertjan van Noord and Dale Gerdemann. 2001. Finite state transducers with predicates and identities. *Grammars*, 4(3):263–286.

Adam Przepiórkowski. 2004. *Korpus IPI PAN. Wersja wstępna*. Institute of Computer Science, Polish Academy of Sciences, Warsaw.

Xiaofei Wang. 2012. *High Performance Stride-based Network Payload Inspection*. Dissertation, Dublin City University.

Synchronous Regular Relations and Morphological Analysis

Christian Wurm, Younes Samih,
{cwurm,samih}@phil.uni-duesseldorf.de

Abstract

We list the major properties of some important classes of subrational relations, mostly to make them easily accessible to computational linguists. We then argue that there are good linguistic reasons for using no class smaller than the class of synchronous regular relations for morphological analysis, and good mathematical reasons for using no class which is larger.

1 Below the Rational Relations

We need not stress the importance of finite state transducers and of rational relations for computational linguistics (see Johnson [1972],Koskenniemi [1983],Kaplan and Kay [1994],Beesley and Karttunen [2003]). So we rather start with stressing the importance of sub-rational relations, that is, classes of relations properly contained in the rational relations. As is well-known in the community, rational relations are not closed under intersection. Furthermore, the equivalence and inclusion problems for rational relations are undecidable. So there are a number of arguments for not using rational relations, but rather some weaker class with more favorable decision properties. The question is: if we want to go below the rational relations, which class should we choose? In the literature, we often find the so called sequential relations; these however are quite restricted and will not be considered here. We rather focus on three classes, the strictly synchronous, the k-bounded (e.g. Roark and Sproat [2007]), and the synchronous regular relations, which are ordered by inclusion. We present their main closure properties, which are partly already known. For some reason the important class of synchronous regular relations, which has attracted a lot of attention in various fields of mathematics,[1] has to our knowledge not gained very much attention in the field of computational linguistics.[2] We argue here that 1. there are good linguistic reasons for using no class smaller than the class of synchronous regular relations; and 2. we do not know of any linguistics evidence in morphology to use the more powerful rational relations instead of synchronous regular relations.

2 Closure Properties and Decision Problems

We will consider the main closure properties for classes of relations. *Union* and *intersection* of two relations R_1, R_2 are defined in the obvious set-theoretic fashion. The *complement* of a relation R is defined wrt. two alphabets Σ, T, where $R \subseteq \Sigma^* \times T^*$, and $\overline{R} := (\Sigma^* \times T^*) - R$. The *inversion* of a word $a_1...a_n \in \Sigma^*$ is defined as $(a_1...a_n)^i := a_n...a_1$. For a relation $R \subseteq \Sigma^* \times T^*$, we put $R^i := \{(w^i, v^i) : (w, v) \in R\}$. Given two relations R_1, R_2, we define their *composition* $R_1 \circ R_2 := \{(x, z) : (x, y) \in R_1, (y, z) \in R_2\}$. Given Two relations $R_1 \subseteq \Sigma_1^* \times T_1^*, R_2 \subseteq \Sigma_2^* \times T_2^*$, we define their *concatenation* $R_1 \cdot R_2 := \{(w_1w_2, v_1v_2) : (w_1, v_1) \in R_1, (w_2, v_2) \in R_2\}$. In general, we

[1] We just mention Frougny and Sakarovitch [1993], and the research on automatic structures, see Rubin [2008]

[2] We have to mention that scholars working on the finite-state manipulation platform Vaucanson have made some efforts in using synchronous regular relations, see Lesaint [2008]

say a class $\mathcal{R}$ is *closed* under a n-ary operation X, if from $R_1, ..., R_n \in \mathcal{R}$ it follows that $X(R_1, ..., R_2) \in \mathcal{R}$.

3 Three Classes and Their Inclusion Relations

We consider three classes as most interesting in this context. The first one is the class of strictly synchronous regular relations (**SSR**). For generality, we present relations of arbitrary arity. R is in **SSR** if 1. R is rational, and 2. if $(w_1, ..., w_i) \in R$, then $|w_1| = ... = |w_i|$. Secondly, a relation R is k-bounded, if 1. R is rational and 2. there is a $k \in \mathbb{N}$ such that for all $(w_1, ..., w_n) \in R$, $max\{|w_1|, ..., |w_n|\} - min\{|w_1|, ..., |w_n|\} \leq k$.[3] Call this class k-**B**. Obviously, k-**B** properly contains **SSR**. As the third class, we present the synchronous regular relations (**SR**): Put $\Sigma_\perp := \Sigma \cup \{\perp\}$, for $\perp \notin \Sigma$. The **convolution** of a tuple of strings $(w_1, ..., w_i) \in (\Sigma^*)^i$, written as $\otimes(w_1, ..., w_i)$ of length $max(\{|w_j| : 1 \leq j \leq i\})$ is defined as follows: the kth component of $\otimes(w_1, ..., w_i)$ is $\langle \sigma_1, ..., \sigma_i \rangle$, where σ_j is the k-th letter of w_j provided that $k \leq |w_j|$, and $\perp$ otherwise. The convolution of a relation $R \subseteq (\Sigma^*)^i$ is defined as $\otimes R := \{\otimes(w_1, ..., w_i)\colon (w_1, ..., w_i) \in R\}$. A relation $R \in (\Sigma^*)^i$ is **synchronous regular**, if there is a finite state automaton over $(\Sigma_\perp)^i$ recognizing $\otimes R$.

Informally, **SR** are the relations computed by finite state transducers which allow ϵ transitions in a component only if no other letter is to follow in this component. It is not obvious that **SR** contains k-**B**; it follows however from the following well-known synchronization lemma (see Frougny and Sakarovitch [1993]):

Lemma 1 *Assume R is an n-ary rational relation, such that there is a $k \in \mathbb{N}$, such that for all $(w_1, ..., w_n) \in R$, $max\{|w_1|, ..., |w_n|\} - min\{|w_1|, ..., |w_n|\} \leq k$. Then R is in* ***SR***.

4 A Logical Characterization of SR

We can actually characterize **SR** with first order logic over the language $\mathcal{L} := (EL, pref, last_a : a \in \Sigma)$ where $EL, pref$ are binary predicates, and all $a : a \in \Sigma$ are unary predicates. We call this logic $\mathsf{FOL}(\mathcal{L})$, and interpret it in the structure $\mathfrak{S} := \langle \Sigma^*, EL, pref, a : a \in \Sigma \rangle$, where Σ^* is our universe, $a : a \in \Sigma \subseteq \Sigma^*$, and $EL, pref \subseteq \Sigma^* \times \Sigma^*$. We have $w \in a$ if and only if $w = w'a$; we have $(w, v) \in pref$ if and only if $v = wv'$, that is, w is a prefix of v; and we have $(w, v) \in EL$ if and only if $|w| = |v|$. For what is to follow, we have to assume that $|\Sigma| \geq 2$. The proof of the following theorem of Eilenberg et al. [1969] is long and complicated, so we cannot even give a sketch at this place.

Theorem 2 *Assume $M \subseteq (\Sigma^*)^i$. Then there is a $\mathsf{FOL}(\mathcal{L})$-formula $\phi(x_1, ..., x_i)$ in the free variables $x_1, ..., x_i$, such that $M := \{w_1, ..., w_i \in \Sigma^* : \mathfrak{S} \models \phi(x_1, ..., x_i)[w_1, ..., w_i]\}$, if and only if $M \in$* ***SR***.

5 Mathematical Properties

5.1 Closure Properties

That **SSR** is closed under union is obvious. Intersection follows from the fact that 1. **SR** is closed under intersection, and 2. if all pairs in R_1 and R_2 have equal length, then surely the pairs in $R_1 \cap R_2$ have equal length. It is easy to see that **SSR** is not closed under complement, as the complement of $R \in$ **SSR** in particular contains all pairs of words of different length. Moreover, **SSR** is closed under inversion, because 1. rational relations are closed under inversion, and 2. equal length is preserved; **SSR** is closed under composition and concatenation for exactly the same reason. So we have quite good closure (and decision) properties; still, **SSR** is very restrictive.

Therefore one might prefer the more powerful class k-**B**. k-**B** is obviously also closed under union, closed under intersection and not under complement, for exactly the same reason as **SSR**. Also, k-**B** is closed under composition, concatenation and inversion, again for the same reasons as **SSR**.

There is a characterization of regular relations in first order logic.[4] From this result it immediately follows that **SR** is closed under union, intersection and complement, by

[3] Note the order of quantifiers: we do not fix the k for the entire class of relations; we can choose it arbitrarily for any given relation, but then it is fixed for all of its elements.

[4] Actually, this only holds for relations over an alphabet Σ with $|\Sigma| \geq 2$; but our claims are easy to show separately for the case where $|\Sigma| = 1$.

logical connectives; moreover, by logical definability we easily obtain closure under composition: put $R_1 := \{(w_1, w_2) \in (\Sigma^*)^2 : \mathfrak{S} \models \phi(x,y)[w_1, w_2]\}$; $R_2 := \{(v_1, v_2) \in (\Sigma^*)^2 : \mathfrak{S} \models \psi(y,z)[v_1, v_2]\}$; then $R_1 \circ R_2 = \{(w_1, w_2) : \mathfrak{S} \models \exists.y\phi(x,y) \wedge \psi(y,z)[w_1, w_2]\}$. We can easily show that **SR** is *not* closed under concatenation: $(a,\epsilon)^* \in$ **SR**, $(b,c)^* \in$ **SR**; but $(a,\epsilon)^* \cdot (b,c)^* \notin$ **SR**.[5] As $(b,c)^* \cdot (a,\epsilon)^*$ is regular, we also know that **SR** is *not* closed under inversion.

5.2 Decision Problems

In general, the question whether for a given characterization of a rational relation R (transducer, rational expression), we have $R = \emptyset$, is decidable. From this and the fact that **SR** is a Boolean algebra it follows that for $R_1, R_2 \in$**SR**, we can decide the questions: given characterizations of R_1, R_2, is $R_1 \subseteq R_2$, and is $R_1 = R_2$? This can be demonstrated using the standard proof for regular languages. So, we have *a fortiori* the same result for **SSR**, k-**B**. For rational relations themselves the latter problems are undecidable.

6 Natural Language Morphology Requires SR

6.1 German Compounding

So which one should we take? As there is no absolutely convincing mathematical argument, we should take a look at linguistic facts. We now present an argument for using the additional power coming with synchronous regular relations.

Compounding is a very productive morphological process in German and many other languages (Dutch, Danish, Finish, Greek etc.). It is a process whereby new words are formed by combining independent words/morphemes, where there is no restriction on the number of morphemes which can be put together to form a single new word. German compounds are strictly right-headed (Toman [1992]), that is, the morphosyntactic features of the compounds are always inherited from the rightmost morpheme. The head of the compound thus determines category, gender, and all morphosyntactic features of the whole compound. For example,the `bahn` in German `Autobahn` (highway) identifies the word as singular feminine. Due to space constraints, we cannot say much about morphological analysis in general or analysis of our particular example; we will say only as much as is needed for our formal argument, which in our view however is of general importance for computational morphology.

6.2 The Compounding Relation is Synchronous Regular

If we want to morphologically analyze a compound, in a first step, we want to transduce a sequence of compounded words $W_1...W_i$ to a sequence of representations of their morphosyntactic features $C_1...C_i$. This relation is synchronous if we use words and feature bundles as atoms. One might object that this is usually not the case, or at least depends on whether we allow complex words as atomic transitions. But mathematically, we are quite safe, as we can always form a new, finite alphabet via a bijection with finite strings over another alphabets.[6] Still, this is not satisfying, as the compound is a single word, and its morphosyntactic features are exactly the same as the one of its head. As the head is rightmost, we thus have a relation of the form $(C_1...C_i, C_i)$, mapping the entire sequence to its last element. We call this the **compounding relation**, which has to be composed with the first relation. As compounding is unbounded and consequently there is no upper bound to i, this relation is *not* in k-**B**. We now show that this relation is however in **SR**. This would be obvious if the head would be the leftmost element; for the head rightmost we need some work.

Let I be a finite set, $L_i : i \in I$ a finite set of regular languages. We say a function $f : (\Sigma \times T)^* \to (\{\epsilon\} \times \{L_i : i \in I\}) \cup (\{L_i : i \in I\} \times \{\epsilon\})$ is regular, if there is a deterministic finite state automaton $(Q, \delta, q_0, \Sigma \times T)$, where δ is extended to strings in the canonical fashion, and a finite function $g : Q \to (\{\epsilon\} \times \{L_i : i \in I\}) \cup (\{L_i : i \in I\} \times \{\epsilon\})$, such that for all $(w,v) \in (\Sigma \times T)^*$, we have $f(w,v) = g \circ \delta(w,v)$.

[5]This follows from the standard proof that rational relations are not closed under intersection, which uses exactly this relation, see Kaplan and Kay [1994].

[6]Still more technically, we would also have to ensure that the bijection defines a *code*, but we leave this aside, noting that this is satisfied in all normal cases.

Lemma 3 *A relation $R \subseteq \Sigma^* \times T^*$ is in* ***SR****, if and only if there is a regular function f, such that for every $(w, v) \in R$, $(w, v) = (w', v') \cdot f(w', v')$, where $|w'| = |v'|$.*[7]

So take the compounding relation $\{(C_1...C_i, C_i) : C_1...C_i$ is a well-formed compound$\}$. We simply put $f(C_1, C_i) = (\{C_1\} \backslash \overline{C}_{C_1}) \times \epsilon$, where $\overline{C}_{C_i}$ is the language of well-formed compounds ending with C_i, and $L_1 \backslash L_2 := \{v : \forall w \in L_1, wv \in L_2\}$; it is well-known that regular languages are closed under this operation, so the compounding relation is synchronous regular, provided that the set of compounds itself is a regular set. This is clearly the case for the languages we considered. And even if there is a language where this is not the case, this would not be an argument in particular against using **SR**, but rather against using finite-state methods in natural language morphology in general.

7 Conclusion

We have summed up the major closure and decision properties of a number of subrational classes of relations which are currently in use. The properties we listed are mostly known, and otherwise relatively easy to obtain. We have undertaken this summarization as there does not seem to be any other literature where one could find it; and in particular in the computational linguistics literature one finds very little on closure and decision properties of subrational classes of relations.

Our main argument however is of linguistic nature: we have shown that the k-bounded (and thus strictly synchronous) relations are unable to allow for morphological analysis of a phenomenon which is as common and widespread as compounding. Synchronous regular relations on the other side are powerful enough to capture this phenomenon. We also argued that synchronous regular relations are preferable over rational relations from a purely mathematical point of view, because they form a Boolean algebra and all their decision problems are decidable.

Of course, there are many finite-state NLP applications for which **SR** is insufficient, such as inserting markup expressions in shallow parsing. Our argument was: for most of standard morphological analysis, **SR** is the smallest class which provides sufficient expressive power.[8]

[7] Actually, this lemma is sometimes even taken to be the definition of **SR**; so we omit the proof.

References

Kenneth R. Beesley and Lauri Karttunen. *Finite state morphology.* CSLI Publ., Stanford, Calif., 2003.

Samuel. Eilenberg, C. C. Elgot, and J. C. Shepherdson. Sets recognized by n-tape automata. *Journal of Algebra*, 13:447–464, 1969.

Christiane Frougny and Jacques Sakarovitch. Synchronized rational relations of finite and infinite words. *Theor. Comput. Sci.*, 108(1): 45–82, 1993.

C. Douglas Johnson. *Formal Aspects of Phonological Description.* Mouton, The Hague, 1972.

Ron M. Kaplan and Martin Kay. Regular Models of Phonological Rule Systems. *Computational Linguistics*, 20:331–378, 1994.

Kimmo Koskenniemi. Two–level morphology. A general computational model for word–form recognition. Technical Report 11, Department of General Linguistics, University of Helsinki, 1983.

Florian Lesaint. Synchronous relations in Vaucanson. Technical Report 0833, Laboratoire de Recherche et Développement de L'Epita, 2008.

Brian Roark and Richard William Sproat. *Computational approaches to morphology and syntax.* Oxford surveys in syntax and morphology ; 4. Oxford Univ. Press, 2007.

Sasha Rubin. Automata presenting structures: A survey of the finite string case. *Bulletin of Symbolic Logic*, 14(2):169–209, 2008.

Jindrich Toman. Compound. In W. Bright, editor, *International Encyclopedia of Linguistics*, volume 1, pages 286 – 288. Oxford Univ. Pr., 1992.

[8] Though there are morphological phenomena which clearly go beyond the expressive power of **SR**, such as reduplication, they seem to be quite rare; and in fact, the latter is equally problematic for finite-state morphology in general as for **SR**.

Parsing Morphologically Complex Words

Kay-Michael Würzner*
University of Potsdam, Psychology Dept.
Karl-Liebknecht-Str. 24-25
14476 Potsdam, Germany
wuerzner@uni-potsdam.de

Thomas Hanneforth
University of Potsdam, Linguistics Dept.
Karl-Liebknecht-Str. 24-25
14476 Potsdam, Germany
thomas.hanneforth@uni-potsdam.de

Abstract

We present a method for probabilistic parsing of German words. Our approach uses a morphological analyzer based on weighted finite-state transducers to segment words into lexical units and a probabilistic context free grammar trained on a manually created set of word trees for the parsing step.

1 Introduction

Most existing systems for automatic, morphological analysis of German focus on flat structures, i.e. the segmentation into morphemes and the identification of their features and the involved operations. But as soon as more than one operation leads to the word in question, possible orderings of these operations can be captured in different hierarchical structures. Consider Ex. (1) from Faaß et al. (2010),

(1) un$_{Pref}$ übersetz$_{V}$ bar$_{Suff}$
un translate able
'untranslatable'

The adjective *unübersetzbar* is analyzed as a combination of the prefix *un*, the verbal stem *übersetz* and the suffix *bar*. This analysis could be assigned two structures (depicted in Fig. 1): either the prefixation (a) or the suffixation (b) occurs first.

Research on human morphological processing has long moved from linear segmentations to more advanced representations of the morphological structure of words (Libben, 1993; Libben, 1994). We aim to provide researchers in this field with hierarchical morphological analyses for all words in our lexical database `dlexDB` (Heister et al., 2011).

In the following, we present an approach for the automatic assignment of hierarchical structures to complex words using flat morphological analyses and a PCFG[1]. As a case study, we apply our method to the parsing of German adjectives. To do so, we created a corpus of manually annotated word trees for 5,000 structurally ambiguous adjectives. We describe types of ambiguity and their distribution in the training set and report results of the parsing process in dependence of various grammar transformations.

1.1 Word Formation and Structures

Word formation is the combination of morphemes to form new words. We distinguish between *inflection* (combination of a free morpheme with one or more affixes to fulfill agreement), *compounding* (combination of several free morphemes) and *derivation* (combination of a morpheme with an affix to change the category and/or the meaning of a word). *Conversion* might be considered a special case of derivation. Here, a change of a word's category occurs without any affixes being involved.

Word formation processes which are involved in the creation of a complex word can be linearly ordered. Multiple possible orderings lead to structural ambiguities. Ex. (2) gives examples for the possible different types of ambiguity[2]: *Compound – Suffix*, *Compound – Compound*, *Prefix – Suffix*, *Prefix – Compound*.

(2) a. Mensch$_{N}$ en Freund$_{N}$ lich$_{Suff}$
human link friend ly
'humanitarian'

b. dunkel$_{A}$ Asche$_{N}$ grau$_{A}$
dark ash gray
'dark ashen'

c. nicht$_{Pref}$ Objekt$_{N}$ iv$_{Suff}$
non object ive
'non-objective'

d. ab$_{Pref}$ Gas$_{N}$ frei$_{A}$
off gas free
'zero-emission'

The decision which ordering is the correct one is driven by morphological as well as semantic restrictions on the involved morphemes. The tree given in Fig. 1a for example could be ruled out by the fact that verbs may

* This author's work was funded by the DFG (grant no. KL 955/19-1).

[1] We assume here the usual definition of a context-free grammar (CFG) $G = (V,T,S,P)$ consisting of non-terminal (V) and terminal symbols (T), a start symbol $S \in V$ and a set of context-free productions P. In a *probabilistic CFG* (PCFG; Booth, 1969), each production is assigned with a probability.

[2] Since inflection in German is triggered by a word's context to ensure agreement and from a productive point of view always takes place last in word formation, we ignore it in our list and for the remainder of this work and restrict ourselves to base forms (*lemmas*) of the words in question.

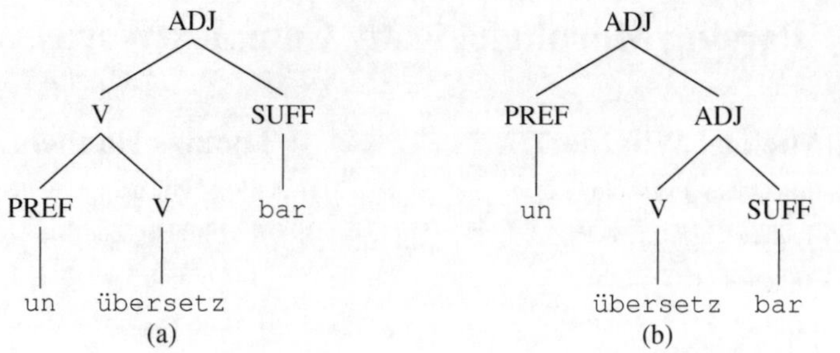

Figure 1: Possible tree structures for the morphological analysis in Example (1).

not be combined with the prefix *un* in German. As an example for semantic restrictions consider the analysis for *antirheumatisch* given in Ex. (3).

(3) anti$_{Pref}$ Rheuma$_N$ t isch$_{Suff}$
anti *rheumatism* link *ish*
'antirheumatic'

Since the concept of "antirheumatism" does not exist, we assume that the suffixation with *isch* takes place first.

1.2 Morphological Analysis

Before parsing, input words must be segmented into their basic units. In addition, the parser needs sufficient categorical annotation to get started. For that purpose, we used the TAGH morphology (Geyken and Hanneforth, 2006), a comprehensive computational morphology system for German based on weighted finite-state transducers.

Computer morphology systems normally suffer from oversegmentation: a sufficiently long enough word gets segmented in all possible ways, resulting in a lot of ambiguous readings most of which are nonsensical. To tackle this problem, the TAGH morphology (TAGH-M) makes use of three strategies:

1. TAGH-M measures morphological complexity by associating each derivation and compounding rule with a context-dependent penalty weight. These weights are taken from a *tropical semiring* weight structure (Kuich and Salomaa, 1986), that is, weights are added along a path in the weighted finite-state automaton representing a set of morphological analyses, and, among the competing analyses, the one with the least weight is selected.

2. TAGH-M is not strictly morpheme-based, but instead more oriented towards semantics. In German, there are a lot of overtly morphologically complex words which nevertheless denote simple concepts. Take for example the exocentric compound *Geizhals* ('scrapepenny'). But it can be also segmented into *Geiz* ('miserliness') and *Hals* ('neck'). TAGH-M's base lexicon now contains morphological simple entries like *Hals*, but morphologically complex ones like *Geizhals* as well. In association with the weighting mechanism, this means, that lexicalized but complex forms will be always given priority.

3. The word formation grammar underlying TAGH-M is very carefully crafted. Looking at adjective formation, the corresponding subgrammar contains approx. 3,000 rules. These rules are divided into groups, responsible for prefixation, suffixation, compounding and conversion. The suffixation part of the grammar is itself divided into further groups, one for each productive adjective suffix like *-isch*, *-ig* or *-lich*.[3] Every suffixation rule is associated with a number of base stems of different category (nouns, names, etc.) which happen to take this particular suffix. The association of affixes and stems is derived from a huge list of entries taken from the German Google books corpus (see also Sec. 2.2).

By incorporating these three strategies, TAGH-M avoids a lot of segmentation ambiguities which would otherwise enter into the subsequent parsing phase.

In addition, TAGH-M inserts marker symbols (for separable and non-separable prefixes, suffixes, linking morphemes and free morphemes), reduces allomorphic variants to their underlying citation form and annotates each segment with a morphological category taken from a set of approx. 20 categories.

Ex. (4) shows the preferred segmentation of the adjective *länderspezifisch* ('country-specific').

(4) `Land` ⟨`N`⟩ `\er` ⟨`l`⟩ `# spezif` ⟨`f`⟩ ~ `isch` ⟨`a`⟩

The symbols enclosed in angle brackets denote the morphosyntactic category of the segment: ⟨`N`⟩ is a free noun, while ⟨`a`⟩ represents a bound adjective (suffix -*isch*); ⟨`f`⟩ denotes a neoclassical formative and ⟨`l`⟩ a linking morpheme. The segmentation symbol # marks a free morpheme boundary, while ~ flags a following suffix. Annotated segments as well as segmentation markers enter the subsequent parsing phase.

[3] In total, the adjective suffixation grammar lists almost 70 of these suffixes.

1.3 Parsing

To get an initial grammar for the training experiments reported on in Sec. 3, we manually derived a context-free grammar based on the grammar underlying TAGH-M. For parsing, this grammar was automatically converted into an unweighted *finite tree automaton, FTA* (Comon et al., 2007). Transitions of FTAs are either of the form

$$w \to q \qquad (1)$$

which introduce the leaves of a tree, or rules of the form

$$f(q_1, q_2, \ldots, q_k) \to q \qquad (2)$$

which describe k-branching tree nodes with label f; the q_is are the states of the FTA. The language of an FTA is the set of trees generated by the FTA.

Finite-tree automata offer an advantage over context-free grammars: their transitions decouple the label (functor) f of the transition (which corresponds to a context-free rule's left-hand side) from the destination state q of the transition (which reflects the context in which the subtree might be inserted). This for example make techniques like parent annotation (see below) easily applicable since annotated categories are represented in the states of the FTA, not its translation labels.

For word structure parsing, we used an intersection based approach (Hanneforth, 2013).

1.3.1 Lexicalization

In lexicalized grammars, individual productions are specialized for certain lexical items. Non-terminal symbols are extended with lexical information as shown in Fig. 2.

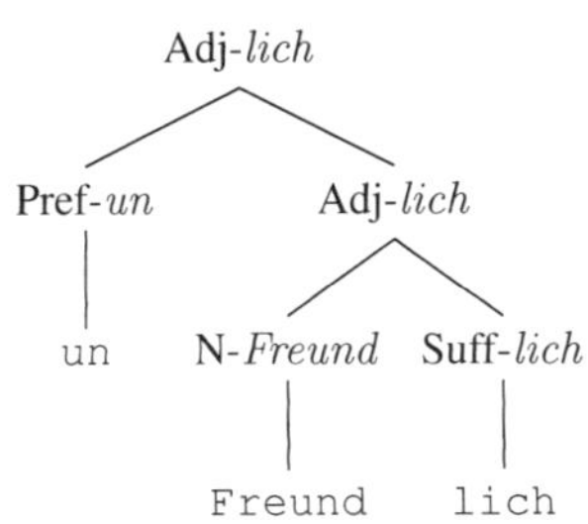

Figure 2: A lexicalized word tree.

This example is an instance of so called *head* lexicalization (Charniak, 1997). Lexical information of the rightmost constituent is percolated through the tree. Lexicalizing a grammar is a way to add some kind of contextual information to *context-free* grammars.

1.3.2 Parent Annotation

Parent annotation (Johnson, 1998) is another way of enriching a CFG with contextual information. The category of some non-terminal is added to the labels of its daughters as shown in Fig. 3.

Extending the grammar as described above increases the number of non-terminals and productions. This can

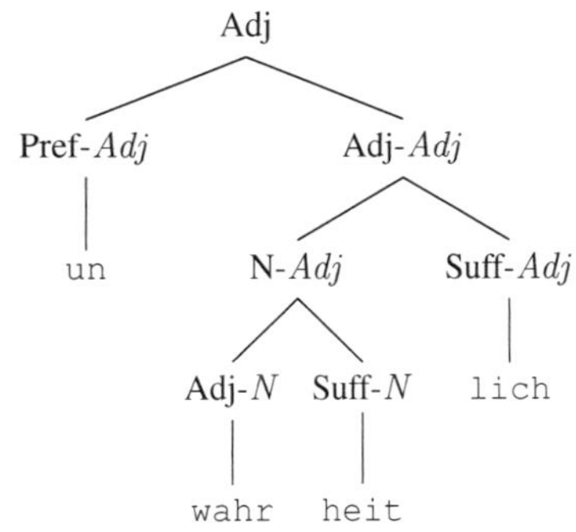

Figure 3: A word tree with parent annotation.

lead to sparseness problems in the probabilistic case. These problems can be dealt with by applying some smoothing method (Collins, 1999).

2 Method

In what follows, we describe our pilot study for the generation of parse trees for morphologically complex words. Our goal is to determine the most likely structure for each item in the test set, namely a large set of German adjectives.

2.1 Procedure

We decided to evaluate a statistical parsing approach using a PCFG. The aforementioned hand-crafted CFG which covers the different types of ambiguity was used to create candidate trees (cf. Fig. 1) for a set of training items (see Sec. 2.2). The design of the grammar also ensured that there is always an unary derivation from the pre-terminal to the terminal level. This allowed us to keep lexical rules separate from the rest of the grammar. The grammar contains no further unary productions.

After the manual annotation step described in Sec. 2.2, we divided the data into 10 equal parts and induced context-free productions from the trees in each part. For each subtree

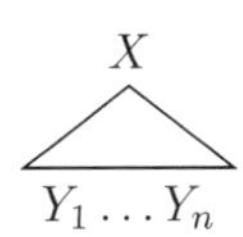

a production $X \to Y_1 \ldots Y_n$ was added to P. We also stored the production's frequency in each of the 10 sub-parts.

Estimation of the probabilities for the productions in P and evaluation of the resulting PCFG was done by iterating over the sub-parts G_i which served as a test set while the rest was used for training.

Probabilities were computed via simple maximum likelihood estimation with add-one smoothing. Here, $c(X \to Y_1 \ldots Y_n)$ denotes the frequency of the rule $X \to Y_1 \ldots Y_n$ in the training materials.

Ambiguity	Number
Compound – Suffix	5,239
Prefix – Suffix	1,136
Compound – Compound	447
Prefix – Compound	0

Table 1: Numbers of different types of structural ambiguities within a set of 20,000 adjectives.

$$\Pr(Y_1 \ldots Y_n|X) = \frac{c(X \rightarrow Y_1 \ldots Y_n) + 1}{c(X \rightarrow (V \cup T)^+) + |P|} \quad (3)$$

In order to capture restrictions as those mentioned above, we applied various transformations on the trees prior to the grammar induction resulting in different grammar versions: (1) specialization of the pre-terminal level for bound morphemes, (2) specialization of the pre-terminal level for frequent free morphemes, (3) lexicalization of adjective suffixes and (4) parent annotation. The specialization of the pre-terminal level may be considered as lexicalization of only the lexical rules.

2.2 Materials

We chose the Google books N-grams (Google Incorporated, 2009) as our source for training and test materials. The list of unigrams contains all words with a frequency greater or equal to ten within the German portion of the Google books corpus (all in all 3,685,340 types). From this list, we extracted a large number of adjectives using a list of known adjective suffixes (see Sec. 1.2) and manually filtered this list for optical character recognition errors and false positives (e.g. verbal forms). This set was extended using known adjectives from various hand-maintained lexical resources resulting in a list of 338,423 adjectives.

Initially, we randomly selected 10,000 words with a length of $8 \leq n \leq 20$ (which were unique for their lemma; i.e., only one instance per lemma was selected) from this list. These words were morphologically analyzed and parsed along the lines of sections 1.2 and 1.3. The resulting analyses were manually checked for errors in the morphological analysis and the word trees. Detected errors led to readjustments of both the morphological analyzer and the grammar. Finally, only roughly a quarter of the items were assigned more than one tree (the main reason for this is that TAGH-M already removes a lot of possible ambiguities). That is why we added another 10,000 words (this time with a length of $10 \leq n \leq 25$) to get more ambiguous forms. Tab. 1 shows the numbers of the different possible types of ambiguity in the test set.

For training and evaluating the PCFG, we manually selected the preferred tree for 5,000 structurally ambiguous adjectives.

2.3 Evaluation

We used `evalb` (Sekine and Collins, 1997) to evaluate the different probabilistic grammars extracted from the training materials as described in Sec. 2.1. We report their performance in terms of (1) *tagging accuracy*, i.e., the proportion of correct pre-terminal to terminal assignments, (2) *bracketing accuracy*, i.e., the proportion of correct rule applications and (3) *complete matches*, i.e. the proportion of identities between manually selected and automatically generated trees.

3 Results and Discussion

Table 2 summarizes the results for the different grammar versions. The corresponding tree transformations are applied in a cumulative way. Due to the inclusion of the morpheme annotation done by TAGH-M into the grammar, tagging accuracy is always 100% and thus omitted in Table 2.

The biggest improvement is gained through the specialization of frequent free morphemes. This transformation helps us to model binding preferences for certain morphemes. Consider for example the noun *Freund* ('friend') which is very often combined with the suffix *lich* in order to form *freundlich* ('friendly'). There are many compounds with *freundlich* as *anwenderfreundlich* where, due to semantic restrictions, the noun compound as first component is not an option.

Head-lexicalization did not improve parsing results with one exception: The test materials contain many coordinative structures like *psychischphysisch* ('psycho-physical'), thus the production *Adj* $\rightarrow$ *Adj Adj* has a fairly high probability. But there is one notable exception to this rule: In words like Ex. (5),

(5) Nation$_N$ al$_{Suff}$ Sozialist$_N$ isch$_{Suff}$
nation al socialist ish
'Nazi'

a coordinative analysis is also available, but adjectives formed with *al* almost always combine with a noun if possible. Lexicalizing *al* successfully models this behavior. It will be subject to further work to systematically test for other equally successful lexicalization patterns.

Parent annotation does not add very much to the performance of the grammar which is due to the relatively simple structures that we encounter during parsing of words compared to the parsing of sentences.

If we look at the remaining errors, it is striking that most of these originate from exceptions from the typical formation patterns. The prefix *über* ('over') is usually combined with adjectives but in some rare cases it operates as a noun prefix (*Übermensch*, 'superman'). Derivations from these nouns are assigned with the wrong analysis by our grammar.

The approach we presented here is a promising first step in the direction of parsing morphologically complex words. Next, we will extend our approach to Ger-

Grammar	Number of prod.	Bracketing acc.	Complete match
baseline	63	91.64%	82.05%
specialized bound morphemes	196	92.20%	83.04%
specialized freq. free morphemes	238	94.92%	89.11%
lexicalized suffix `al`	274	96.26%	92.02%
parent annotation	481	95.91%	93.34%

Table 2: Number of non-lexical productions as well as proportions of correct bracketing and complete matches for different PCFGs.

man nouns where the great number of compounds will be the major challenge.

Acknowledgements

We would like to thank Edmund Pohl for creating the web-based tree training tool (`http://www.dlexdb.de/wordstruct`) and the anonymous reviewers for their helpful remarks.

References

Taylor L. Booth. 1969. Probabilistic Representation of Formal Languages. In *IEEE Conference Record of 10th Annual Symposium on Switching and Automata Theory*, pages 74–81.

Eugene Charniak. 1997. Statistical Techniques for Natural Language Parsing. *AI Magazine*, 18(4):33–43.

Michael John Collins. 1999. *Head-Driven Statistical Models for Natural Language Parsing*. Ph.D. thesis, University of Pennsylvania.

Hubert Comon, Max Dauchet, Remi Gilleron, Christof Löding, Florent Jacquemard, Denis Lugiez, Sophie Tison, and Marc Tommasi. 2007. Tree Automata Techniques and Applications. Available on: `http://www.grappa.univ-lille3.fr/tata`. release October, 12th 2007.

Gertrud Faaß, Ulrich Heid, and Helmut Schmid. 2010. Design and Application of a Gold Standard for Morphological Analysis: SMOR as an Example of Morphological Evaluation. In Nicoletta Calzolari, Khalid Choukri, Bente Maegaard, Joseph Mariani, Jan Odijk, Stelios Piperidis, Mike Rosner, and Daniel Tapias, editors, *Proceedings of the seventh LREC conference*, pages 803–810.

Alexander Geyken and Thomas Hanneforth. 2006. TAGH: A Complete Morphology for German based on Weighted Finite State Automata. In *Finite State Methods and Natural Language Processing*, volume 4002 of *Lecture Notes in Computer Science*, pages 55–66, Berlin, Heidelberg. Springer.

Google Incorporated. 2009. Google Books Ngrams. http://books.google.com/ngrams.

Thomas Hanneforth. 2013. An Efficient Parsing Algorithm for Weighted Finite-tree Automata. *In preparation.*

Julian Heister, Kay-Michael Würzner, Johannes Bubenzer, Edmund Pohl, Thomas Hanneforth, Alexander Geyken, and Reinhold Kliegl. 2011. dlexDB – eine lexikalische Datenbank für die psychologische und linguistische Forschung. *Psychologische Rundschau*, 62(1):10–20.

Mark Johnson. 1998. PCFG Models of Lingusitic Tree Representations. *Computational Linguistics*, 24(4):612–632.

Werner Kuich and Arto Salomaa. 1986. *Semirings, Automata, Languages*, volume 5 of *EACTS Monographs on Theoretical Computer Science*. Springer.

Gary Libben. 1993. Are Morphological Structures Computed During Word Recognition? *Journal of Psycholinguistic Research*, 22(5):533–544.

Gary Libben. 1994. Computing Hierarchical Morphological Structure: A Case Study. *Journal of Neurolinguistics*, 8(1):49–55.

Satoshi Sekine and Michael John Collins. 1997. evalb – Bracket Scoring Program. http://nlp.cs.nyu.edu/evalb/.

Optimizing Rule-Based Morphosyntactic Analysis of Richly Inflected Languages — a Polish Example

Dominika Pawlik
University of Warsaw
Institute of Mathematics

Aleksander Zabłocki
University of Warsaw
Institute of Informatics

Bartosz Zaborowski
Polish Academy of Sciences
Institute of Computer Science

{dominika, olekz}@mimuw.edu.pl, b.zaborowski@ipipan.waw.pl

Abstract

We consider finite-state optimization of morphosyntactic analysis of richly and ambiguously annotated corpora. We propose a general algorithm which, despite being surprisingly simple, proved to be effective in several applications for rulesets which do not match frequently.

1 Introduction

Morphosyntactic analysis of natural language texts is commonly performed as an iterative process of applying pre-defined syntactical rules to a previously tokenised and morphologically annotated input (Aït-Mokhtar and Chanod, 1997). We consider two of its sub-tasks: shallow parsing and disambiguation.

As stated in (Mohri, 1997), such tasks can often be efficiently realized with finite-state transducers (FST), which allow time savings by the classical operations of determinization, minimization and composition (Roche and Schabes, 1995). However, the applicability of the FST model may depend on the richness of annotation and on the expressive power of the rules. These both tend to complicate in richly inflected languages, including Baltic and most of Slavic.

Motivated by the needs which arose during the development of the National Corpus of Polish (NCP, (Przepiórkowski et al., 2012)), we aim at a high-efficiency rule-based morphosyntactic analysis framework suitable for such languages. Despite the existence of many formal methods and tools for this task, we are not aware of any previous result meeting all our needs, listed in Section 2. We discuss the state of the art in Section 3.

Our solution to the problem, though surprisingly single, performs well under the assumption that the rules match *rarely*, i.e. the average number of matches per rule per sentence is significantly below 1. In the case of rules designed for analyzing the Polish corpora (Przepiórkowski, 2008a), this was about 0.05–0.1, depending on the particular corpus and ruleset.

2 Problem statement

Richly inflected languages often require complex annotation as in the Constraint Grammar model (Karlsson, 1990): each token is assigned a list of potentially correct *readings*, each of which specifies the lemmatized form and a *tag* consisting of the values of syntactic attributes (PoS, case, gender etc.). For example, the English word *found* could have the following readings:[1]

found:`VB`	(The king would *found* a new city.)
find:`VBD`	(He *found* no money for that.)
find:`VBN`	(The robber has not been *found*.)

while the Polish word *drogi* the following ones:

drogi:`adj:m3:sg:nom`	/It is an *expensive* house./
drogi:`adj:m3:sg:acc`	/I see an *expensive* house./
drogi:`adj:m2:sg:nom`	/It is an *expensive* dog./
droga:`noun:f:sg:gen`	/I do not see that *road*./
droga:`noun:f:pl:acc`	/I see these *roads*./
... (6 other readings[2])	

In this setting, *unification* becomes a key tool in morphosyntactic analysis. For example, since a noun must agree with its modifying adjectives upon case, number and gender, unifying the values of these attributes can be used to remove all but the first two readings of *drogi* in

drogi	*dom*
drogi:`adj:m3:sg:nom`	dom:`noun:m3:sg:nom`
drogi:`adj:m3:sg:acc`	dom:`noun:m3:sg:acc`
drogi:`adj:m2:sg:nom`	

[1] In the examples for English language, we use the PoS tags of the Brown corpus. Tagging for Polish roughly follows the National Corpus of Polish, though has been simplified.

[2] This is the number of practically possible readings (with disregard of the context). Note that in general, the complex morphology of Polish forces the morphological analyzers to either under- or over-generate token readings. While the latter choice is often considered as better for the accuracy, it makes the syntactic analysis even more complicated.

... (8 other readings)

/an expensive house/

Hence, we desire at least the following features:

1. Functionality. Our rules should support disambiguation by unifying selected attributes in (selected of) the tokens matched by a regexp, e.g.

[pos~vb] A:([pos~adj]*) B:[pos~noun]
⇒ unify(case number gender, A B)

should look for a sequence consisting of a verb[3], a number of adjectives and a noun, and unify three attributes of the two latter. As for shallow parsing, we should allow creating syntactic structures depending on whether such unification has been successful (e.g. a noun and an adjective can be marked as a nominal group if they agree).

2. (Practical) determinism. By this we mean that single rules should run in an (almost) linear time in the input size. This clearly holds in models relying on FST determinization[4], but we would equally appreciate e.g. deterministic pushdown automata or other not purely finite-state tools.

3. (Practical) composition. By this we mean obtaining the ability to execute a cascade of rules significantly faster than it would take to execute them separately.

Clearly, a trade-off between time and memory efficiency is involved in both conditions 2 and 3.

3 Related work

Building FSTs for given replace rules, their determinization and minimization have been extensively described in theory (see (Roche and Schabes, 1995) and (Mohri, 1997)) and efficiently implemented, e.g. in the XFST toolkit (Beesley and Karttunen, 2003). However, as many authors notice, these methods turn out to be inapplicable in some situations. In our case, this happens for more than one reason.

First, a FST may be not determinizable; as discussed in (Roche and Schabes, 1996, Sec. 3.8) and (van Noord and Gerdemann, 2001), this tends to happen for replace rules acting over unbounded ranges of tokens, including both rule types discussed in Section 2. Trying to by-pass this problem — by assuming that a rule will not have a match longer than n tokens — typically leads to an exponential number of states wrt. n, which practically makes composing the results impossible. As explained in (van Noord and Gerdemann, 2001, Sec. 3.6), the explosion of states can be avoided by equipping FSTs with a queue; however, such devices no longer admit the standard composition (and no other composition method is given).

Apparently, the most commonly chosen solution of the problem is to abandon determinism for the rules which turn out to be too complex. This is the case in FASTUS (Hobbs et al., 1997), JAPE (Cunningham et al., 2000) (at least, in its full expressive power) and most probably also in SProUT (Becker et al., 2002), as its authors do not at all discuss the issue, while they refer to the standard methods which we discussed above.

In our situation, the second obstruction to using FSTs is a (yet another) explosion of states caused by unification rules for rich inflection. In order to compute the result of a unification, a determinized FST must remember its temporary result (in the current state) while processing consecutive tokens. This means increasing a part of the state space by a factor of N, where N is the number of possible unification results; in the case of Polish case-number-gender agreement, this is about 100.[5]

The scale of this problem depends on the representation of the input. Choosing a naive string encoding of the form

found/found:VB/find:VBD/find:VBN# (∗)

will increase N hopelessly since the result of unification will be a *set* of tags rather than a single value. This is not the case in the more common model for ambiguous annotation, Finite-State Intersection Grammar (FSIG) (Koskenniemi, 1990). In this approach, the input is represented as a finite-state automaton (FSA) so that alternative readings give rise to parallel paths, e.g. *he found that* will be represented as

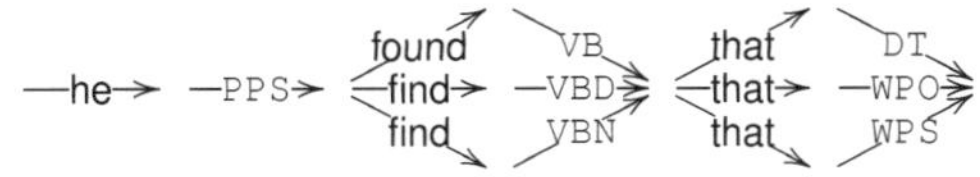

The rules are applied by intersecting the above automaton with FSTs representing them. This means that the FSTs operate on the *paths* of the

[3] To be more precise, a *potential* verb, i.e. a token having some verbal reading. The same applies in the sequel.

[4] As in (Roche and Schabes, 1995), by FST *determinization* we mean building an equivalent subsequential form, i.e. a form not which does not backtrack during the execution.

[5] The number of possible values of these three attributes is $7 \cdot 2 \cdot 5 = 70$ in NCP but more than 200 in some other tagsets used for Polish.

input FSA, each of which contains exactly one reading of each token, e.g.

he `PPS` find `VBN` that `WPO`

In this setting, unification leads to at most N-fold increase of the state space even in compound FSTs, which allows hoping for composition. However, the FSIG model has the disadvantage that the execution time is not linear in terms of the input size, particularly for high ambiguity (cf. (Tapanainen, 1999)). Hence, the model does not ensure our efficiency requirements.

Efficient unification seems to be achievable by equipping the FST with additional memory for the temporary result, even though this means leaving the pure finite-state formalism. Note also that this is analogous to introducing a queue in (van Noord and Gerdemann, 2001). These observations have motivated the solution proposed below.

4 The solution

Basic model. We follow the idea present in the old Spejd as well as in JAPE: each rule is split into a simple *match pattern* and a list of more complex *actions* performed outside of the finite-state formalism. In our case, match patterns are regular expressions[6], while the actions can be virtually arbitrary, provided that they operate within a given match. The match patterns are compiled into deterministic automata (DFA). Rather than following the FSIG approach, we traditionally run these DFAs on single strings encoding the input, as in the example ($*$) on page 2, which enables finding matches without backtracking.

Whenever a match is found, we stop the DFA which found it and apply the pre-defined routines corresponding to the actions. For the example input *drogi dom* discussed in Section 2, the routine for unify would scan and store all the readings of *drogi*, do the same for *dom*, intersect the two sets of readings and save the result.[7]

Single-pattern DFAs. Even though our patterns are regular expressions, compiling them to DFAs is not straightforward since the actions may refer to *sub-matches* (e.g. A, B in the example in Section 2). In general, a single run of a classical DFA cannot unambiguously determine the positions of all such sub-matches (Friedl, 2002). For this purpose, we use the enhanced *tagged DFAs* (TDFAs) from (Laurikari, 2000) which use additional integer registers (which Laurikari calls *tags*) to store the references to potential sub-match boundaries.

TDFAs are asymptotically fast as they do not backtrack, but several times slower than the classical DFAs. Hence we adopt the *double pass* technique of (Cox, 2010): we process the input first with a classical DFA deciding solely whether it contains a match for a given rule; only when it does, we execute a more complex TDFA localizing the match and the desired sub-matches, and finally apply the rule actions. In this way, every sentence containing a match is processed twice; however, our assumption that the matches are (averagely) rare guarantees that in total this variant is faster than using only TDFAs.

Practical composition. We have already met the first two requirements from Section 2. It remains to provide means for practical composition. At this point, the (average) rareness of the matches becomes crucial. Intuitively, it means that many rules do not change the input, and it should be advantageous to compose *these* rules together. Among several possible realizations of this idea, we have chosen the following simple algorithm.

Let $M_1, \ldots, M_n$ denote the match specifications of the rules to be applied. We build:

- for each i, a TDFA T_i recognizing M_i;
- a DFA D recognizing $M_1|M_2|\ldots|M_n$.

Then, we slightly modify D in Laurikari's spirit by equipping it with two integer registers, L and R, used as follows: whenever a match for some M_i is found, D shall set $R := i$ provided that $L < i \leq R$. Hence, running D on the whole input with initial $R = \infty$ results in setting R to the least $i > L$ such that M_i has some match.

The main algorithm proceeds as follows:

1. Set $L := 0$. (Start with all rules.)
2. Set $R := \infty$ and run D on the whole input.
3. If $R = \infty$ (no M_i with $i > L$ matched), halt.
4. Run T_R on the whole input. For every match found, apply to it the actions of the R-th rule.
5. Set $L := R$ and jump to step 2.
   (M_L done; proceed only with $\{M_i : i > L\}$.)

[6] A match pattern is a regular expression over token specifications. These are built of attribute requirements, combined by logical connectives and quantifiers over readings, e.g. "there is a reading in which both `pos` equals `noun` and `case` equals `nom`". For the input encoding of the form ($*$), such patterns clearly translate to character-level regular expressions.

[7] This might be non-linear in terms of the match size but will happen rarely due to the rareness of the matches.

Avoiding explosion. Even though the number of constructed states is clearly smaller than in the FST models (as we have avoided states arising from sophisticated rule actions), it is still very high. We reduced it significantly[8] by a simple technique of *lazy construction*: the transitions and their target states are built only during the execution, just before their first use.

In practice, for a large number of rules, we fix a *composition width* k and apply the above algorithm to groups of k consecutive rules. To achieve best performance, k should be chosen possibly large but so that the states still fit into memory. This makes the running time asymptotically linear in the number of rules; nevertheless, the third requirement from Section 2 has been met.

5 Evaluation

Our approach has been applied to optimize Spejd, a syntactic parser of broad functionality which has been used for corpus development, valence extraction (Przepiórkowski, 2008b), and also sentiment analysis (Buczyński and Wawer, 2008).

composition width	**avg. speed** [tokens/s]	**memory** [MB]
N/A (old Spejd)	802	184
1	6,013	292
10	18,536	488
30	21,746	3,245

Table 1: The speed and memory usage of Spejd in terms of the composition width.

Table 1 presents the overall efficiency of the system. In the tests, performed on a computer with 3.1 GHz AMD FX processor, 467 handwritten rules of (Przepiórkowski, 2008a) were applied to a 15 million token sample from the IPI Corpus (Przepiórkowski, 2004).

Notably, the use of lazy construction increased the achievable width from about 3–4 to about 30.[9]

Conclusion

We have described a variation of the finite-state approach which, although it may seem strange in comparison with the classical solutions, seems to be a good choice for infrequently matching complex morphosyntactic rules, particularly for highly ambiguous rich annotation. In practice, it has allowed over 25-fold acceleration of the Spejd system while preserving its rich functionality.

[8]In some TDFAs in our applications, less than 5% of states are reachable in practice, even for megabytes of input.

[9]Further state space reduction techniques, which are out of scope of this paper, have allowed us to work with widths exceeding 1000. Due to the overhead involved in them, this resulted "only" in about 10-fold acceleration in comparison with $k = 30$.

References

Salah Aït-Mokhtar and Jean-Pierre Chanod. 1997. Incremental finite-state parsing. In *ANLP*, pages 72–79.

Markus Becker, Witold Drożdżyński, Hans-Ulrich Krieger, Jakub Piskorski, Ulrich Schäfer, and Feiyu Xu. 2002. SProUT — shallow processing with typed feature structures and unification. In *Proceedings of the International Conference on NLP (ICON 2002)*, Mumbai, India.

Kenneth R. Beesley and Lauri Karttunen. 2003. *Finite State Morphology*. CSLI Studies in Computational Linguistics. CSLI Publications.

Aleksander Buczyński and Aleksander Wawer. 2008. Shallow parsing in sentiment analysis of product reviews. In Sandra Kübler, Jakub Piskorski, and Adam Przepiórkowski, editors, *Proceedings of the LREC 2008 Workshop on Partial Parsing*, pages 14–18, Marrakech. ELRA.

Russ Cox. 2010. Regular expression matching in the wild. `http://swtch.com/~rsc/regexp/regexp3.html`.

Hamish Cunningham, Diana Maynard, and Valentin Tablan. 2000. JAPE: a java annotation patterns engine (second edition). Technical Report Technical Report CS–00–10, of Sheffield, Department of Computer Science.

Jeffrey E. F. Friedl. 2002. *Mastering Regular Expressions*. O'Reilly & Associates, Inc., Sebastopol, CA, USA, 2 edition.

Jerry R. Hobbs, Douglas E. Appelt, John Bear, David J. Israel, Megumi Kameyama, Mark E. Stickel, and Mabry Tyson. 1997. FASTUS: A cascaded finite-state transducer for extracting information from natural-language text. *CoRR*, cmp-lg/9705013.

Fred Karlsson. 1990. Constraint grammar as a framework for parsing running text. In *Proceedings of the 13th conference on Computational linguistics - Volume 3*, pages 168–173, Stroudsburg, PA, USA. Association for Computational Linguistics.

Kimmo Koskenniemi. 1990. Finite-state parsing and disambiguation. In *Proceedings of the 13th conference on Computational linguistics - Volume 2*, pages 229–232, Stroudsburg, PA, USA. Association for Computational Linguistics.

Ville Laurikari. 2000. NFAs with tagged transitions, their conversion to deterministic automata and application to regular expressions. In *In Proceedings of the 7th International Symposium on String Processing and Information Retrieval*, pages 181–187.

Mehryar Mohri. 1997. Finite-state transducers in language and speech processing. *Computational Linguistics*, 23(2):269–311.

Gertjan van Noord and Dale Gerdemann. 2001. Finite state transducers with predicates and identities. *Grammars*, 4(3):263–286.

Adam Przepiórkowski, Mirosław Bańko, Rafał L. Górski, and Barbara Lewandowska-Tomaszczyk, editors. 2012. *Narodowy Korpus Języka Polskiego [Eng.: National Corpus of Polish]*. Wydawnictwo Naukowe PWN, Warsaw.

Adam Przepiórkowski. 2004. *The IPI PAN Corpus: Preliminary version*. Institute of Computer Science, Polish Academy of Sciences, Warsaw.

Adam Przepiórkowski. 2008a. *Powierzchniowe przetwarzanie języka polskiego*. Akademicka Oficyna Wydawnicza EXIT, Warsaw.

Adam Przepiórkowski. 2008b. Towards a partial grammar of Polish for valence extraction. In *Grammar & Corpora 2007: Selected contributions from the conference Grammar and Corpora, Sept. 25–27, 2007, Liblice*, pages 127–133. Academia, Prague.

Emmanuel Roche and Yves Schabes. 1995. Deterministic part-of-speech tagging with finite-state transducers. *Comput. Linguist.*, 21:227–253, June.

Emmanuel Roche and Yves Schabes. 1996. Introduction to finite-state devices in natural language processing. Technical report, Mitsubishi Electric Research Laboratories.

Pasi Tapanainen. 1999. *Parsing in Two Frameworks: Finite-state and Functional Dependency Grammar*. University of Helsinki, Department of General Linguistics.

Finite State Morphology Tool for Latvian

Daiga Deksne
Tilde
Vienības gatve 75a, Riga, Latvia
daiga.deksne@tilde.lv

Abstract

The existing Latvian morphological analyzer was developed more than ten years ago. Its main weaknesses are: low processing speed when processing a large text corpus, complexity of adding new entries to the lexical data base, and limitations for usage on different operational platforms. This paper describes the creation of a new Latvian morphology tool. The tool has the capability to return lemma and morphological analysis for a given word form; it can generate the required word form if lemma and form description is given; it can also generate all possible word forms for a given lemma. As Finite state transducer (FST) technology is used for the morphology tool, it is easy to extend the lexicon, the tool can be reused on different platforms and it has good performance indicators.

Introduction

An efficient way to generate forms and obtain morphological information about a word in a text is to apply morphological analysis tools. Such tools and their efficient implementation are especially important for languages that have a rich morphology. In this paper, we describe a new morphological processing tool for the Latvian language.

The Latvian language is an inflectional language. As described in (Skadiņa et al., 2012), words change form according to grammatical function. Most word forms are built by adding an affix to the stem of the word. The endings are ambiguous. The same lexical ending can symbolize several grammatical word forms. There can also be changes in a stem – regular consonant changes at the end of a stem, or a stem can be completely different for a word form. For example, for the verbs of the first conjugation, the full set of inflectional word forms is generated using three different stems - infinitive, present tense, and past tense stems. To describe the morphological lexicon, the relationships between stems and different affixes must be defined.

The existing Latvian morphological analyzer was developed more than ten years ago. It is based on a relational lexical data base of contemporary Latvian language. Prefixes, stems, and endings are stored in separate tables and are marked by different predefined declension groups. The relationship tables define eligible combinations of affixes. To be used by the morphological analyzer, this data base is compiled into a proprietary format. The same data base is used for building a spelling checker data file for Latvian. The main weaknesses of the existing Latvian morphological analyzer are: low processing speed when processing a large text corpus, complexity of adding new entries to the lexical data base, and limitations on platforms (it works only on the Windows platform). These factors promoted the search for a new solution.

In next chapters, we describe in detail the proposed solution.

1 Substantiation for chosen architecture

Existing morphological analysis tools for different languages and ways to describe the morphological lexicon were analyzed. There are many morphology tools for different languages that use FST technology. A good example from which to borrow ideas about morphologically tagged lexicon representation in finite state format is

SMOR (Schmid et al., 2004) – a morphological analyzer for German. Concatenation is used to concatenate previously defined prefixes, stems, suffixes, and inflectional endings. As these parts are marked with agreement features, filters are applied to eliminate invalid sequences.

There are several toolkits available which help in developing FST based solutions: Stuttgart Finite-State Transducer Tools[1], OpenFst library[2], Foma finite state library[3], Helsinki Finite-State Transducer Technology toolkit[4], Lttoolbox[5].

To describe the lexicon, we use the Stuttgart Finite-State Transducer Toolkit (SFST) as its extended regular expressions based transducer specification language allows to clearly describe the lexicon, to define variables, to apply concatenation, composition, insertion, and other operators needed for transducer implementation (Schmid, 2005). For transducer compilation, we use OpenFst as it supports weighted finite state transducers, and its source code can be compiled on Linux and Windows platforms. Examples in text are presented in SFST syntax.

2 Designing finite state morphology tool

There are three different transducers in the morphology tool: morphological analysis, form synthesis, and all word form generation for a given lemma. Table 1 shows the input and the output strings produced by every transducer. The files for the synthesis transducer are generated from the all form generation transducer. Only the last symbol differs in the transducer. For synthesis, the empty symbol on the input level changes to form ID on the output level (1), but for all word form generation, the form ID on the input level changes to the part-of-speech tag on the output level (2). The transducer for analysis is the inverted version of the transducer for synthesis.

(1) <>:<1397>
(2) <1397>:<m>

Analysis	
Input	piecu
Output	pieci<m0fpg000c0000000> pieci<m0mpg000c0000000>
Synthesis	
Input	pieci<m0fpd000c0000000>
Output	piecām
All forms	
Input	pieci<m>
Output	pieci<m0mpn000c0000000> piecu<m0mpg000c0000000> pieciem<m0mpd000c0000000> piecus<m0mpa000c0000000> piecos<m0mpl000c0000000> piecas<m0fpn000c0000000> piecu<m0fpg000c0000000> piecām<m0fpd000c0000000> piecas<m0fpa000c0000000> piecās<m0fpl000c0000000>

Table 1: Different transducer input and output for the numeral 'five'

For form description, the original form identifiers are used as they are in the lexical data base of contemporary Latvian language. When further compiling transducers with OpenFst, they are remapped to form descriptions which are based on a tagset developed in MUTEXT-East (Erjavec, 2011). Both (3) and (4) describe the same form – numeral, feminine, plural, genitive case, cardinal numeral.

(3) <1397>
(4) < m0fpg000c0000000>

The input for analysis is a word form, the output – one or more lemmas and form description tags. The input for synthesis is a lemma and a form description tag, and the output is one or several word forms. The input for full paradigm generation is a lemma with a part-of-speech tag, and the output is all word forms and their form descriptions.

The transducers are created incrementally. The final transducer is represented as a union of separate part-of-speech transducers.

(5) $morph$ = $Pronouns$ | $Numerals$ | $Others$ | $Adjectives$ | $Nouns$ | $Verbs$

1 http://www.ims.uni-stuttgart.de/projekte/gramotron/SOFTWARE/SFST.htm
2 http://www.openfst.org
3 http://foma.sourceforge.net/dokuwiki/doku.php
4 http://www.ling.helsinki.fi/kieliteknologia/tutkimus/hfst
5 http://wiki.apertium.org/wiki/Lttoolbox

Words belonging to a different part-of-speech are represented in a slightly different way. Words from non-inflected part-of-speech, such as conjunction, exclamation, particle, abbreviation, preposition, are represented as a lexical entry followed by one or several form IDs on the input level which changes to a part-of-speech value on the output level. All such entries are joined by union operators (6).

```
(6) $Others$ = bravo<1574>:<i> | ...
```

Every numeral and pronoun is represented as an inflected form on the input level and a lemma on the output level followed by one or several form IDs on the input level which changes to a part-of-speech value on the output level. All such entries are joined by union operators. If the inflected form and the lemma start with the same characters, they are represented as a character sequence. In example (7), the word "man" (to me) has the lemma "es" (I), and the word "citam" (to other) has the lemma "cits" (other).

```
(7) $Pronouns$ = {man}:{es}<1474>:<p> |
    cit{am}:{s}<1634>:<p> | ...
```

The ending classes, the lists of inflections, and stems are defined separately for nouns, adjectives, and verbs. In the future, the morphological lexicon will be extended mostly by adding adjective, verb, or noun stems of new words. The ending classes contain a full set of possible noun, adjective, and verb endings and will not require further changes. Before every adjective and verb ending is a prefix tag which marks with which prefix a particular ending can be used. As the nouns and verbs can have several inflected stems for a lemma, the special ending tag marks with which stem a particular ending can be used. In example (8), the ending tags are "<altEnd1>" and "<normEnd>". The ending on the output level changes to the corresponding lemma's ending. All ending groups are joined by union operator (9), and before every ending group is an ending group tag which will be used in a filter for filtering out the combinations of stems and endings marked with the different ending group tags. There are 15 ending groups for adjectives, 26 ending groups for verbs and 69 ending groups for nouns.

```
(8) $Verb2$ = \
 <normEnd><PrefOther>{sim}:{t}<643>:<v> |
 <altEnd1><PrefOther>{a}:{t}<624>:<v> | ...
```

```
(9) $VInfl$ = \
<>:<Verbmodal>$Verbmodal$ |
<>:<Verb2>$Verb2$ |
<>:<Verb3_aam_refl>$Verb3_aam_refl$ ...
```

As nouns and verbs can have several stems to form a full paradigm, it is hard to write FST transformations by hand. There is a special file format for editing – the stems of the same paradigm are on the same line. This file contains two information blocks – one about predefined ending groups (10) and the other about the actual lexical entries, stems (11). The predefined ending group block is fixed; to improve the verb's morphological analysis, the editors will make changes in the lexical entries block. In the predefined ending group block, every line contains a predefined ending group tag, the maximal number of stems for a word marked with this ending group tag, and ending tags for every stem. All verb groups have infinitive and present stems, some might also have past stem, second present stem, participle stems. In example (10) ending group '<Verb2>' requires two stems but '<Verbmodal>' – four stems. In (11) verb 'barot' of ending group '<Verb2>' has two stems but word 'iet' of ending group '<Verbmodal>' - four.

```
(10)
<Verb2>        2 |t<normEnd> |u<altEnd1>
<Verbmodal>  4 |t<normEnd>
  |u<normEnd1><altEnd1>
  |u<normEnd2><altEnd2> |<altEnd3>
```

```
(11)
<Verb2>              baro|t baroj|u
<Verbmodal>          ie|t ej|u gāj|u iet|
```

The script changes lines to SFST representation and adds required tags for every stem (12).

```
(12)
ie<normEnd><Verbmodal>
ej<normEnd1><Verbmodal>
e:ij:e<altEnd1><Verbmodal>
gāj<normEnd2><Verbmodal>
g:iā:ej:<><altEnd2><Verbmodal>
iet:<><altEnd3><Verbmodal>
```

Verbs and adjectives are represented as a concatenation of prefixes, stems, and endings, and nouns are represented as a concatenation of stems and endings.

(13)
```
$Verbs$ = $VPrefix$ $VStems$ $VInfl$
$Adjectives$ = $APrefix$ $AStems$ $AInfl$
$Nouns$ = $NStems$ $NInfl$
```

At this stage, every verb consists of three parts – prefix part, stem part, and ending part (14).

(14)
```
<PrefJa>jā
lob<>:ī<altEnd1><Verb3>
<Verb3><altEnd1><PrefJa>{a}:{t}<649>:<v>
```

The wrong forms are filtered out by composing transducers with filters which accept the same prefix, ending, and ending group tags between word constituents.

3 Evaluation

We evaluated 37 964 words from the Latvian part of the Latvian-English dictionary (Veisbergs, 2005). These words were morphologically analyzed on a computer with Windows 7 operating system (Intel® Core™ i7-2600 3.40 GHz processor, 8 GB RAM). The existing morphology tool spent 2 minutes on this task, e.g., 316 words per second, while the FST based morphology tool completed it in 4 seconds, e.g., 9491 words per second. The similar performance speed for this task also on a computer with Ubuntu GNU/Linux operating system (Intel® Core™ 2 CPU 6300 1.86 GHz processor, 7.74 GB RAM). The outputs of the two systems slightly differ as some errors in lexicon where fixed. The functionality of all form generation for a given lemma and part of speech was tested on the same data. First the word was analyzed, then the lemma and part of speech were extracted from the analysis output and passed on to the form generation transducer. The existing morphology tool spent 7 minutes and 25 seconds on this task, while the FST based morphology tool – 27 seconds. The speed of the all form generation functionality should be viewed only as a comparison between the previous and the new FST morphology tools as extra tasks are performed by the script while processing analysis results.

4 Conclusion and future work

In comparison with the existing morphology tool, FST technology is the better choice for morphology tool development. The new solution is faster; it works not only on Windows, but also on the Linux platform; it makes it easy to add new stems to predefined declension groups.

For now, all stems are listed in the transducer, except for nouns with suffixes '–tāj', '–um', '–ēj', '–šan', which are derived from verb stems. Future work will be to reduce the size of the lexicon by generating stems that have regular consonant changes. This task is not simple. Phonological changes occur only for words of certain inflectional classes and only in certain grammatical forms. For example, for nouns of the fifth and the sixth declension in plural genitive and for nouns of the second declension in singular genitive and all plural cases stem's last or two last consonants change to one or two different consonants (15). However, some stems do not follow this pattern.

(15)
```
$nounAlt$ = ({b}:{bj} | {c}:{č} | {d}:{ž} | {dz}:{dž} | {l}:{ļ} | {ln}:{ļņ} | {m}:{mj} | {n}:{ņ} | {p}:{pj} | {s}:{š} | {sl}:{šļ} | {sn}:{šņ} | {t}:{š} | {v}:{vj} | {z}:{ž} | {zl}:{žļ} | {zn}:{žņ} | {ll}:{ļļ} | {nn}:{ņņ})
```

Not all words are listed in the lexicon. Time by time new words are introduced into a language. Mostly these are foreign words and domain-specific terms, and many are formed as compounds. Compounding rules should be added to the transducer, which will increase its coverage.

Acknowledgments

The research leading to these results has received funding from the research project "Information and Communication Technology Competence Center" of EU Structural funds, contract nr. L-KC-11-0003 signed between ICT Competence Centre and Investment and Development Agency of Latvia, Research No. 2.8 "Research of automatic methods for text structural analysis".

References

Erjavec T. 2012. MULTEXT-East: Morphosyntactic Resources for Central and Eastern European Languages. *Language Resources and Evaluation*, 46/1, pp. 131-142.

Skadiņa I., Veisbergs A., Vasiļjevs A., Gornostaja T., Keiša I., Rudzīte A. 2012. http://www.meta-net.eu/whitepapers/e-book/latvian.pdf. Springer.

Schmid. H. 2005. A Programming Language for Finite State Transducers. *Proceedings of the 5th International Workshop on Finite State Methods in Natural Language Processing (FSMNLP 2005)*, Helsinki, Finland.

Schmid H., Fitschen A. and Heid U. 2004. SMOR: A German Computational Morphology Covering Derivation, Composition, and Inflection. *Proceedings of the IVth International Conference on Language Resources and Evaluation (LREC 2004)*, p. 1263-1266, Lisbon, Portugal.

Veisbergs A. 2005. Jaunā latviešu-angļu vārdnīca = the new Latvian-English dictionary. Rīga : Zvaigzne ABC, c2005

Modeling Graph Languages with Grammars Extracted via Tree Decompositions

Bevan Keeley Jones[*,†] B.K.Jones@sms.ed.ac.uk
Sharon Goldwater[*] sgwater@inf.ed.ac.uk
Mark Johnson[†] mark.johnson@mq.edu.au

* School of Informatics
University of Edinburgh
Edinburgh, UK

† Department of Computing
Macquarie University
Sydney, Australia

Abstract

Work on probabilistic models of natural language tends to focus on strings and trees, but there is increasing interest in more general graph-shaped structures since they seem to be better suited for representing natural language semantics, ontologies, or other varieties of knowledge structures. However, while there are relatively simple approaches to defining generative models over strings and trees, it has proven more challenging for more general graphs. This paper describes a natural generalization of the n-gram to graphs, making use of Hyperedge Replacement Grammars to define generative models of graph languages.

1 Introduction

While most work in natural language processing (NLP), and especially within statistical NLP, has historically focused on strings and trees, there is increasing interest in deeper graph-based analyses which could facilitate natural language understanding and generation applications. Graphs have a long tradition within knowledge representation (Sowa, 1976), natural language semantics (Titov et al., 2009; Martin and White, 2011; Le and Zuidema, 2012), and in models of deep syntax (Oepen et al., 2004; de Marneffe and Manning, 2008). Graphs seem particularly appropriate for representing semantic structures, since a single concept could play multiple roles within a sentence. For instance, in the semantic representation at the bottom right of Figure 1 *lake* is an argument of both *rich-in* and *own* in the sentence, "The lake is said to be rich in fish but is privately owned." However, work on graphs has been hampered, due, in part, to the absence of a general agreed upon formalism for processing and modeling such data structures. Where string and tree modeling benefits from the wildly popular Probabilistic Context Free Grammar (PCFG) and related formalisms such as Tree Substitution Grammar, Regular Tree Grammar, Hidden Markov Models, and n-grams, there is nothing of similar popularity for graphs. We need a slightly different formalism, and Hyperedge Replacement Grammar (HRG) (Drewes et al., 1997), a variety of context-free grammar for graphs, suggests itself as a reasonable choice given its close analogy with CFG. Of course, in order to make use of the formalism we need actual grammars, and this paper fills that gap by introducing a procedure for automatically extracting grammars from a corpus of graphs.

Grammars are appealing for the intuitive and systematic way they capture the compositionality of language. For instance, just as a PCFG could be used to parse "the lake" as a syntactic subject, so could a graph grammar represent *lake* as a constituent in a parse of the corresponding semantic graph. In fact, picking a formalism that is so similar to the PCFG makes it easy to adapt proven, familiar techniques for training and inference such as the inside-outside algorithm, and because HRG is context-free, parses can be represented by trees, facilitating the use of many more tools from tree automata (Knight and Graehl, 2005). Furthermore, the operational parallelism with PCFG makes it easy to integrate graph-based systems with syntactic models in synchronous grammars (Jones et al., 2012).

Probabilistic versions of deep syntactic models such as Lexical Functional Grammar and HPSG (Johnson et al., 1999; Riezler et al., 2000) are one grammar-based approach to modeling graphs represented in the form of feature structures. However, these models are tied to a particular linguistic paradigm, and they are complex, requiring a great deal of effort to engineer and annotate the necessary grammars and corpora. It is also not obvious how to define generative probabilistic models with such grammars, limiting their utility in certain applications.

In contrast, this paper describes a method of automatically extracting graph grammars from a corpus of graphs, allowing us to easily estimate rule probabilities and define generative models. The class of grammars we extract generalize the types of regular string and tree grammars one might use to define a bigram or similar Markov model for trees. In fact, the procedure produces regular string and tree grammars as special cases when the input graphs themselves are strings or trees.

There is always overhead in learning a new formalism, so we will endeavor to provide the necessary background as simply as possible, according to the following structure. Section 2 introduces Hyperedge Replacement Grammars, which generate graphs, and their probabilistic extension, weighted HRGs. Section 3 explains how each HRG derivation of a graph induces a tree decomposition of that graph. Given a tree decomposition of a graph, we use that mapping "in reverse" to induce an HRG that generates that graph (section 4). Section 4 also introduces four different strategies for finding tree decompositions of (and hence inducing HRGs from) a set of graphs. Section 5 applies these strategies to the LOGON corpus (Oepen et al., 2004) and evaluates the induced weighted HRGs in terms of held-out perplexity. Section 6 concludes the paper and discusses possible applications and extensions.

2 Graphs and Hyperedge Replacement Grammars

Hyperedge Replacement Grammar (HRG) is a generalization of CFG to graph languages (see Drewes et al. (1997) for an overview). Where a CFG builds up strings by replacing symbols with new substrings, an HRG builds graphs by replacing edges with subgraphs. As a context-free formalism, HRG derivations can be described by trees, similar to CFG parses. Thus, in the case of probabilistic HRG, it is possible to assign rule weights to define easily factorizable probability distributions over graphs, just as PCFGs do for strings.

We start by defining a hypergraph, a generalization of a graph where edges may link any finite number of vertices. Formally, a hypergraph is a tuple $(\mathcal{V}, \mathcal{E}, \alpha, \ell, x)$. $\mathcal{V}$ and $\mathcal{E}$ are finite sets of vertices and hyperedges, respectively. The *attachment function* $\alpha : \mathcal{E} \to \mathcal{V}^*$ maps each hyperedge $e \in \mathcal{E}$ to a sequence of pairwise distinct vertices from $\mathcal{V}$, where we call the length of $\alpha(e)$ the *arity* of e. The *labeling function* $\ell : \mathcal{E} \to \Sigma$ maps each hyperedge to a symbol in some ranked alphabet Σ, where the rank of $\ell(e)$ is e's arity. Vertices are unlabeled, but they can be simulated by treating unary hyperedges (i.e., hyperedges with a single vertex) as vertex labels. Finally, each graph has a set of zero or more *external vertices*, arranged in a sequence $x \in \mathcal{V}^*$ (pairwise distinct), which plays an important role in the rewriting mechanism of HRG. Just as hyperedges have an arity, so too do hypergraphs, defined as the length of x.

We are primarily interested in languages of simple directed graphs, hypergraphs where each edge is either binary or, for vertex labels, unary. In this case, we can indicate visually the ordering on a binary edge with vertex sequence $v_0 v_1$ by an arrow pointing from vertex v_0 to v_1. We may make use of hyperedges of arbitrary arity, though, for intermediate rewriting steps during derivations. The semantic dependency graph at the bottom right of Figure 1, taken from the Redwoods corpus (Oepen et al., 2004), is an example of a simple graph. It has both unary edges for expressing predicates like 'private' and 'own' and binary edges for specifying their relations. In principle, any vertex can have more than one unary edge, a fact we make use of in HRG rule definitions, such as in the graph on the right-hand side of rule $r4$ in Figure 1 where vertex 2 has two unary edges labeled 'rich-in' and $N_{\text{rich-in}}$.

A weighted HRG is an edge rewriting system for generating hypergraphs, also defined as a tuple $(\Sigma, \mathcal{N}, S, \mathcal{R})$. Σ is a ranked alphabet of edge labels, $\mathcal{N} \subset \Sigma$ a set of nonterminal symbols, $S \in \mathcal{N}$ a special start symbol, and $\mathcal{R}$ is a finite set of weighted rules. Each rule in $\mathcal{R}$ is of the form $[A \to h].w$, where h is a hypergraph with edge labels from Σ, $A \in \mathcal{N}$ has rank equal to the arity of h, and weight w is a real number. As with PCFGs, a weighted HRG is probabilistic if the weights of all rules with the same ranked symbol A on the left-hand side sum to one. In the case of probabilistic HRG, the probability of a derivation is the product of the weights of the rules in the derivation, just as for PCFG. Figure 1 shows an example of an HRG and a sample derivation. The external vertices of the right-hand side graphs have been shaded, and their sequence should be read top to bottom (e.g., 0 to 5 in rule $r1$). Vertices have been identified by numbers, but these identifiers are included only to make it easier to refer to them in our discussion; strictly speaking, vertices are unlabeled, and these numbers are irrelevant to the operation of the grammar. Nonterminal edges are dashed to make them easier to identify.

Hyperedge replacement, the basic rewriting mechanism of HRG, is an operation where a hypergraph is substituted for an edge. If g is a hypergraph containing edge e, and h is another hypergraph with the same arity as e, edge e can be replaced with h by first removing e from g and then "fusing" h and g together at the external vertices of h and the vertices of $\alpha(e)$. So, if $\alpha(e) = v_0 v_1 \ldots v_k$ and h has external vertices $u_0 u_1 \ldots u_k$, we would fuse each u_i to the corresponding v_i.

Much like with CFG, where each step of a derivation replaces a symbol by a substring, each step of an HRG derivation replaces an edge with a certain nonterminal symbol label by the right-hand side graph of some rule with the same symbol on its left-hand side. For instance, in the application of rule $r3$ in the fourth step of Figure 1, the edge $1 \overset{N_{\text{say}}}{\to} 5$ is replaced by the graph $1 \overset{\text{arg2}}{\to} 2 \overset{N_{\text{arg2}}}{\to} 5$ by removing the red N_{say} edge and then attaching the new subgraph. Rule $r3$ has an external vertex sequence of 1 to 5, and these are fused to the incident vertices of the nonterminal edge $1 \overset{N_{\text{say}}}{\to} 5$. The edge to be replaced in each step has been highlighted in red to ease reading.

3 Tree Decompositions

We now introduce one additional piece of theoretical machinery, the *tree decomposition* (Bodlaender, 1993). Tree decompositions play an important role in graph theory, feature prominently in the junction tree algorithm from machine learning (Pearl, 1988), and have proven valuable for efficient parsing (Gildea, 2011; Chiang et al., 2013). Importantly, Lautemann (1988) proved that every HRG parse identifies a particular tree decomposition, and by restricting ourselves to a certain type of tree we will draw an even tighter relationship, allowing us to identify parses given tree decompositions.

A tree decomposition of a graph g is a tree whose nodes identify subsets of the vertices of g which satisfy the following three properties:[1]

- **Vertex Cover**: Every vertex of g is contained by at least one tree node.
- **Edge Cover**: For every edge e of the graph, there is a tree node η such that each vertex of $\alpha(e)$ is in η.
- **Running Intersection**: Given any two tree nodes η_0 and η_1, both containing vertex v, all tree nodes on the unique path from η_0 to η_1 also contain v.

Figure 2 presents four different tree decompositions of the graph shown at the bottom right of Figure 1. Consider (d). Vertex cover is satisfied by the fact that every vertex of the graph appears in at least one tree node. Graph vertex 0, for example, is covered by two nodes $\{0, 1, 5\}$ and $\{0, 3, 5\}$. Similarly, every edge is covered by at least one of the nodes. Node $\{0, 1, 5\}$ covers one binary edge, $0 \overset{\text{arg1}}{\to} 1$, and three unary edges: $\overset{\text{but}}{0}$, $\overset{\text{say}}{1}$, and $\overset{\text{lake}}{5}$.

We focus on a particular class called *edge-mapped* tree decompositions, defined by pairs (t, μ) where t is a tree decomposition of some graph g and μ is a bijection from the nodes of t to the edges of g, where a node also covers the edge it maps to. Every graph has at least one edge-mapped tree decomposition; Figure 2(a)-(c) illustrates three such edge-mapped decompositions for a particular graph, where the mapping is shown by the extra labels next to the tree nodes. The edge mapping simplifies the rule extraction procedure described in Section 4 since traversing the tree and following

[1]To avoid confusion, we adopt a terminology where *node* is always used in respect to tree decompositions and *vertex* and *edge* to graphs.

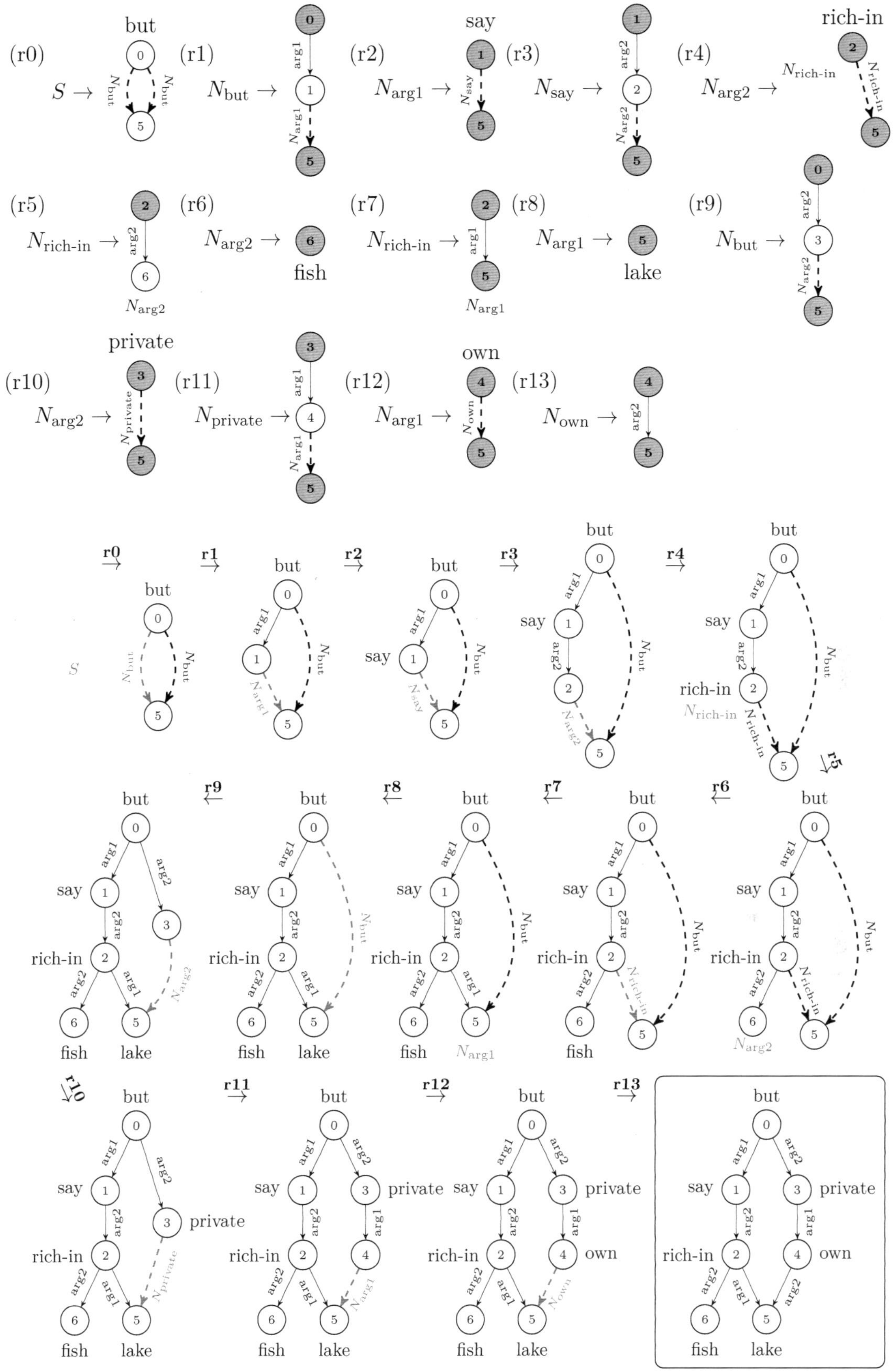

Figure 1: An HRG and a derivation of the semantic dependency graph for "the lake is said to be rich in fish but is privately owned." External vertices are shaded and ordered top to bottom, nonterminal edges are dashed, and the one being replaced is highlighted in red.

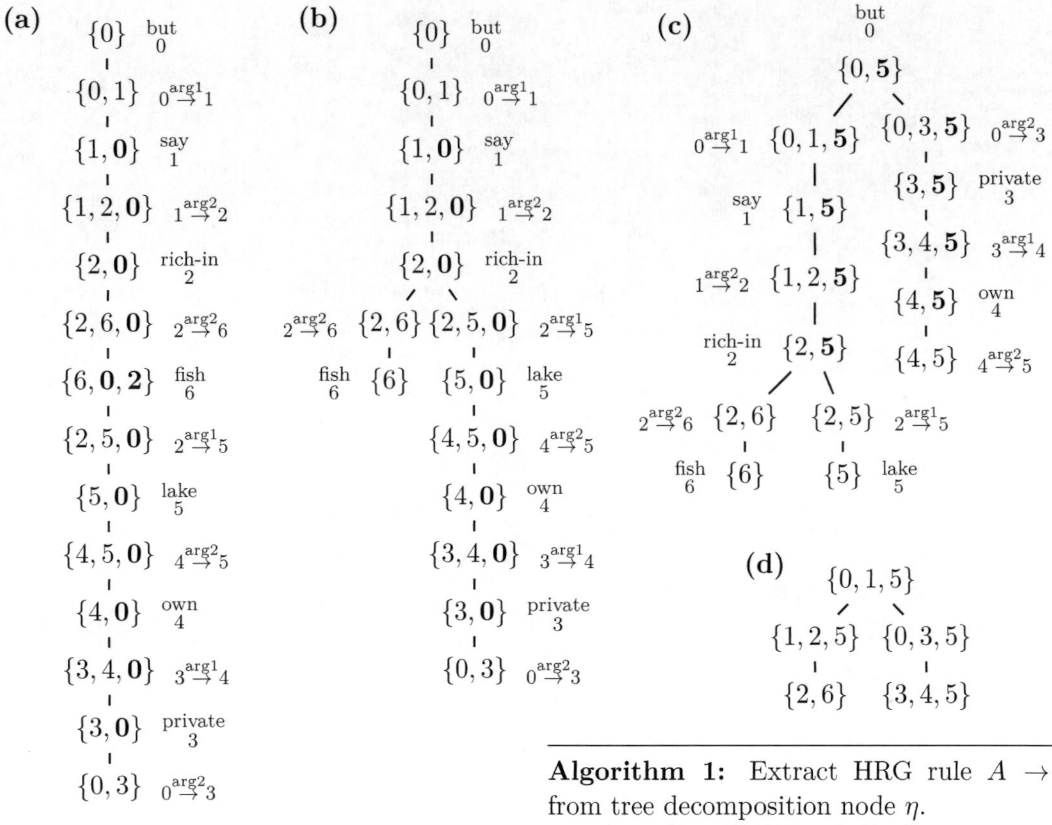

Figure 2: Edge-mapped (a-c) and non-edge-mapped (d) tree decompositions for the graph at the bottom right of Figure 1.

this mapping μ guarantees that every graph edge is visited exactly once.

Running intersection will also prove important for rule extraction, since it tracks the tree violations of the graph by passing down the end points of edges that link edges in different branches of the decomposition. This same information must be passed down the respective paths of the HRG derivation tree via the external vertices of rule-right hand sides. Figure 2 uses bold face and vertex order to highlight the vertices that must be added to each node beyond those needed to cover its corresponding edge. In the decomposition shown in (b), vertex 0 must be passed from the node mapping to $\overset{\text{but}}{0}$ down to the node mapping to $0 \overset{\text{arg2}}{\to} 3$ because the two edges share that vertex. Any HRG derivation will need to pass down vertices in a similar manner to specify which edges get attached to which vertices.

As suggested by the four trees of Figure 2, there are always many possible decompositions

Algorithm 1: Extract HRG rule $A \to h$ from tree decomposition node η.

function EXTRACT(η)
  $A \leftarrow$ label(parent(η), $|$parent(η) $\cap\, \eta|$)
  $h.x \leftarrow$ order(η, parent(η) $\cap\, \eta$)
  add terminal edge $\mu(\eta)$ to h
  for all $\eta_i \in$ children(η) **do**
    add nonterminal edge u_i to h
    $\alpha(u_i) \leftarrow$ order($\eta_i, \eta \cap \eta_i$)
    $\ell(u_i) \leftarrow$ label($\eta, |\eta \cap \eta_i|$)
  return $[A \to h]$

for any given graph. In the next section we describe three methods of producing tree decompositions, each leading to distinct grammars with different language modeling properties.

4 HRG Extraction

Rule extraction proceeds by first selecting a particular tree decomposition for a graph and then walking this tree to extract grammar rules in much the same way as one extracts n-grams or Regular Tree Grammars (RTG) from a corpus of strings or trees. The procedure (Algorithm 1) extracts a single rule for each node of the decomposition to generate the associated terminal edge plus a set of nonterminals which can be subsequently expanded to generate the subgraphs corresponding to each subtree of the decomposition node. In particular, given the tree decomposition in Figure 2(c), the procedure produces the grammar in Figure 1. Rule extraction works for any connected simple graph and can be easily adapted for arbitrary hypergraphs.

Start by assigning the left-hand side nonterminal symbol according to

$$\text{label}(\text{parent}(\eta), r),$$

which returns a symbol determined by η's parent with rank r, the number of vertices in common between η and its parent. The external vertices of h are assigned by sorting the vertices that η shares with its parent. Any ordering policy will work so long as it produces the same ordering with respect to a given decomposition node. What is important is that the order of the external vertices of a rule match that of the vertices of the nonterminal edge it expands.[2] The algorithm then constructs the rest of h by including terminal edge $\mu(\eta)$, and adding a nonterminal edge for each child η_i of η, with vertices assigned according to an ordering of the vertices that η shares with η_i, again labeled according to *label.*

The function *label* just returns a nonterminal symbol of a given rank, chosen to match the number of external vertices of the right-hand side. There are many possible choices of *label*; it can even be a function that always returns the same symbol for a given rank. For purposes of language modeling, it is useful to condition rule probabilities on the label of the edge associated with the parent node in the decomposition (analogous to conditioning on the preceding word in a bigram setting). It is also useful to distinguish the direction of that preceding edge. For instance, we would expect 'rich-in' to have a different probability based on whether it is being generated as the argument of predicate 'say' vs. as a descendant of its own argument 'lake'. Thus, each nonterminal encodes (1) the label of the preceding edge and (2) its direction with respect to the current edge as defined according to the *head-to-tail* relation, where we say edge e_j is head-to-tail with preceding edge e_i iff the last vertex of $\alpha(e_i)$ is the first of $\alpha(e_j)$. For instance, $\overset{\text{lake}}{5}$ is in head-to-tail relation with $2 \overset{\text{arg1}}{\to} 5$, while $2 \overset{\text{arg1}}{\to} 5$ is not head-to-tail with $4 \overset{\text{arg2}}{\to} 5$.

[2] We experimented with various orderings, from preorder traversals of the tree decomposition to simply sorting by vertex identity, all with similar results.

The grammar in Figure 1 is extracted according to the tree decomposition in Figure 2(c). Consider how rule $r4$ is constructed while visiting the node $\eta = \{2, 5\}$ which maps to unary edge $\overset{\text{rich-in}}{2}$. The left-hand side symbol N_{arg2} comes from the label of the edge $1 \overset{\text{arg2}}{\to} 2$ associated with η's parent node $\{1, 2, 5\}$ and has a rank of $|\{2, 5\} \cap \{1, 2, 5\}| = 2$. The rule right-hand side is constructed so that it contains $\overset{\text{rich-in}}{2}$ and two nonterminal edges. The first nonterminal edge comes from the intersection of η with left child $\{2, 6\}$, yielding unary sequence 2 and edge $\overset{N_{\text{rich-in}}}{2}$. The second nonterminal edge is constructed similarly by ordering the vertices in the intersection of η with its right child $\{2, 5\}$ to get the binary sequence 2 to 5, producing $2 \overset{N_{\text{rich-in}}}{\to} 5$. Finally, the external vertex sequence comes from ordering the members of $\{2, 5\} \cap \{1, 2, 5\}$.

The particular edge-mapped tree decomposition plays a key role in the form of the extracted rules. In particular, each branching of the tree specifies the number of nonterminals in the corresponding rule. For example, decompositions such as Figure 2(a) result in linear grammars, where every rule right-hand side contains at most one nonterminal.

We experiment with three different strategies for producing edge-mapped tree decompositions. In each case, we start by building a node-to-edge map by introducing a new tree node to cover each edge of the graph, simultaneously ensuring the vertex and edge cover properties. The strategies differ in how the nodes are arranged into a tree. One simple approach (linear) is to construct a linearized sequence of edges by performing a depth first search of the graph and adding edges when we visit incident vertices. This produces nonbranching trees such as Figure 2(a). Alternatively, we can construct the decomposition according to the actual depth first search *tree* (dfs), producing decompositions like (b). Finally, we construct what we call a topological sort tree (top), where we add children to each node so as to maximize the number of head-to-tail transitions, producing trees such as (c). For rooted DAGs, this is easy; just construct a directed breadth first search tree of the graph starting from the root vertex. It is more involved for other graphs but still straightforward, accomplished by finding a minimum spanning tree of a newly constructed weighted directed graph representing head-to-tail transitions as arcs with weight 0 and all other contiguous transitions as arcs of weight 1. Once the edge-mapped nodes are arranged in a tree all that is left is to add vertices to each to satisfy running intersection.

One attractive feature of *top* is that, for certain types of input graphs, it produces grammars of well-known classes. In particular, if the graph is a string (a directed path), the grammar will be a right-linear CFG, i.e., a regular string grammar (a bigram grammar, in fact), and if it is a rooted tree, the unique topological sort tree leads to a grammar that closely resembles an RTG (where trees are edge-labeled and siblings are un-ordered). The other decomposition strategies do not constrain the tree as much, and their grammars are not necessarily regular.

Another nice feature of *top* is that subtrees of a parse tend to correspond to intuitive modules of the graph. For instance, the grammar first generates a predicate like 'rich-in' and then it proceeds to generate the subgraphs corresponding to its arguments 'fish' and 'lake', much as one would expect a syntactic dependency grammar to generate a head followed by its dependents. The linear grammar derived from Figure 2(a), on the other hand, would generate 'lake' as a descendant of 'fish'.

We also explore an augmentation of *top* called the *rooted* topological sort tree (r-top). Any graph can be converted to a rooted graph by simply adding an extra vertex and making it the parent of every vertex of in-degree zero (or if there are none, picking a member of each connected component at random). We exploit this fact to produce a version of *top* that generates all graphs as though they were rooted by starting off each derivation with a rule that generates every vertex with in-degree zero. We expect rooted graphs to produce simpler grammars in general because they reduce the number of edges that must be generated in non-topological order, requiring fewer rules that differ primarily in whether they generate an edge in head-to-tail order or not. In particular, if a graph is acyclic, all edges will be generated in head-to-tail relation and the corresponding grammar will contain fewer nonterminals.

5 Evaluation

We experiment using 5564 elementary semantic dependency graphs taken from the LOGON portion of the Redwoods corpus (Oepen et al., 2004). From Table 1, we can see that, while there are a few tree-shaped graphs, the majority are more general DAGs. Nevertheless, edge density is low; the average graph contains about 15.4 binary edges and 14.9 vertices. We set aside every 10th graph for the test set, and estimate the models from the remaining 5,008, replacing terminals occurring ≤ 1 times in the training set with special symbol *UNK*.

Model parameters are calculated from the frequency of extracted rules using a mean-field Variational Bayesian approximation of a symmetric Dirichlet prior with parameter β (Bishop, 2006). This amounts to counting the number of times each rule r with left-hand side symbol A is extracted and then computing its weight θ_r according to

$$\theta_r = \exp\left(\Psi(n_r + \beta) - \Psi(\sum_{r':r'=A\to h} n_{r'} + \beta)\right),$$

where n_r is the frequency of r and Ψ is the standard digamma function. This approximation of a Dirichlet prior offers a simple yet principled way of simultaneously smoothing rule weights and incorporating a soft assumption of sparsity (i.e., only a few rules should receive very high probability). Specifically, we somewhat arbitrarily selected a value of 0.2 for β, which should result in a moderately sparse distribution.

We evaluate each model by computing perplexity: $2^{-\sum_{i=1}^{N}\frac{1}{N}\ln_2 p(g_i)}$, where N is the number of graphs in the test set, g_i is the ith graph, and $p(g_i)$ is its probability according to the model, computed as the product of the weights of the rules in the extracted derivation. Better models should assign higher probability to g_i, thereby achieving lower perplexity.

(a) Graphs

strings	0
r-trees	682
r-dags	51
dags	4831
total	**5564**

(b) Edges

	unary	binary
types	5626	10
tokens	83061	85737

Table 1: LOGON corpus. (a) Graph types (r stands for rooted). (b) Edge types and tokens.

model	perplexity	size
linear	505,061	59,980
dfs	341,336	14,443
top	22,484	20,985
r-top	40,504	19,052

Table 2: Model perplexity and grammar size.

Table 2 lists the perplexities of the language models defined according to our four different tree decomposition strategies. *Linear* is relatively poor since it makes little distinction between local and more distant relations between edges. For instance, the tree in Figure 2(a) results in a grammar where $2 \overset{\text{arg2}}{\rightarrow} 5$ is generated as the child of distantly related $\overset{\text{fish}}{6}$ but as a remote descendant of neighboring edge $\overset{\text{rich-in}}{2}$. *Dfs* is better, but suffers from similar problems. Both *top* and *r-top* perform markedly better, but *r-top* less so because the initial rule required for generating all vertices of in-degree zero is often very improbable. There are 1562 different such rules required for describing the training data, many of which appear only once. We believe there are ways of factorizing these rules to mitigate this sparsity effect, but this is left to future work.

Grammar sizes are also somewhat telling. The linear grammar is quite large, due to the extra rules required for handling the long-distance relations. The other grammars are of a similar, much smaller size, but *dfs* is smallest since it tends to produce trees of much smaller branching factor, allowing for greater rule reuse. As predicted, the *r-top* grammar is somewhat smaller than the vanilla *top* grammar, but, as previously noted, the potential reduction in sparsity is counteracted by the introduction of the extra initial rules.

6 Conclusion & Discussion

Graph grammars are an appealing formalism for modeling the kinds of structures required for representing natural language semantics, but there is little work in actually defining grammars for doing so. We have introduced a simple framework for automatically extracting HRGs, based upon first defining a tree decomposition and then walking this tree to extract rules in a manner very similar to how one extracts RTG rules from a corpus of trees. By varying the kinds of tree decomposition used, the procedure produces different types of grammars. While restricting consideration to a broad class of tree decompositions where visiting tree nodes corresponds to visiting edges of the graph, we explored four special cases, demonstrating that one case, where parent-to-child node relations in the tree maximize head-to-tail transitions between graph edges, performs best in terms of perplexity on a corpus of semantic graphs. This topological ordering heuristic seems reasonable for the corpus we experimented on since such parent-child transitions are equivalent to predicate-argument transitions in the semantic representations.

Interesting questions remain as to which particular combinations of graph and decomposition types lead to useful classes of graph grammars. In our case we found that our topological sort tree decomposition leads to regular grammars when the graphs describe strings or particular kinds of trees, making them useful for defining simple Markov models and also making it possible to perform other operations like language intersection (Gecseg and Steinby, 1984). We have presented only an initial study and there are potentially many interesting combinations.

Acknowledgments

We thank Mark-Jan Nederhof for his comments on an early draft and the anonymous reviewers for their helpful feedback. This research was supported in part by a prize studentship from the Scottish Informatics and Computer Science Alliance, the Australian Research Council's Discovery Projects funding scheme (project numbers DP110102506 and DP110102593) and the US Defense Advanced Research Projects Agency under contract FA8650-11-1-7151.

References

Christopher M. Bishop. 2006. *Pattern Recognition and Machine Learning*. Springer.

Hans L. Bodlaender. 1993. A tourist guide through treewidth. *Acta Cybernetica*, 11(1-2):1–21.

David Chiang, Jacob Andreas, Daniel Bauer, Karl Moritz Hermann, Bevan Jones, and Kevin Knight. 2013. Parsing graphs with hyperedge replacement grammars. In *Proceedings of the 51st Meeting of the ACL*.

Marie-Catherine de Marneffe and Christopher D. Manning. 2008. The stanford typed dependencies representation. In *Proceedings of COLING Workshop on Cross-framework and Cross-domain Parser Evaluation*.

Frank Drewes, Annegret Habel, and Hans-Jorg Kreowski. 1997. Hyperedge replacement graph grammars. *Handbook of Graph Grammars and Computing by Graph Transformation*, pages 95–1626.

Ferenc Gecseg and Magnus Steinby. 1984. *Tree Automata*. Akademiai Kiado, Budapest.

Daniel Gildea. 2011. Grammar factorization by tree decomposition. *Computational Linguistics*, 37(1):231–248.

Mark Johnson, Stuart Geman, Stephen Canon, Zhiyi Chi, and Stefan Riezler. 1999. Estimators for stochastic 'unification-based' grammars. In *Proceedings of the 37th Meeting of the ACL*, pages 535–541.

Bevan Jones, Jacob Andreas, Daniel Bauer, Karl-Moritz Hermann, and Kevin Knight. 2012. Semantics-based machine translation with hyperedge replacement grammars. In *Proceedings of COLING*.

Kevin Knight and Jonathon Graehl. 2005. An overview of probabilistic tree transducers for natural language processing. In *Proceedings of the 6th International Conference on Intelligent Text Processing and Computational Linguistics*.

Clemens Lautemann. 1988. Decomposition trees: Structured graph representation and efficient algorithms. In M. Dauchet and M. Nivat, editors, *CAAP '88*, volume 299 of *Lecture Notes in Computer Science*, pages 28–39. Springer Berlin Heidelberg.

Phong Le and Willem Zuidema. 2012. Learning compositional semantics for open domain semantic parsing. In *Proceedings of COLING*.

Scott Martin and Michael White. 2011. Creating disjunctive logical forms from aligned sentences for grammar-based paraphrase generation. In *Proceedings of the Workshop on Monolingual Text-To-Text Generation (MTTG)*, pages 74–83.

Stephan Oepen, Dan Flickinger, Kristina Toutanova, and Christopher D. Manning. 2004. Lingo redwoods. *Research on Language and Computation*, 2(4):575–596.

Judea Pearl. 1988. *Probabilistic Reasoning in Intelligent Systems: Networks of Plausible Inference*. Morgan Kaufmann, San Francisco, CA, 2 edition.

Stefan Riezler, Detlef Prescher, Jonas Kuhn, and Mark Johnson. 2000. Lexicalized stochastic modeling of constraint-based grammars using log-linear measures and em. In *Proceedings of the 38th Meeting of the ACL*.

John F. Sowa. 1976. Conceptual graphs for a data base interface. *IBM Journal of Research and Development*, 20(4):336–357.

Ivan Titov, James Henderson, Paola Merlo, and Gabriele Musillo. 2009. Online graph planarisation for synchronous parsing of semantic and syntactic dependencies. In *Proceedings of IJCAI*, pages 1562–1567.

Finite State Methods and Description Logics

Tim Fernando
Trinity College Dublin, Ireland
Tim.Fernando@tcd.ie

Abstract. The accepting runs of a finite automaton are represented as concepts in a Description Logic, for various systems of roles computed by finite-state transducers. The representation refines the perspective on regular languages provided by Monadic Second-Order Logic (MSO), under the Büchi-Elgot-Trakhtenbrot theorem. String symbols are structured as sets to succinctly express MSO-sentences, with auxiliary symbols conceived as variables bound by quantifiers.

1 Introduction

As declarative specifications of sets of strings accepted by finite automata (i.e. regular languages), regular expressions are far and away more popular than the formulas of *Monadic Second-Order Logic* (MSO), which, by a fundamental theorem due to Büchi, Elgot and Trakhtenbrot, pick out the regular languages (e.g. Thomas, 1997). Computational semantics, however, can hardly ignore MSO's model-theoretic perspective on strings with its computable notions of entailment. Furthermore, regular expressions lack the succinctness that MSO's Boolean connectives support. Both negation and conjunction blow up the size of regular expressions by an exponential or two (Gelade and Neven, 2008). A symptom of the problem is the exponential cost of mapping a finite automaton $\mathbb{A}$ to a regular expression denoting the language $\mathcal{L}(\mathbb{A})$ accepted by $\mathbb{A}$ (Ehrenfeucht and Zeiger, 1976; Holzer and Kutrib, 2010). A more economical declarative representation of $\mathcal{L}(\mathbb{A})$ is afforded by pairing a string $a_1a_2 \cdots a_n$ in $\mathcal{L}(\mathbb{A})$ with a string $q_1q_2 \cdots q_n$ of $\mathbb{A}$'s (internal) states q_i in the course of a run (by $\mathbb{A}$) accepting $a_1a_2 \cdots a_n$. This representation involves expanding the alphabet of the strings, and subsequently contracting the alphabet. A simple way to carry this out is by forming strings $\alpha_1\alpha_2 \cdots \alpha_n$ of sets α_i that we can, for instance, intersect with a fixed set B, defining a string homomorphism ρ_B for componentwise intersection with B

$$\rho_B(\alpha_1 \cdots \alpha_n) := (\alpha_1 \cap B) \cdots (\alpha_n \cap B).$$

For example, assuming *no* state q_i belongs to the alphabet Σ of $\mathcal{L}(\mathbb{A})$,

$$\rho_\Sigma(\boxed{a_1, q_1} \cdots \boxed{a_n, q_n}) = \boxed{a_1} \cdots \boxed{a_n}$$

where we draw boxes instead of curly braces for sets used as string symbols.

The homomorphisms ρ_B are linked below to the treatment of variables in MSO. Given a finite alphabet A, MSO$_A$-sentences are formed from a binary relation symbol S (encoding successor) and a unary relation symbol U_a, for each $a \in A$. We then interpret an MSO$_A$-sentence against a string over the alphabet 2^A of subsets of A, deviating ever so slightly from the custom of interpreting against strings in A^+. Expanding the alphabet from A to 2^A accommodates a form of underspecification that, among other things, facilitates the interpretation of MSO$_A$-formulas relative to variable assignments. As for the homomorphisms ρ_B, the idea is that B picks out a subset of A, leaving each $a \in A$ that is *not* in B as an "auxiliary marker symbol" — a staple of finite-state language processing (Beesley and Karttunen, 2003; Yli-Jyrä and Koskenniemi, 2004; Hulden, 2009).

By focusing on the accepting runs of a finite automaton, the present paper strives to be relevant to finite-state language processing in general. But to understand its difference with say (Hulden, 2009), a few words about the language applications motivating it might be helpful. These applications concern not morphology, phonology, speech or even syntax but semantics — in particular, temporal semantics. The convenience of equating succession in a string with temporal succession is yet another reason to step from A up to 2^A (reading a boxed subset of A as a snapshot). It is a trivial enough matter to build a finite-state transducer between $(2^A)^*$ and $(A \cup \{[,]\})^*$ unwinding say, the string

$$\boxed{a, a'}\boxed{a'} \text{ of length 2 over the alphabet } 2^{\{a,a'\}}$$

to the string

$$[aa'][a'] \text{ of length 7 over the alphabet } \{a, a', [,]\}$$

and if we are to apply ρ_B, it is natural to choose the alphabet 2^A over $A \cup \{[,]\}$. There are, in any case, many more regular relations apart from ρ_B to consider for temporal semantics (Fernando, 2011), including those that change string length and the notion of temporal succession, i.e. granularity. A simple but powerful way of building a regular language from a regular relation R is by forming the inverse image of a regular language L under R, which we write $\langle R \rangle L$, following dynamic logic (e.g. Fischer and Ladner, 1979). The basic thrust of the present paper is to extend regular expressions by adding connectives for negation, conjunction and inverse images under certain regular relations.

This extension is dressed up below in *Description Logic* (DLs; Baader et al. 2003), with the languages $\mathcal{L}(\mathbb{A})$ accepted by automata $\mathbb{A}$ as DL-concepts (unary relations), and various regular relations including ρ_B (for different sets B) as DL-roles (binary relations). As in the *attributive language with complement* $\mathcal{ALC}$, DL-concepts C are closed under conjunction $C \wedge C'$, negation $\neg C$, and inverse images under DL-roles R, the usual DL notation for which, $(\exists R)C$, we replace by $\langle R \rangle C$ from dynamic logic, with

$$[\![\langle R \rangle C]\!] \; := \; \{s \mid (\exists s' \in [\![C]\!]) \; s[\![R]\!]s'\}.$$

Since DL-concepts and DL-roles in the present context, have clear intended interpretations, we will often drop the semantic brackets $[\![\cdot]\!]$, conflating an expression with its meaning.

MSO is linked to DL by a mapping of MSO-sentences φ to DL-concepts C_φ that reduces MSO-entailments $\models_{MSO}$ to concept inclusion

$$\varphi \models_{MSO} \psi \iff C_\varphi \subseteq C_\psi \, . \qquad (1)$$

Let us take care *not* to read (1) as stating MSO is *interpretable* in DL in the sense of (Tarski et al., 1953); no formal DL theory is mentioned in (1), only a particular (intended) interpretation over strings. What we vary is not the interpretation $[\![\cdot]\!]$ but the mapping $\varphi \mapsto C_\varphi$ establishing (1). Many different definitions of C_φ will do, and the main aim of the present work is to explore these possibilities, expressed as particular DL concepts and roles. In its account of regular languages, the Büchi-Elgot-Trakhtenbrot theorem says nothing about finite-state transducers, which are nonetheless instrumental in establishing the theorem. Behind the move to Description Logics is the view that the role of finite-state transducers in constructing regular languages merits scrutiny.

To dispel possible confusion, it is perhaps worth remarking that a relation computable by a finite-state transducer may have a transitive closure that no finite-state transducer can compute. A simple example is the function f that leaves all strings unchanged except those of the form $1^n0^{m+2}2^k$ which it maps to $1^{n+1}0^m2^{k+1}$. The intersection

$$1^*2^* \; \cap \; \{f^k(0^n) \mid k, n \geq 0\}$$

is the non-regular language $\{1^n2^n \mid n \geq 0\}$, precluding a finite-state transducer from computing the transitive closure of f. Commenting on the Description Logic counterpart $\mathcal{ALC}_{reg}$ to Propositional Dynamic Logic (Fischer and Ladner, 1979), Baader and Lutz write

> many of today's most used concept languages do not include the role constructors of $\mathcal{ALC}_{reg}$. The main reason is that applications demand an implementation of description logic reasoning, and the presence of the reflexive-transitive closure constructor makes obtaining efficient implementations much harder.

There should be no mistaking the interpretations of concepts and roles below for models of $\mathcal{ALC}_{reg}$. Most every role considered below (from ρ_B on) is, however, transitive and indeed can be viewed as some notion of "part of."

The remainder of this paper is organized as follows. The accepting runs of a finite automaton are expressed as a DL-concept in section 2. This is then used to present MSO's semantic set-up in section 3. A feature of that set-up is the expansion of MSO_A-models from A^+ to $(2^A)^+$, opening up possibilities of underspecification which section 4 explores alongside non-deterministic DL-roles (in addition to the inverse of ρ_B). Section

5 looks at more DL-roles that, unlike ρ_B, change length, and section 6 concludes, returning to auxiliary symbols, which are subject not only to ρ_B but the various regular relations formulated above as DL-roles.

2 Accepting runs as a DL-concept

One half of the aforementioned Büchi-Elgot-Trakhtenbrot theorem turns finite automata to MSO-sentences. This section adapts the idea behind that half in a DL setting, deferring details about MSO to the next section. An *accepting run of* a finite automaton $\mathbb{A}$ is a string $\boxed{a_1, q_1}\boxed{a_2, q_2}\cdots\boxed{a_n, q_n}$ such that

$$q_0 \overset{a_1}{\leadsto} q_1 \overset{a_2}{\leadsto} q_2 \overset{a_3}{\leadsto} \cdots \overset{a_n}{\leadsto} q_n \in F$$

where q_0 is $\mathbb{A}$'s initial state, $\leadsto$ is $\mathbb{A}$'s set of transitions (labeled by symbols), and F is $\mathbb{A}$'s set of final/accepting states. (Note $\mathbb{A}$ may be identified with such a triple $\langle \leadsto, q_0, F\rangle$.) Let us assume that $\mathbb{A}$'s set Q of states is disjoint from the alphabet Σ, and treat $\boxed{a_i, q_i}$ as a 2-element subset of $\Sigma \cup Q$, making an accepting run a string over the alphabet $2^{\Sigma\cup Q}$ of subsets of $\Sigma \cup Q$. Clearly, for any finite automaton $\mathbb{A}$, the set *AccRuns*$(\mathbb{A})$ of accepting runs of $\mathbb{A}$ is regular — simply modify $\mathbb{A}$'s transitions to

$$\{(q, \boxed{a, q'}, q') \mid q \overset{a}{\leadsto} q'\} \; .$$

The language $\mathcal{L}(\mathbb{A})$ accepted by $\mathbb{A}$ can then be formed applying ρ_Σ to $\mathbb{A}$'s accepting runs (setting aside the cosmetic difference between $\boxed{a}$ and a)

$$\begin{aligned} \mathcal{L}(\mathbb{A}) &\approx \{\rho_\Sigma(s) \mid s \in \mathit{AccRuns}(\mathbb{A})\} \\ &= \langle {\rho_\Sigma}^{-1}\rangle \, \mathit{AccRuns}(\mathbb{A}) \; . \end{aligned}$$

It remains to express the language *AccRuns*$(\mathbb{A})$ through conjunctions and negations of a small number of languages $\langle R\rangle L$ for certain (particularly simple) choices of R and L. One such R is componentwise inclusion $\unrhd$ between strings of sets of the same length

$$\unrhd \; := \; \{(\alpha_1 \cdots \alpha_n, \beta_1 \cdots \beta_n) \mid \alpha_i \supseteq \beta_i \text{ for } 1 \leq i \leq n\}$$

(Fernando, 2004). For example, $s \unrhd \rho_B(s)$ for all strings s of sets, and $\alpha \unrhd \boxed{}$ for all sets α. Returning to *AccRuns*$(\mathbb{A})$, let us collect

(i) strings with final position containing an $\mathbb{A}$-final state in

$$L_F \; := \; \langle \unrhd \rangle \sum_{q \in F} \boxed{}^{*} \boxed{q}$$

(ii) strings whose first position contains a pair a, q such that $q_0 \overset{a}{\leadsto} q$ in

$$L_{q_0 \leadsto} \; := \langle \unrhd \rangle \sum_{q_0 \overset{a}{\leadsto} q} \boxed{a, q}\boxed{}^{*}$$

and

(iii) (bad) strings containing $\boxed{q}\boxed{a, q'}$, for some triple $(q, a, q') \in Q \times \Sigma \times Q$ *out*side the set $\leadsto$ of transitions in

$$L_{\not\leadsto} \; := \; \langle \unrhd \rangle \sum_{q \overset{a}{\not\leadsto} q'} \boxed{}^{*} \boxed{q}\boxed{a, q'}\boxed{}^{*}$$

Also, for any set B, let *Spec*(B) be the set

$$\mathit{Spec}(B) \; := \; \langle \rho_B \rangle (\sum_{b \in B} \boxed{b})^{*}$$

of strings with exactly one element of B in each string position.

Proposition 1. *Let $\mathbb{A}$ be a finite automaton with transitions $\leadsto \subseteq Q \times \Sigma \times Q$, final states $F \subseteq Q$ and initial state q_0. The set AccRuns$(\mathbb{A}) - \{\epsilon\}$ of non-null accessible runs of $\mathbb{A}$ is*

$$\mathit{Spec}(\Sigma) \cap \mathit{Spec}(Q) \cap L_F \cap L_{q_0 \leadsto} - L_{\not\leadsto}$$

intersected with the set $(2^{\Sigma\cup Q})^*$ of strings over the alphabet $2^{\Sigma\cup Q}$ of subsets of the finite set $\Sigma \cup Q$.

Given any finite set A, the restrictions to $(2^A)^*$ of the relations ρ_B and $\unrhd$

$$\begin{aligned} \rho_B^A &:= \rho_B \cap ((2^A)^* \times (2^A)^*) \\ \unrhd_A &:= \unrhd \cap ((2^A)^* \times (2^A)^*) \end{aligned}$$

are computable by finite-state transducers. That is, the intersection mentioned in Proposition 1 with $(2^{\Sigma\cup Q})^*$ can be built into the relations ρ_Σ, ρ_Q and $\unrhd$ for a characterization of *AccRuns*$(\mathbb{A})$ as well as $\mathcal{L}(\mathbb{A})$ within a description logic, all concepts in which are regular languages, and all roles in which are computable by finite-state transducers (keeping $\langle R\rangle L$ regular). The obvious question is how that characterization compares with MSO, to which we turn next.

3 MSO-models and reducts from ρ_B

Given a finite set A, let us agree that an *MSO_A-model* M is a tuple $\langle [n], S_n, \{[\![U_a]\!]\}_{a\in A}\rangle$ for some positive integer $n > 0$,[1] where

(i) $[n]$ is the set $\{1, 2 \ldots, n\}$ of positive integers from 1 to n

(ii) S_n is the relation encoding the successor/next relation on $[n]$

$$S_n := \{(i, i+1) \mid i \in [n-1]\}$$

and for each $a \in A$,

(iii) $[\![U_a]\!]$ is a subset of $[n]$ interpreting the unary relation symbol U_a.

We can form MSO_A-models from strings over the alphabets A and (2^A) as follows. Given a string $s = a_1 a_2 \cdots a_n \in A^n$, let $\text{Mod}(s)$ be the MSO_A-model $\langle [n], S_n, \{[\![U_a]\!]\}_{a\in A}\rangle$ interpreting U_a as the set of string positions i occupied by a

$$[\![U_a]\!] = \{i \in [n] \mid a_i = a\}$$

for each $a \in A$. Expanding the alphabet A to 2^A, a string $\alpha_1\alpha_2 \cdots \alpha_n \in (2^A)^n$ induces the MSO_A-model $\langle [n], S_n, \{[\![U_a]\!]\}_{a\in A}\rangle$ interpreting U_a as the set of positions i filled by boxes containing a

$$[\![U_a]\!] = \{i \in [n] \mid a \in \alpha_i\}$$

for each $a \in A$. Conversely, given an MSO_A-model $M = \langle [n], S_n, \{[\![U_a]\!]\}_{a\in A}\rangle$, let $\mathit{str}(M)$ be the string $\alpha_1 \cdots \alpha_n \in (2^A)^n$ where

$$\alpha_i := \{a \in A \mid i \in [\![U_a]\!]\}.$$

That is, for all $a \in A$ and $i \in [n]$,

$$a \in \alpha_i \iff i \in [\![U_a]\!]$$

making the map $M \mapsto \mathit{str}(M)$ a bijection between MSO_A-models and $(2^A)^+$.

Proposition 2. *Given an MSO_A-model M, the following are equivalent.*

(i) M is $\text{Mod}(s)$ *for some $s \in A^+$*

(ii) M satisfies the MSO_A-sentence

$$(\forall x) \bigvee_{a\in A} (U_a(x) \wedge \bigwedge_{a'\in A-\{a\}} \neg U_{a'}(x))$$

(saying the non-empty $[\![U_a]\!]$'s partition the universe)

(iii) $\mathit{str}(M) \in \mathit{Spec}(A)$

(iv) $\mathit{str}(M) = \boxed{a_1} \cdots \boxed{a_n}$ for some $a_1 \cdots a_n \in A^+$.

While the Büchi-Elgot-Trakhtenbrot theorem (BET) concerns MSO_A-models $\text{Mod}(s)$ given by strings $s \in A^+$, the wider class of MSO_A-models (isomorphic to $(2^A)^+$) is useful for encoding variable assignments crucial to the second half of BET, asserting the regularity of MSO-sentences. More precisely, the remainder of this section is devoted to defining regular languages $\mathcal{L}_A(\varphi)$ for MSO_A-sentences φ establishing

Proposition 3. *For every MSO_A-sentence φ, there is a regular language $\mathcal{L}_A(\varphi)$ such that for every MSO_A-model M,*

$$M \models \varphi \iff \mathit{str}(M) \in \mathcal{L}_A(\varphi).$$

Insofar as the models $\text{Mod}(s)$ given by strings $s \in A^+$ differ from those given by strings over (2^A) via str^{-1}, Proposition 3 differs from the half of BET saying MSO-sentences define regular languages. There is no denying, however, that the difference is slight.

Be that as it may, I claim the expansion of A to 2^A leads to a worthwhile simplification, as can be seen by proving Proposition 3 as follows. Given a positive integer n, an *n-variable assignment* f is a function whose domain is a finite set $\mathit{Var} = \mathit{Var}_1 \cup \mathit{Var}_2$ of first-order variables $x \in \mathit{Var}_1$ that f maps to an integer $f(x) \in [n]$ and second-order variables $X \in \mathit{Var}_2$ that f maps to a set $f(X) \subseteq [n]$. Then if M is a MSO_A-model over $[n]$,

$$M, f \models U_a(x) \iff f(x) \in [\![U_a]\!]$$

and

$$M, f \models X(x) \iff f(x) \in f(X).$$

[1] There is, of course, a rich theory of infinite MSO-models, given by infinite strings (e.g. Thomas, 1997). We focus here on finite models/strings, which suffice for many applications; more in section 6 below.

We can package the pair M, f as the $\mathrm{MSO}_{A \cup Var}$-model M^f over $[n]$ identical to M on U_a's for $a \in A$, with interpretations

$$[\![U_X]\!] = f(X) \qquad \text{for } X \in \mathit{Var}_2$$
$$[\![U_x]\!] = \{f(x)\} \qquad \text{for } x \in \mathit{Var}_1.$$

Note $[\![U_x]\!]$ intersects $[\![U_X]\!]$ if $M, f \models X(x)$, which is to say $X(x)$ entails the negation of *spec*$(\{X, x\})$, where *spec*(A) is the MSO_A-sentence that Proposition 2 mentions in (ii)

$$(\forall x) \bigvee_{a \in A} (U_a(x) \wedge \bigwedge_{a' \in A - \{a\}} \neg U_{a'}(x)).$$

In other words, to treat a pair M, f as an $\mathrm{MSO}_{A \cup Var}$-model (and an MSO_A-formula φ with free variables in *Var* as an $\mathrm{MSO}_{A \cup Var}$-sentence), the step from A to 2^A is essential. Turning model expansions around, given $B \subseteq A$, we define the *B-reduct of* an MSO_A-model M to be the MSO_B-model M_B obtained from M after throwing out all interpretations $[\![U_a]\!]$ for $a \in A - B$. It is easy to see that the homomorphisms ρ_B yield B-reducts:

$$\mathit{str}(M_B) = \rho_B(\mathit{str}(M))$$

(for all MSO_A-models M). Proceeding now to the languages $\mathcal{L}_A(\varphi)$ in Proposition 3, observe that we can picture $U_a(x)$ as the language

$$L(a, x) := (\square + \boxed{a})^* \boxed{a, x} (\square + \boxed{a})^*$$

inasmuch as

$$M, f \models U_a(x) \iff \rho^{A \cup Var}_{\{a,x\}}(\mathit{str}(M^f)) \in L(a, x).$$

For the remainder of this section, let $A' \subseteq A \cup \mathit{Var}$. We put, for $a, x \in A'$,

$$\mathcal{L}_{A'}(U_a(x)) := \langle \rho^{A'}_{\{a,x\}} \rangle \, L(a, x).$$

Similarly, for $X, x \in A'$, let $\mathcal{L}_{A'}(X(x))$ be

$$\langle \rho^{A'}_{\{X,x\}} \rangle \, (\square + \boxed{X})^* \boxed{X, x} (\square + \boxed{X})^*$$

and for $x, y \in A'$,

$$\mathcal{L}_{A'}(x = y) := \langle \rho^{A'}_{\{x,y\}} \rangle \, \square^* \boxed{x, y} \square^*$$
$$\mathcal{L}_{A'}(S(x, y)) := \langle \rho^{A'}_{\{x,y\}} \rangle \, \square^* \boxed{x}\boxed{y} \square^*.$$

We also put

$$\mathcal{L}_{A'}(\varphi \wedge \psi) := \mathcal{L}_{A'}(\varphi) \cap \mathcal{L}_{A'}(\psi)$$
$$\mathcal{L}_{A'}(\neg\varphi) := (2^{A'})^+ - \mathcal{L}_{A'}(\varphi).$$

As for quantification, for $v \in \mathit{Var}$, let $\sigma^{A'}_v$ be the inverse of $\rho^{A' \cup \{v\}}_{A'}$,[2] and set

$$\mathcal{L}_{A'}(\exists X.\varphi) := \langle \sigma^{A'}_X \rangle \, \mathcal{L}_{A' \cup \{X\}}(\varphi)$$
$$\mathcal{L}_{A'}(\exists x.\varphi) := \langle \sigma^{A'}_x \rangle \, (\mathcal{L}_{A' \cup \{x\}}(\varphi) \cap \mathcal{L}_{A' \cup \{x\}}(x = x))$$

where the intersection with $\mathcal{L}_{A' \cup \{x\}}(x = x)$ insures that x is treated as a first-order variable in φ (occurring in exactly one string position).

Taking stock, to define the regular language $\mathcal{L}_A(\varphi)$ required by Proposition 3 for an MSO_A-sentence φ with variables from a finite set *Var* of variables, we form $\mathcal{ALC}$-concepts from

(i) the primitive concepts

$$L(a, x), \ L(X, x),$$
$$\square^* \boxed{x, y} \square^*, \ \square^* \boxed{x}\boxed{y} \square^*, \ (2^B)^+$$

for $a \in A$ and $x, X, y \in \mathit{Var}$ and $B \subseteq A \cup \mathit{Var}$, and

(ii) the roles

$$\rho^{A'}_B, \ \sigma^{A'}_v$$

for $B \subseteq A' \subseteq A \cup \mathit{Var}$ and $v \in \mathit{Var}$.

4 B-specified strings and containment $\sqsupseteq$

Recall that *spec*(B) is the MSO_B-sentence saying every string position has exactly one symbol from B

$$(\forall x) \bigvee_{b \in B} (U_b(x) \wedge \bigwedge_{b' \in B - \{b\}} \neg U_{b'}(x))$$

and observe that there is no trace of σ^A_x or complementation or intersection (interpreting $\neg\exists x$ and $\wedge$) in the language

$$\mathit{Spec}_A(B) := \langle \rho^A_B \rangle (\sum_{b \in B} \boxed{b})^*$$

of strings encoding MSO_A-models satisfying *spec*(B), for $B \subseteq A$. That is, although $\mathit{Spec}_A(B)$ and $\mathcal{L}_A(\mathit{spec}(B))$ from the previous section specify the same set of strings, they differ as expressions, suggesting different automata. Section 2 provides yet more expressions for automata, drawing on a different pool of primitive concepts and roles.

[2] We could instead move the inverse out of the relation R, allowing $\langle R \rangle$ to go not only to the left of L as in $\langle R \rangle L$ but also to its right for the image $L\langle R \rangle$ of L under R.

In addition to componentwise inclusion $\trianglerighteq$ (a non-deterministic generalization of the functions ρ_B that dispenses with the subscript B), it is useful to define relations between strings of different lengths, including those that pick out prefixes

$$\mathit{prefix}_A \;:=\; \{(ss', s) \mid s, s' \in (2^A)^*\}$$

and suffixes

$$\mathit{suffix}_A \;:=\; \{(ss', s') \mid s, s' \in (2^A)^*\}.$$

Leaving out the subscripts $A = \Sigma \cup Q$ for notational simplicity, we can describe three of the languages in Proposition 1 (section 2) as

$$\begin{aligned} L_F &= \langle\trianglerighteq\rangle\langle\mathit{suffix}\rangle \sum_{q\in F} \boxed{q} \\ L_{q_0\rightsquigarrow} &= \langle\trianglerighteq\rangle\langle\mathit{prefix}\rangle \sum_{q_0 \overset{a}{\rightsquigarrow} q} \boxed{a, q} \\ L_{\not\rightsquigarrow} &= \langle\trianglerighteq\rangle\langle\mathit{suffix}\rangle\langle\mathit{prefix}\rangle \sum_{q \overset{a}{\not\rightsquigarrow} q'} \boxed{q}\boxed{a, q'} \end{aligned}$$

zeroing in on the substrings of length ≤ 2 that are of interest. It is convenient to abbreviate $\langle\trianglerighteq\rangle\langle\mathit{suffix}\rangle\langle\mathit{prefix}\rangle L$ (equivalently, $\langle\trianglerighteq\rangle\ \square^* L \square^*$)) to $\langle\sqsupseteq\rangle L$, effectively defining *containment* $\sqsupseteq$ to be the relational composition of componentwise inclusion $\trianglerighteq$ with *suffix* and *prefix*

$$\sqsupseteq \;:=\; \trianglerighteq\, ;\ \mathit{suffix}\ ;\ \mathit{prefix}$$

(and $\sqsupseteq_A$ as $\trianglerighteq_A; \mathit{suffix}_A; \mathit{prefix}_A$). Writing $\mathcal{E}_A(x)$ for the set

$$\mathcal{E}_A(x) \;:=\; \mathcal{L}_A(x = x)$$

of strings in $(2^A)^+$ in which x occurs exactly once, we have

$$\begin{aligned} \mathcal{L}_A(U_a(x)) &= \mathcal{E}_A(x) \cap \langle\sqsupseteq\rangle\boxed{a, x} \\ \mathcal{L}_A(X(x)) &= \mathcal{E}_A(x) \cap \langle\sqsupseteq\rangle\boxed{X, x} \\ \mathcal{L}_A(x = y) &= \mathcal{E}_A(x) \cap \mathcal{E}_A(y)\ \cap\ \langle\sqsupseteq\rangle\boxed{x, y} \\ \mathcal{L}_A(S(x, y)) &= \mathcal{E}_A(x) \cap \mathcal{E}_A(y)\ \cap\ \langle\sqsupseteq\rangle\boxed{x}\boxed{y} \end{aligned}$$

and apart from $\mathcal{E}_A(x)$, primitive concepts given by strings of length ≤ 2 will do. The locality (in such short strings) is obscured in our ρ^A_B-based analysis of $\mathcal{L}_A(\varphi)$ in the previous section, under which

$$\begin{aligned} \mathcal{E}_A(x) &= \langle\rho^A_{\{x\}}\rangle\square^*\boxed{x}\square^* \\ &= \langle\sqsupseteq_A\rangle\boxed{x}\ -\ \langle\sqsupseteq\rangle\boxed{x}\square^*\boxed{x}. \end{aligned} \qquad (2)$$

An existence predicate of sorts, $\mathcal{E}_A(x)$ is presuppositional in the same way for MSO that $\mathit{Spec}_A(B)$ is for the accepting runs of finite automata; $\mathcal{E}_A(x)$ and $\mathit{Spec}_A(B)$ are general, non-local background requirements imposed indiscriminately on models and automata, in contrast to assertions (in the foreground) that focus on short substrings, picking out specific models and automata.

An instructive test case is provided by the transitive closure $<$ of S; an $\mathrm{MSO}_{\{x,y\}}$-sentence saying that $x < y$ is

$$\begin{aligned} \exists X\ ((\forall u, v)(X(u) \wedge S(u, v) \supset X(v)) \\ \wedge\, X(y) \wedge \neg X(x)). \end{aligned}$$

Second-order quantification aside, the obvious picture to associate with $x < y$ is $\boxed{x}\square^*\boxed{y}$, which is built into the representation

$$\begin{aligned} \mathcal{L}_A(x < y) &= \mathcal{E}_A(x) \cap \mathcal{E}_A(y) \cap \\ &\quad \langle\sqsupseteq\rangle\boxed{x}\square^*\boxed{y} \end{aligned} \qquad (3)$$

of MSO_A-models satisfying $x < y$ (with $x, y \in A$). In both lines (2) and (3) above, arbitrarily long substrings from $\square^*$ occur, that we will show how to compress next.

5 Intervals and compression

Given $e \in A$, we can state that the set $[\![U_e]\!]$ represented by a symbol $e \in A$ is an interval through the $\mathrm{MSO}_{\{e\}}$-sentence

$$\exists x\ U_e(x) \wedge \neg\exists y\ \mathrm{gap}_e(y) \qquad (4)$$

where $\mathrm{gap}_e(y)$ abbreviates the $\mathrm{MSO}_{\{e,y\}}$-sentence

$$\neg U_e(y) \wedge \exists u \exists v\ (u < y \wedge y < v \wedge U_e(u) \wedge U_e(v)).$$

We can translate (4) into a regular language, applying the recipes above. But a more concise and perspicuous representation is provided by defining a function bc that compresses a string s as follows. Let $bc(s)$ compress blocks β^n of $n > 1$ consecutive occurrences in s of the same symbol β to a single β, leaving s otherwise unchanged

$$bc(s) \;:=\; \begin{cases} bc(\beta s') & \text{if } s = \beta\beta s' \\ \alpha\ bc(\beta s') & \text{if } s = \alpha\beta s' \text{ with } \alpha \neq \beta \\ s & \text{otherwise.} \end{cases}$$

For example,

$$bc(\boxed{\ }\boxed{e}\boxed{e}\boxed{e, y}\boxed{e}) \;=\; \boxed{\ }\boxed{e}\boxed{e, y}\boxed{e}$$

and in general, bc outputs only stutter-free strings, where a string $\beta_1\beta_2\cdots\beta_n$ is *stutter-free* if $\beta_i \neq \beta_{i+1}$ for i from 1 to $n-1$. Observe that $[\![U_e]\!]$ is an interval precisely if

$$\mathit{bc}(\rho_{\{e\}}(\mathit{str}(M))) \in (\square + \epsilon)\boxed{e}(\square + \epsilon).$$

Compressing further, we can delete initial and final empty boxes through *unpad*

$$\mathit{unpad}(s) := \begin{cases} \mathit{unpad}(s') & \text{if } s = \square s' \text{ or} \\ & \text{else } s = s'\square \\ s & \text{otherwise} \end{cases}$$

and collect all strings in $(2^A)^+$ representing MSO_A-models in which e is an interval in

$$\mathit{Interval}_A(e) := \langle \rho^A_{\{e\}} \rangle \langle \mathit{bc} \rangle \langle \mathit{unpad} \rangle \boxed{e}.$$

Defining π^A_B to be the composition of ρ^A_B with bc and *unpad*

$$\pi^A_B(s) := \mathit{unpad}(\mathit{bc}(\rho^A_B(s)))$$

we have

$$\mathit{Interval}_A(e) = \langle \pi^A_{\{e\}} \rangle \boxed{e}$$

and, as promised at the end of section 4, we can eliminate $\square^*$ from (2)

$$\mathcal{E}_A(x) = \langle \pi^A_{\{x\}} \rangle \boxed{x} - \langle \sqsupseteq \rangle \boxed{x}\boxed{x}$$

and from (3)

$$\mathcal{L}_A(x < y) = \mathcal{E}_A(x) \cap \mathcal{E}_A(y) \cap \langle \pi_{\{x,y\}} \rangle \left(\boxed{x}\boxed{y} + \boxed{x}\square\boxed{y}\right)$$

(dropping the superscript A on π^A_B when possible). Stepping from one interval e to a finite set E of such, let

$$\begin{aligned} \mathit{Interval}(E) &:= \{\pi^E_E(s) \mid (\forall e \in E)\ \pi^E_{\{e\}}(s) = \boxed{e}\} \\ &= \langle \mathit{unpad}^{-1} \rangle \langle \mathit{bc}^{-1} \rangle \bigcap_{e \in E} \langle \pi^E_{\{e\}} \rangle \boxed{e} \end{aligned}$$

so that $\mathit{Interval}(\{e\}) = \boxed{e}$, and for $e \neq e'$, the set $\mathit{Interval}(\{e, e'\})$ consists of thirteen strings, one per interval relation in (Allen, 1983). We can organize these strings as follows (Fernando, 2012). For any finite set E, a string $s \in \mathit{Interval}(E)$ determines a triple $\langle E, \bigcirc_s, \prec_s \rangle$ with binary relations on E of *overlap* $e \bigcirc_s e'$ when $\pi^E_{\{e,e'\}}(s)$ is one of the nine strings in $\mathit{Interval}(\{e, e'\})$ that contain the pair $\boxed{e, e'}$

$$\begin{aligned} \bigcirc_s := \{(e, e') \mid \pi^E_{\{e,e'\}}(s) \in & \left(\boxed{e} + \boxed{e'} + \epsilon\right) \\ & \boxed{e, e'}\left(\boxed{e} + \boxed{e'} + \epsilon\right)\} \end{aligned}$$

and *precedence* $e \prec_s e'$ when $\pi^E_{\{e,e'\}}(s)$ is either $\boxed{e}\boxed{e'}$ or $\boxed{e}\square\boxed{e'}$

$$\prec_s := \{(e, e') \mid \pi^E_{\{e,e'\}}(s) \in \boxed{e}\boxed{e'} + \boxed{e}\square\boxed{e'}\}$$

leaving the two other strings in $\mathit{Interval}(\{e, e'\})$ for $e' \prec_s e$. The triple $\langle E, \bigcirc_s, \prec_s \rangle$ satisfies the axioms for an *event structure* in the sense of (Kamp and Reyle, 1993), and conversely, every such event structure over E can be obtained as $\langle E, \bigcirc_s, \prec_s \rangle$ for some $s \in \mathit{Interval}(E)$.

6 Discussion: simplifying where possible

Few would argue against representing information as simply as possible. Among strings, there is nothing simpler than the null string ϵ, and ϵ is the starting point for refinements given by the system of string functions π^A_B insofar as

$$\epsilon = \pi^A_B(\alpha_1 \cdots \alpha_n) \quad \text{for all } \alpha_1 \cdots \alpha_n \in (2^A)^* \text{ such that } B \cap \bigcup_{i=1}^{n} \alpha_i = \emptyset\ .$$

We have taken pains above to motivate the construction of $\pi^A_B := \rho^A_B; \mathit{bc}; \mathit{unpad}$ from

(i) ρ^A_B, linked in section 3 to MSO and regular languages via the Büchi-Elgot-Trakhtenbrot theorem

and from

(ii) bc and *unpad*, linked in section 5 to event structures for the Russell-Wiener construction of temporal moments from events (or temporal intervals).

A familiar example is provided by a calendar year, represented as the string

$$\text{year}_{mo} := \boxed{\text{Jan}}\boxed{\text{Feb}}\cdots\boxed{\text{Dec}}$$

of length 12, one box per month from the set $mo := \{\text{Jan, Feb, Mar, \ldots, Dec}\}$. A finer-grained representation is given by the string

$$\text{year}_{mo,dy} := \boxed{\text{Jan,d1}}\boxed{\text{Jan,d2}}\cdots\boxed{\text{Jan,d31}}\ \boxed{\text{Feb,d1}}\cdots\boxed{\text{Dec,d31}}$$

of length 365, one box per day, featuring unordered pairs from mo and $dy := \{\text{d1, d2, \ldots, d31}\}$. As the homomorphisms ρ^A_B see only what is in B,

$$\rho^{mo \cup dy}_{mo}(\text{year}_{mo,dy}) = \boxed{\text{Jan}}^{31}\boxed{\text{Feb}}^{28}\cdots\boxed{\text{Dec}}^{31}$$

which $\pi^{mo \cup dy}_{mo}$ then compresses to

$$\mathit{bc}(\boxed{\text{Jan}}^{31}\boxed{\text{Feb}}^{28}\cdots\boxed{\text{Dec}}^{31}) = \text{year}_{mo}$$

making $\pi^{mo \cup dy}_{mo}(\text{year}_{mo,dy}) = \text{year}_{mo}$. If ρ^A_B provides the key to establishing the regularity of MSO-formulas, block compression bc captures the essence of the slogan "no time without change" behind the Russell-Wiener conception of time. Whereas ρ^A_B limits what can be observed to what is in B, bc minimizes the time (space) over which to make these observations. Note that there are finite-state transducers that compute ρ^A_B and bc (over a finite alphabet). Thus, we may form the inverse image of a regular language under either ρ^A_B or bc without worrying if the result is still regular. (It is.)

Were we to leave *unpad* out and make do with $\mathit{bc}^A_B := \rho^A_B; \mathit{bc}$, we need only start our bc^A_B-based refinements from the string $\boxed{}$ of length one consisting of the empty set (rather than ϵ, as in the case of π^A_B) insofar as

$$\boxed{} = \mathit{bc}^A_B(\alpha_1 \cdots \alpha_n) \qquad \text{for all } \alpha_1 \cdots \alpha_n \in (2^A)^+ \text{ such that } B \cap \bigcup_{i=1}^{n} \alpha_i = \emptyset\,.$$

Indeed, $\boxed{}$ has the advantage over ϵ of qualifying as a model of MSO, which ϵ does not, under the usual convention that models of predicate logic have non-empty domains.

And even if one were to construct temporal spans from (say, closed intervals of) the real line $\mathbb{R}$ as in (Klein, 2009), the string $\boxed{}$ is a fine (enough) representation of $\mathbb{R}$, unbroken and virgin. The influential analysis of tense and aspect in (Reichenbach, 1947) positions the speech s and described event e relative to a reference time r. For instance, in the simple past (e.g. *it rained*), r coincides with e but precedes s

$$\text{simplePast}(e, r, s) := \boxed{e,r}\boxed{s} + \boxed{e,r}\boxed{}\boxed{s}$$

while in the present perfect (e.g. *it has rained*), r comes after e but coincides with s

$$\text{presentPerfect}(e, r, s) := \boxed{e}\boxed{s,r} + \boxed{e}\boxed{}\boxed{s,r}.$$

Factoring out the reference time, the simple past and present perfect become identical

$$\begin{aligned}\rho^{\{e,r,s\}}_{\{e,s\}}(\text{simplePast}(e, r, s)) &= \boxed{e}\boxed{s} + \boxed{e}\boxed{}\boxed{s} \\ &= \rho^{\{e,r,s\}}_{\{e,s\}}(\text{presentPerfect}(e, r, s)).\end{aligned}$$

$\boxed{e}\boxed{s} + \boxed{e}\boxed{}\boxed{s}$ is a simple example of "the expression of time in natural language" relating "a clause-internal temporal structure to a clause-external temporal structure" (Klein, 2009, page 75). The clause-internal structure $\boxed{e}$ and clause-external structure $\boxed{s}$ can be far more complex, subject to elaborations from lexical and grammatical aspect. Elaborations in interval temporal logic made in (Dowty, 1979) are formulated in terms of strings in (Fernando, 2013).

The finiteness and discreteness of strings arguably mirrors the bounded granularity of natural language statements (rife with talk of "the next moment"). Boundaries drawn to analyze, for example, telicity become absurd if they separate arbitrarily close pairs of real numbers (as they would, applied to the real line). It is customary to view a model M as an *index* that the Carnap-Montague *intension* of a formula φ maps to one of two truth values, indicating whether or not $M \models \varphi$. But the construal of a string as an underspecified representation suggests viewing it not only as an index but also as an *extension* (or denotation) of φ (Fernando, 2011). In this connection, a proposal from (Bach, 1986) is worth recalling — namely, that we associate an event type such as KISSING with a function EXT(KISSING) that maps histories to subparts that are temporal manifestations of KISSING (with input histories as indices, and output manifestations as extensions). Relativizing notions of indices and extensions to a bounded granularity, it is natural to assume at the outset not indices but extensions, which are then enlarged, as required, to more detailed and larger indices. The relation EXT(KISSING) then becomes a relation between strings (contained in $\sqsupseteq$) which a finite-state transducer might compute. For refinements of granularity, we start with an undifferentiated piece (viz. ϵ or $\boxed{}$) rather than a multitude of fully fleshed out possible histories. From ϵ or $\boxed{}$, the ingredients we require are a set of auxiliary symbols, and a suitable system R^A_B of regular relations, for finite sets A and $B \subseteq A$ of auxiliary symbols, projecting indices over the alphabet 2^A to indices over 2^B — e.g., bc^A_B or, as in (Fernando, 2013), π^A_B.

References

James F. Allen. 1983. Maintaining knowledge about temporal intervals. *Communications of the Association for Computing Machinery*, 26(11):832–843.

F. Baader, D. Calvanese, D. L. McGuinness, D. Nardi, P. F. Patel-Schneider. 2003. *The Description Logic Handbook: Theory, Implementation, Applications*. Cambridge University Press.

Franz Baader and Carsten Lutz. 2006. Description logic. In Patrick Blackburn, Johan van Benthem, and Frank Wolter, editors, *The Handbook of Modal Logic*, pages 757–820. Elsevier.

Emmon Bach. 1986. Natural language metaphysics. In R. Barcan Marcus, G.J.W. Dorn, and P. Weingartner, editors, *Logic, Methodology and Philosophy of Science VII*, pages 573 – 595. Elsevier.

Kenneth R. Beesley and Lauri Karttunen. 2003. *Finite State Morphology*. CSLI,Stanford,

David R. Dowty. 1979. *Word Meaning and Montague Grammar*. Reidel, Dordrecht.

Andrzej Ehrenfeucht and Paul Zeiger. 1976. Complexity measures for regular expressions. *J. Comput. Syst. Sci.*, 12(2):134–146.

Tim Fernando. 2004. A finite-state approach to events in natural language semantics. *Journal of Logic and Computation*, 14(1):79–92.

Tim Fernando. 2011. Regular relations for temporal propositions. *Natural Language Engineering*, 17(2):163184.

Tim Fernando. 2012. A finite-state temporal ontology and event-intervals. Proceedings of the 10th International Workshop on Finite State Methods and Natural Language Processing, pages 80–89, Donostia/San Sebastian (ACL archive).

Tim Fernando. 2013. Segmenting temporal intervals for tense and aspect. 13th Mathematics of Language meeting. Sofia, Bulgaria.

Michael J. Fischer and Richard E. Ladner. 1979. Propositional dynamic logic of regular programs. *Journal of Computer and System Sciences*, 18:194–211.

Wouter Gelade and Frank Neven. 2008. Succinctness of the complement and negation of regular expressions. In *Symposium on Theoretical Aspects of Computer Science*, pages 325–336.

Markus Holzer and Martin Kutrib. 2010. The complexity of regular(-like) expressions. In *Developments in Language Theory*, pages 16–30. Springer.

Mans Hulden. 2009. Regular expressions and predicate logic in finite-state language processing. In *Finite-State Methods and Natural Language Processing*, pages 82–97. IOS Press.

Hans Kamp and Uwe Reyle. 1993. *From Discourse to Logic*. Kluwer.

Wolfgang Klein. 2009. How time is encoded. In *The Expression of Time*, pages 39–82. Mouton De Gruyter.

Hans Reichenbach. 1947. *Elements of Symbolic Logic*. MacMillan Company, NY.

Alfred Tarski, Andrzej Mostowski, and Raphael Robinson. 1953. *Undecidable Theories*. North-Holland.

Wolfgang Thomas. 1997. Languages, automata and logic. In *Handbook of Formal Languages: Beyond Words*, volume 3, pages 389–455. Springer-Verlag.

Anssi Yli-Jyrä and Kimmo Koskenniemi. 2004. Compiling Contextual Restrictions on Strings into Finite-State Automata. In *Proceedings of the Eindhoven FASTAR Days*.

Using NooJ for semantic annotation of Italian language corpora in the domain of motion: a cognitive-grounded approach

Edoardo Salza
LiCoTT - Università del Piemonte Orientale
Vercelli,Italy
edoardo.salza@gmail.com

Abstract

In this paper we propose a system to parse and annotate motion constructions expressed in Italian language. We used NooJ as a software tool to implement finite-state transducers in order to recognize linguistic elements constituting motion events. In this paper we describe the model we adopted for semantic description of events (grounded on Talmy's Cognitive Semantics theories) and then we illustrate how the system works with a domain-specific corpus, the structure of annotation that our system will perform, some annotation structures of example sentences expressing motion and then an attempt to evaluate the system's performance.

1 Introduction

The building of models of semantic knowledge to be implemented in language recognition and analysis systems shares some features with the theory of perception (Piotrowski and Palibina, 1973). In a Cognitive Linguistics paradigm this task should be viewed as the modelling of the human ability to map concepts onto syntactic-semantic constructs. The aim of this contribution is to describe an approach to the annotation of expressions of motion in Italian. The set of concepts (i.e. the semantic model) is grounded on a cognitive semantics theory where knowledge representation constitute both the basis of the construction process of meaning and also the goal of the proposed application. From the computational point of view we make use of recursive transition networks (RTNs) used for recognition and subsequent annotation of text with the domain's concepts. To implement RTNs we used NooJ development environment (Silberztein, 2004). We used NooJ because in this way we can easily write local grammars describing the elements to be recognized. From the technical point of view, at the dawn of NLP research on pattern recognition, experimentation started using the so-called rule-based paradigm. This entailed the processing of a large amount of grammar rules and the need of storage-consuming electronic dictionaries. These drawbacks caused these methods to be substantially impractical thus shifting rapidly the mainstream to the now widespread statistical corpus-based approach. In this paper we then propose a system that, using a cascade of transducers, deterministically recognizes semantic patterns describing motion events (Abney, 1996). These patterns show a large variety of diverse expressions and lexical choices (in one word lexicalization patterns) to describe motion. Such a variety is easily accounted for by a set of finite-state automata. The formalism used here to extract semantic components of the patterns is grounded on cognitive semantics theories attempting to describe the lexicalization processes that underlie the production of the syntactic and semantic structures expressing concepts related to motion and, consequently, to space.

2 Theoretical Framework

Spatial notions form the *kernel* of linguistic knowledge from which all other concepts are derived from, giving to the spatial knowledge a primary role on the conceptualization of the reality. This stance is called *localism*. Localism is the "*hypothesis that spatial expressions are more basic, grammatically and semantically, than various kind of spatial expressions [. . .] spatial organization is of central importance in human cognition*" (Lyons, 1977) and such approaches date back to the early comparative studies on prepositions and cases (Wüllner, 1827), where their meaning is viewed as grounded on spatial subjective intuition. Concepts related to space hold a basic role in the conceptualization process of the human's mind (and in child's development of concepts) and they serve as a major source of lexicalization of more abstract ones. These views regained importance with the rise of cognitive science in the 1970's, with the dominance of universalist studies on categorization. According to these theories, abstract concepts are thought to be derived from spatial primitives by using cognitive tools like *conceptual* metaphor (Lakoff, 1980) or derivation from universal representations like *image-schemata* (Johnson, 1987). Space-related constructs can thus refer also to a wider semantic area than just concepts closely related to space and motion: in this way a system extracting motion events will recognize also events other than motion-related ones, if expressed metaphorically with motion verbs. Sentences expressing motion events are generally characterized by a set of thematic roles from the semantic domain of concepts related to motion. Our purpose is to parse simple sentence constructs, more specifically we focus on compound nouns and predicate-argument structures, which bear most of the meaning (Surdeanu et al., 2003). Our final goal is to recognize the type of motion described and to semantically annotate the text with the related concepts.

3 The proposed system

The system implements semantic role labeling techniques (Gildea and Jurafsky, 2002) to parse predicate-arguments structures. Lexical constructs are connected to their corresponding roles selected by the verb. These latter will be recognized and annotated with their respective information elements related to the motion event. Predicate-argument structures are constituted by a main verb and a set of nouns or prepositional phrases specifying the meaning of the verb, which works as the head of the structure. Semantic model maps lexical elements into their respective semantic roles. In the following section we will describe the model we used for structure detection and annotation, we then detail the mapping layers implemented according to the annotation to be performed and finally we will illustrate some of the transducers used for the recognition of lexical elements and also we give some examples of possible practical uses of our system.

3.1 Semantic model of the motion event

To choose a suitable representation of motion events we need to consider different semantic roles expressed by lexical elements in order to map the predicate-argument structures onto elements of the semantic model of the event (Exner and Nugues, 2011). The model is thus constituted by a set of domain-specific semantic roles belonging to motion. To choose them we have considered the notion of *motion event* as introduced by Talmy (1985) where motion events are described as *"situation containing movement or the maintenance of a stationary location [...]. The basic motion event consists of one object (the Figure) moving or located with respect to another object (the reference-object or Ground)"*. Talmy's approach is based on perception and on neuropsychological theories: *Figure* and *Ground* are, for example, concepts borrowed from the so-called *Gestalt Theory*, a theory of mind opposed to structuralist and behaviorist approaches aiming to describe the mind/brain through holistic, analog and emergent mechanisms. This has led to choose a semantic model that is both cognitive-grounded and comprehensive of all necessary conceptual elements (Mosca, 2010). In Table 1 are listed the elements we choose to extract. As Italian is a pro-drop language, subject is often omitted and then FIGURE is seldom lexicalized.

Element	Description
FIGURE	The object that moves or is located with respect to another object.
GROUND	The reference object with respect to with the motion takes place or another object is located to.
SOURCE	The place where the described motion event starts.
GOAL	The place where the described motion event ends.
DIRECTION	The relative direction taken with respect to a ground or reference point (as *left, right, north, west, ...*).
VECTOR	The axis along which the motion take place and/or the absolute direction of the moving element.
PATH	The type of path performed by the moving element involving a ground element (*inwards, outwards, crossing, passing through*).
SHAPE	The shape of movement performed. (*circular, straight, curvilinear*)
PROXIMALITY	The distinctive feature of motion with respect to a ground or reference point (*near, along or throughout*)
MANNER	The manner of performed motion (*walking, running, wandering,...*)

Table 1: Elements of motion

3.2 Description of the system

The elements previously listed constitute the set of semantic roles of our model. They can be beared by the verb itself or explicitly lexicalized as syntactic elements of the sentence as direct objects, indirect objects or adverbial phrases (i.e. they are *satellites* of the verb). We need to implement a set of lexico-syntactic transducers to parse every single semantic elements.According to Mosca (2010), motion event sentences can be grouped in eight syntactic patterns with increasing analyticity. For our purposes we select the following ones:

1. Motion verbs that can stand alone with no adjoints.
2. Motion verbs accepting a noun phrase as direct object.
3. Motion verbs accepting a prepositional phrase as object.
4. Motion verbs expressed with a generic motion verb with prepositional phrases(s) plus one or more satellites to specify motion event roles.
5. Motion events analytically expressed with support verbs[1]

Verbs of the first type bear a lot of information and accept none or few satellites: according to Talmy's terminology they *conflate* semantic elements. A verb like *fiancheggiare* "conflates"all the information about the fact that a figure is moving in proximity to a reference ground. Conflation is "*any syntactic process [...] whereby a more complex construction turns into a simpler one.*" (Talmy, 2000). More analytic verbs bear few information and devolves their meaning to their *satellites*[2]. Satellites are lexicalized with different syntactic constructs. Our system recognizes locative adverbial phrases representing position or direction, deictic elements expressing proximality or distality (frequently referred to a reference ground) and so on. The system also maps satellites to the corresponding semantic roles and "deflates" the meaning of the verbs making it explicit.

Motion verbs are grouped in *semantic clusters* according to their meaning (Mosca, 2007). For each cluster we need to implement a set of transducers. We have considered motion verbs with the meaning of a generic motion from and/or to a ground object, verbs indicating a continuing motion along the same direction (called *source-destination verbs*), verbs indicating motion along a direction or towards something that specifies the followed path (*direction verbs*), verbs with the meaning of passing beyond, crossing, exiting or entering a ground, or with the meaning of moving along a direction or near a ground (*path verbs*), verbs indicating a proximal motion passing near a ground (*proximity verbs*), verbs specifying the shape of a path (curvilinear, circular, straight, etc.) (called *shape verbs*) and verbs that specifies the manner of motion (*manner verbs*).

Semantic patterns are represented with formalisms involving lexical, syntactic and semantic elements (*local grammars*) implemented on NooJ [3]. Local grammars are formal descriptions of morpho-syntactic and/or semantic regularities represented with finite-state transducers (Harris, 1991; Gross, 1993).

3.2.1 Annotation layers

The annotation is performed using a cascade of transducers. Parsing is done incrementally: annotations at one level make use of the ones performed on previous levels. We have implemented seven different layers, each defined by the type of structure(s) recognized, as described below.

Simple compound nouns This layer recognizes compound nouns with patterns like *N+Adj* (e.g. *lago blu*), *Adj+N* (e.g. *nuovo sentiero*), *N+N* (e.g. *piazza Garibaldi*, *N+Prep+N* (e.g. *casa di pietra*). These listed above are the most frequent patterns in Italian (Voghera, 2004). Below is reported the corresponding local grammar reported in NooJ's format[4].

```
SC::= NA | AN | NPN | NPV | NN | NeN
AN::= <A> <N>
NA::= <N> <A>
NPN::= <N> P <N>
NPV::= <N> (a|da|per) <V+Inf>
NN::= <N> <N>
P::= (di|a|da|in|con|su|per|tra|fra) <DET>*
```

Complex compound nouns The second layer refers to complex compound nouns: this layer recognizes compound nouns corresponding to forms as *strada ripida sterrata, bivio segnalato da bolli gialli, casa vicino all'incrocio di tre strade, versante occidentale della catena montuosa.* The head can be one of the cases listed

[1]Support verbs are constructions where the predicative role is taken by the noun (object) and the verb lose its meaning as *fare una curva VS curvare*

[2]They are "*the grammatical category of any constituent other than a noun-phrase or prepositional phrase complement that is in a sister relation to the verb root*"

[3]NooJ standard dictionary with other resources for Italian are developed and maintained by Simonetta Vietri of Università di Salerno and are available at *http://www.nooj4nlp.net/pages/italian.html.* (Elia and Vietri, 2002).

[4]Angle brackets denote a POS element of standard dictionary and asterisk refers to optional elements.

above and the modifier can be an adjectival or a prepositional phrase. Corresponding transducers are shown in Figure 1 and below is presented the related local grammar. As the former, this layer recognizes structure type, number, gender and head of the extracted nouns.

```
CCN::= (<N>|SC> (A_modifier | P_modifier | N_modifier))
A_modifier::= <AVV>* <A> ((e|ed) <A>)*
P_modifier::= P ( (<V+Inf>|<AVV>*)|(<N>|SC) )
N_modifier::= N
```

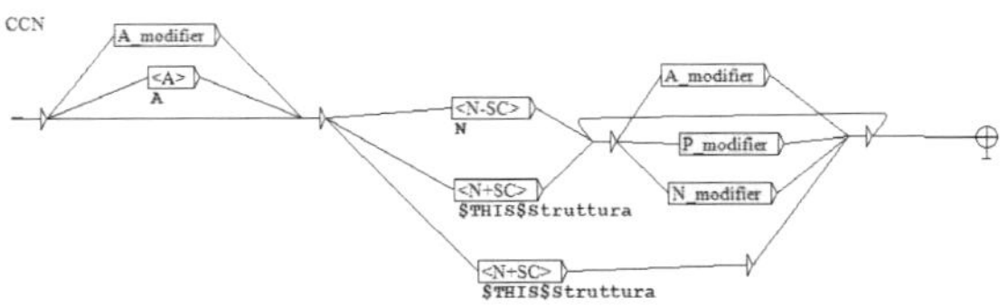

Figure 1: Transducer recognizing complex compound nouns

Noun phrases This layer annotates noun phrases and extracts their head. Transducer is shown in Figure 2.

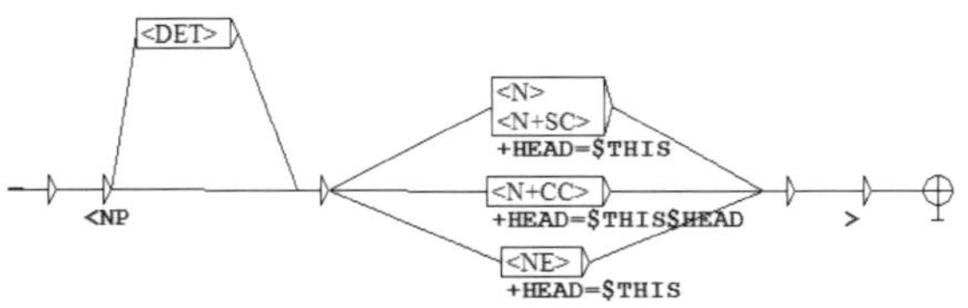

Figure 2: Transducer recognizing noun phrases

Prepositional phrases This layer annotates prepositional phrases and extracts their prepositional head and the dependent noun (or noun phrase). Respective transducer is shown in Figure 3.

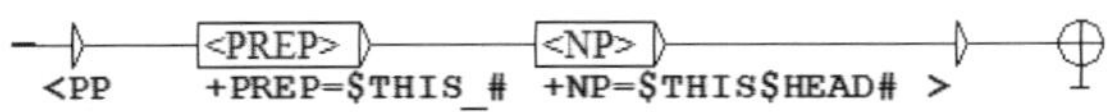

Figure 3: Transducer recognizing prepositional phrases

Motion verbs This layer recognizes motion verbs. The ones recognized by our system are extracted from a list compiled through a statistical analysis of a corpus of spoken Italian. This corpus was collected from experiments for which the goal is to solve a spatial description task. Verbs forming this list are a set of frequently used verbs while describing motion events in Italian. We adopted the classification and the set of lemmas proposed in Mosca (2007). The local grammar that recognizes motion verbs is reported in Figure 4. Transducers are shown in Figure 5.

```
MOTION-VERBS::=V-SD-GEN |V-SD-A|V-SD-CONT|V-SD-DA
        |V-SD-CONT|V-DIRECTION-GEN|V-DIRECTION-BACK
        |V-DIRECTION-DEV|V-DIRECTION-DOWN|
        |V-DIRECTION-UP|V-PATH-THROUGH|V-PATH-IN
        |V-PATH-OUT|V-PATH-ACROSS|V-PROXY-NEAR
        |V-PROXY-ALONG|V-PROXY-OVER|V-SHAPE-CIRC
        |V-SHAPE-CURV|V-SHAPE-STRAIGHT|V-MANNER
V-SD-GEN::=<andare>|<tornare>|<venire>|<spostarsi>
V-SD-A::=<arrivare>|<giungere>|<raggiungere>|<trovare>
            |<incontrare>|<finire>|<trovare>|<sbattere> contro|
         |<trovarsi>|<fermarsi>
V-SD-CONT::=<andare> avanti|<continuare>|<procedere>
      |<proseguire>
V-SD-DA::=<partire>
V-DIRECTION-GEN::=<puntare>|<riandare>|<tenere>|<avvicinarsi>
                     |<dirigersi>|<inoltrarsi>|<muoversi>
        |<tenersi>
V-DIRECTION-BACK::=<tornare> indietro
V-DIRECTION-DEV::=<abbandonare>|<inclinare>|<piegare>
        |<scansare>|<rientrare>|<abbassarsi>
        |<allargarsi>|<alzarsi>|<inclinarsi>
V-DIRECTION-DOWN::=<discendere>|<scendere>
V-DIRECTION-UP::=<salire> su*
V-PATH-THROUGH::=<attraversare>|<incrociare>|<intersecare>
      |<tagliare>
V-PATH-IN::=<entrare>|<infilare>|<imboccare>|<prendere>
     |<immettersi>
V-PATH-OUT::=<sbucare>|<uscire>
V-PATH-ACROSS::=<passare>|<percorrere>|<seguire>
V-PROXY-NEAR::=<rimanere>|<lasciare>|<sfiorare>
V-PROXY-ALONG::=<costeggiare>|<rasentare>|<sfiorare>|<seguire>
V-PROXY-OVER::=<oltrepassare>|<saltare>|<sorpassare>|<superare>
V-SHAPE-CIRC::=<accerchiare>|<aggirare>|<cerchiare>
      |<circondare>|<circoscrivere>|<circumnavigare>
V-SHAPE-CURV::=<curvare>|<girare>|<svoltare>|<virare>
      |<voltare>
V-SHAPE-STRAIGHT::=<tirare>|<proseguire>|<andare>
        |<continuare>
V-MANNER::=<camminare>
```

Figure 4: Grammar recognizing of motion verbs

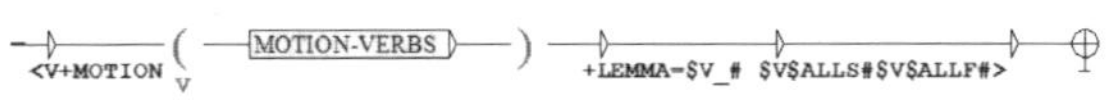

Figure 5: Transducers recognizing motion verbs

Verb phrases This layer recognizes different syntactic realizations of motion verb phrases distinguishing between active and passive form. The corresponding transducer is shown in Figure 6.

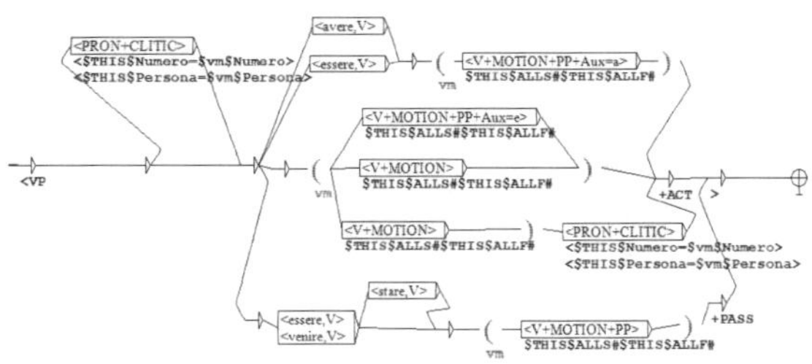

Figure 6: Transducer recognizing verb chunks

4 Motion Events' elements recognition

The two upper layers (i.e. the last processed ones) are used for recognizing the different elements of motion event: the first is dedicated to the recognition of satellites. They consist mainly of prepositions expressing information about motion (Mosca, 2012) such as Prepositional Case-Markers (PCM) and satellites-prepositions. Prepositional Case-Markers are prepositions with a weak or no meaning that serve to introduce a prepositional phrase as in *salire **su** sul tetto*. Satellite-preposition *Satpreps* are intended as prepositional particles fulfilling both the functions described before. For our purposes we have distinguished the following satellite types:

- DIRECTION: satellites expressing direction. They can be specified using an absolute or an intrinsic frame or reference Levinson (2003) (as *in direzione est* or *a destra*). The system also recognizes deictic relative reference grounds to/from an *origo*[5].
- POSITION: satellites expressing locations with an absolute or relative reference as *di fronte, a destra, sopra sotto, a est, qui, l.*
- PROXIMITY: satellites expressing *proximality*, i.e. object located in areas expressed with respect to a ground (*lungo, accanto, di fianco, nei pressi, vicino*).
- STRAIGHT: satellites expressing motion events in which the taken direction is straight (as *dritto*).
- CIRCULAR: satellites expressing motion events where the motion is circular (as *intorno,attorno*).
- THROUGH: satellites expressing motion events whose GOAL is reached via a path (as *attraverso*) or through a reference ground (as *in fondo, a fine*).

These transducers recognize FIGURE and GROUND elements, satellites and PCM (see Figure 7).

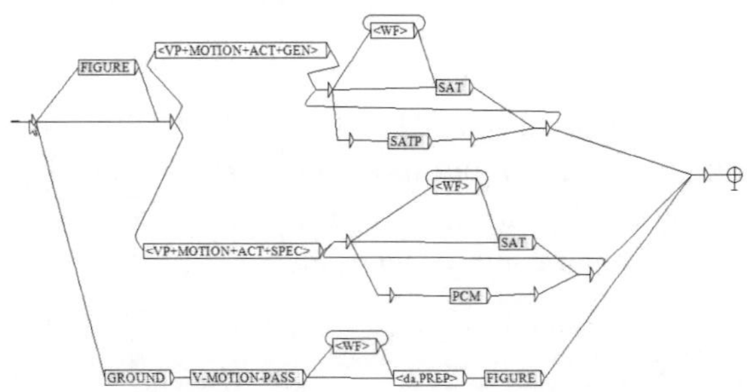

Figure 7: Transducers for recognizing satellites, figure, ground, PCM and Satpreps elements

We have also distinguished five types of lexicalization structures according to the meaning of the verb:

1. Structures expressing a generic motion with a source and/or a destination explicitly expressed.

<table>
<tr><td>Layer 1</td><td><N></td><td>+SC</td></tr>
<tr><td>Layer 2</td><td><N></td><td>+CC</td></tr>
<tr><td>Layer 3</td><td><PP></td><td>+PREP=preposition +DET+ NP=noun_phrase</td></tr>
<tr><td>Layer 4</td><td><NP></td><td>+HEAD</td></tr>
<tr><td>Layer 5</td><td><V></td><td>+LEMMA=lemma
+(SD_GEN|SD_A|SD_DA|SD_CONT|DIRECTION_GEN|DIRECTION_BACK|
|DIRECTION_DOWN|DIRECTION_UP|DIRECTION_DEV|PATH_IN|PATH_OUT|
|PATH_ATTR|PATH_PER|SHAPE_CURV|SHAPE_CIRC|SHAPE_STRAIGHT
|MANNER)
+TERM</td></tr>
<tr><td>Layer 6</td><td><VP></td><td>+ACT | +PASS (+AUX=essere|avere)</td></tr>
<tr><td>Layer 7</td><td><SAT></td><td>(SATP | PCM
| SAT
+DIR (
+ABS +DIRECTION=(NORTH|NORTHEAST|SOUTH|SOUTHWEST|WEST|NORTHEAST)
| +REL +DIRECTION=(RIGHT|LEFT|BACKWARD|FORWARD|UPWARD|DOWNWARD
|OUTWARD|INWARD)
| +DEICTIC +DIRECTION=(TO_ORIGO|FROM_ORIGO|TO_GROUND))
+POS (
+ABS +POSITION=(NORTH|NORTHEAST|SOUTH|SOUTHWEST|WEST|NORTHEAST)
| +REL +POSITION = (FRONT|BACK|LEFT_FROM|RIGHT_FROM|ON|UNDER|INTO
|OUT_FROM)
| +DEICTIC +POSITION=(NEAR_ORIGO|FAR_FROM_ORIGO))
+CIRC
+PROXY=(NEAR|OVER|ALONG)
+STRAIGHT
+THROUGH +THROUGH_GROUND</td></tr>
<tr><td>Layer 8</td><td><ME></td><td>+SD (+TO |+FROM | +CONT)
+GROUND
+SOURCE
+GOAL
+PATH=(CROSSING|INTO|OUT_FROM|THROUGH)
+SHAPE=(CIRCULAR|CURVILINEAR +ENABLEMENT|STRAIGHT|custom)
+FIGURE_POSITION=<SAT+POSITION> +CHANGE_VECTOR
+VECTOR=(BACKWARDS|UPWARDS|DOWNWARDS)
+DIRECTION=<SAT+DIRECTION>
+PROXIMITY +PROXY_TYPE=(PASS|NEAR|ALONG)
+MANNER=manner</td></tr>
</table>

Figure 8: Annotations performed by our system

2. Structures describing a movement in a particular direction and/or along a particular vector. The direction can be expressed by a conflation of the directional element of meaning in the verb root (as in *scendere, salire, indietreggiare*) or by a satellite.
3. Structures expressing a motion along a path where the moving element can enter, exit, pass over or going through a the reference ground (verbs as *entrare, attraversare, percorrere, sbucare*).
4. Structures expressing proximal motion. We distinguish a motion along (*costeggiare, seguire*), near (*sfiorare, toccare*) or passing through a GROUND (*sorpassare, superare*).
5. Structures expressing a straight or round shape of the motion path. A round path can be a complete circular loop, a circle arc (*circoscrivere, aggirare*) or a curved trajectory as in *curvare, svoltare*. Note that in this latter case the motion will change vector so the system will note this explicitly with a dedicated annotation (+VECTOR_CHANGE).

Note that if the elements about motion are conflated in the verb root the information should be extracted by putting an empty-string transducer before the matching element with the desired annotation in output (see Figure 9).

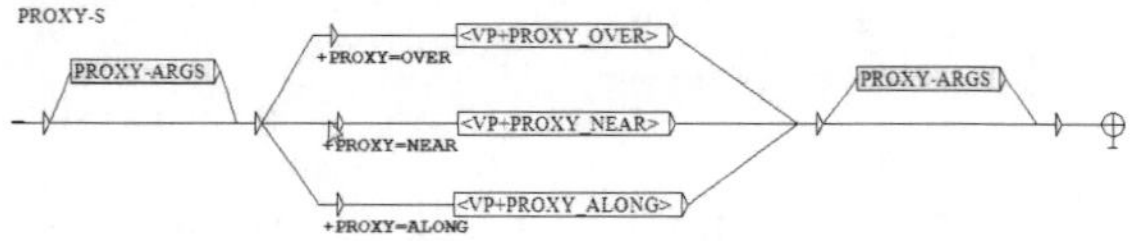

Figure 9: Example of a transducer recognizing motion elements lexicalized in verb root

Arguments of the verbs are extracted with the transducer shown in Figure 10. Elements lexicalized by satellites are extracted using transducers as the one shown in Figure 11. These latter have been designed according to the structure of related verb(s).

[5] With respect to Levinson (2003) we use here a slightly different terminology adopting the term *relative* for an intrinsic frame of reference in Levinson's sense and the term *deictic* for Levinson's relative frame of reference to express a direction with respect to a reference point or ground object

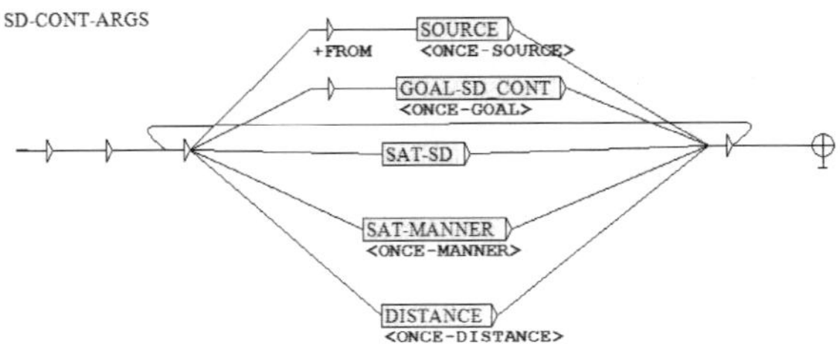

Figure 10: Example of a transducer recognizing motion structures arguments

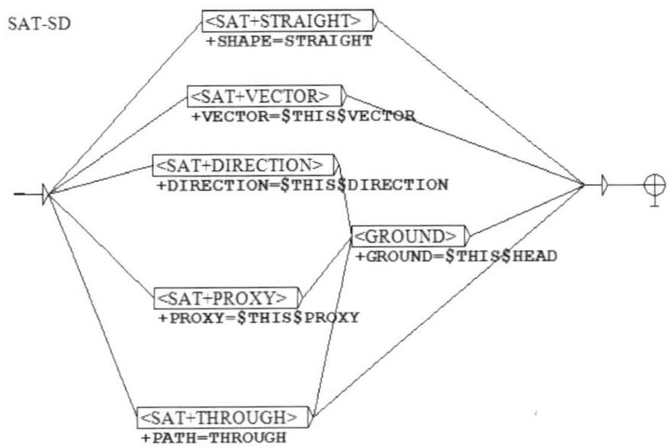

Figure 11: Transducer recognizing motion elements lexicalized in satellites

Transduction is performed when we need to annotate text chunks: annotation is given in the NooJ's XML-like form, i.e. using a node-label and a series of attribute-value pair specifying motion elements. Annotation and extraction are done simultaneously for every stage of the transducers' cascade. A comprehensive list of the annotations performed by our system is shown in Figure 8 where, for every layer, the annotation tree is detailed (annotations introduced by the standard dictionary are not reported).

4.1 Source-destination

These automata describe basic motion events (annotated as +SD) starting from a SOURCE and ending in a GOAL. These can be described by verbs as *andare, venire, spostarsi, tornare*. SOURCE and GOAL can be of different types: we have considered the following three cases:

1. The simplest case where the SOURCE and/or the GOAL are reference grounds expressed with prepositional phrases as *partire da casa* or *andare a casa*.

2. The case where the SOURCE and/or the GOAL are areas defined with respect to a reference ground as in *parti davanti la stazione*. The GOAL can be reached via a path or through a reference ground (*spostarsi in fondo al viale, andare alla fine della strada, partire da davanti la stazione*).

A generic motion should be expressed with a verb whose meaning focuses alternatively on different phases of the event as the reaching of a point or a place (+TO), the leaving from a point or a place (+FROM) as in *partire* or the continuing (+CONT) of the motion along a path as in *proseguire, continuare, andare avanti*. The system also distinguishes from terminative verbs +TERM involving the reaching of a goal (*raggiungere, arrivare, giungere*) or the reaching of a generic point along a translation process (*ritrovarsi, incontrare*). Examples of extracted structures are shown in Figure 12.

SD

Motion event construction	Related annotation
[...] si raggiunge il colletto sottostante.	<ME+SD+TO+GOAL=colletto sottostante>
la mulattiera proseque a destra [...]	<ME+FIGURE=mulattiera+SD+CONT+DIRECTION=RIGHT>
spostandosi alla destra verso un lungo contrafforte davanti al versante ovest	<ME+SD+DIRECTION=RIGHT+DIRECTION=TO_GROUND+GROUND=lungo contrafforte+FIGURE_POSITION=FRONT+GOAL=davanti al versante ovest
partendo dalla destra del parcheggio [...]	<ME+SD+FROM+TO+SOURCE=destra del parcheggio>
[...] si ritrova il passaggio	<ME+SD+TO+GOAL=passaggio>
Arriviamo sotto un ultimo gradino [...]	<ME+SD+TO+FIGURE_POSITION=UNDER+GOAL=ultimo gradino>
[...] si incontra il Ru de Montjovet	<ME+SD+TO+GOAL=Ru de Montjovet>
[...] si proseque a destra verso il bivio	<ME+SD+CONT+DIRECTION=RIGHT+DIRECTION=TO_GROUND+GROUND=bivio
[...] si proseque a sinistra attraverso una umida valletta verso un saliscendi boscoso	<ME+SD+CONT+DIRECTION=LEFT+PATH=THROUGH+GROUND=umida valletta+DIRECTION=TO_GROUND+GROUND=saliscendi boscoso>
[...] si continua verso i pendii superiori [...]	<ME+SD+CONT+DIRECTION=TO_GROUND+GROUND=pendii superiori>
[...] si proseque dritto	<ME+SD+CONT+SHAPE=straight>

Figure 12: Samples of source-destination structures with related annotations

4.2 Path

The system distinguishes four types of paths (+PATH), involving four different configurations of the motion:

1. A motion event which PATH entails that the FIGURE moves THROUGH a GROUND. The reference ground can be a road, a trail or a path (verbs as *passare, percorre, seguire*).

2. A motion event in which the FIGURE goes ACROSS a GROUND element (i.e. a river, a crossing, a wood). It can be described by verbs as *incrociare, tagliare, attraversare*.

3. A motion event in which the FIGURE *enters* in a GROUND element as a house, a road or a new path. It is described by verbs as *entrare, imboccare, immettersi* (INTO).

4. A motion event in which the FIGURE *exits* from a GROUND element (verbs as *sbucare, uscire*) (+OUT_FROM).

Examples of annotated structures are shown in Figure 13.

PATH

Motion event construction	Related annotation
[...] percorri il sentiero a destra per il laghetto	<ME+PATH=THROUGH+PROXY=ALONG+GROUND=sentiero+DIRECTION=RIGHT +TO+GOAL=laghetto>
[...]imboccare a sinistra una strada	<ME+PATH=INTO+CHANGE_VECTOR+DIRECTION=RIGHT+GROUND=strada>
Il sentiero, ora pianeggiante, percorre il bordo di una conca sassosa.	<ME+FIGURE=sentiero+PATH=THROUGH+PROXY=ALONG +GROUND=bordo di una conca sassosa>
[...] si entra nel desolato vallone	<ME+PATH=INTO+GROUND=desolato vallone>
[...] si sbuca fra i ripidi prati	<ME+PATH=OUT_FROM+GROUND=ripidi prati>
[...] attraversata a sinistra un piccolo greto	<ME+PATH=ACROSS+DIRECTION=LEFT+GROUND=piccolo greto>
[...] tagliando il ripido versante di conifere	<ME+PATH=ACROSS+GROUND=ripido versante di conifere>

Figure 13: Samples of path structures with related annotation

4.3 Proximality

The system extracts motion events' structures where the FIGURE moves near a GROUND object (+PROXY). We call this feature *proximality*. Transducers extracting these structures are shown in Figure 9 and examples of annotated structures are shown in Figure 14. Our system distinguishes three cases:

1. The case in which the FIGURE passes NEAR a GROUND object (verbs as *rimanere, sfiorare, toccare*).

2. The case where the FIGURE moves ALONG a reference GROUND (as a border). (as verbs *costeggiare, fiancheggiare*).

3. The case where the FIGURE passes OVER a reference ground (overstepping an obstacle or moving beyond a landmark). This is expressed with verbs as (*oltrepassare, superare*).

PROXIMITY

Motion event construction	Related annotation
[...] oltrepassato un canale di frana [...]	<ME+PROXY=OVER+GROUND=canale di frana>
[...] si lasciano a sinistra le Baite di Rocher	<ME+PROXY=NEAR+DIRECTION=RIGHT+GROUND=Baite di Rocher>
[...] costeggiando sulla destra un rado boschetto [...]	<ME+PROXY=ALONG+DIRECTION=RIGHT+GROUND=rado boschetto>

Figure 14: Samples of proximality structures with related annotation

4.4 Direction

The system recognizes five different cases in respect to the lexicalization of DIRECTION and VECTOR features of motion:

1. The case where the FIGURE has to go back (+DIRECTION_BACK) in respect to the direction already taken (+VECTOR=BACKWARDS). Event is described by verbs like *tornare (indietro), indietreggiare*.

2. The case (+DIRECTION_DOWN) where the FIGURE moves downwards (+VECTOR=DOWNWARDS) (verb *scendere*).

3. The case (+DIRECTION_UP) where the FIGURE moves upwards (verb *salire*).

4. The case (+DIRECTION_DEV) where the FIGURE changes direction (+CHANGE_DIRECTION) (verbs as *abbandonare, inclinarsi, rientrare, alzarsi*). This case can involve the change of direction and/or vector of the FIGURE.

5. The case (+DIRECTION_GEN) where the direction of the FIGURE is explicitly expressed by a generic verb (as *punta, dirigiti, muoviti*) using a direction satellite with respect to a reference ground. The system recognizes the case where DIRECTION is taken toward a reference ground (+DIRECTION=TO_GROUND).

Examples of annotated structures are shown in Figure 15.

4.5 Shape

There are also cases where the motion involves a straight or a circular movement (+SHAPE). The motion can take place with respect to a GROUND following a circular trajectory (verbs *aggirare, circondare, circoscrivere*) or just a direction change, usually with a turn (verbs *girare, curvare, svoltare*). Examples are shown in Figure 16.

DIRECTION

Motion event construction	Related annotation
[...] tornati in casa [...]	<ME+DIRECTION_BACK+VECTOR=BACKWARDS+TO+PATH=INTO+GOAL=casa>
[...] si punta verso un alpeggio in alto sotto la dorsale	<ME+DIRECTION_GEN+DIRECTION=TO_GROUND+GROUND=alpeggio> +VECTOR=UPWARDS+TO+FIGURE_POSITION=under+GROUND=dorsale>
[...] dal fondo del parcheggio si sale alla destra verso i dolci pendii	<ME+DIRECTION_UP+FROM+SOURCE=fondo del parcheggio +VECTOR=UPWARDS+DIRECTION=RIGHT+PATH=THROUGH +GROUND=dolci pendii>
[...] torna indietro attraverso il sentiero grande	<ME+DIRECTION_BACK+VECTOR=BACKWARDS+PATH=THROUGH +GROUND=sentiero grande>
[...] piegando a sinistra [...]	<ME+DIRECTION_DEV+CHANGE_VECTOR+DIRECTION=LEFT>
la traccia scende verso le costruzioni abbandonate	<ME+FIGURE=traccia+DIRECTION_DOWN+VECTOR=DOWNWARDS+TO +GOAL=costruzioni abbandonate+DIRECTION=TO_GROUND>

Figure 15: Samples of direction structures

SHAPE

Motion event construction	Related annotation
[...] si volge a destra [...]	<ME+SHAPE=CURVILINEAR+CHANGE_VECTOR +DIRECTION=RIGHT>
[...] la strada vira a sinistra [...]	<ME+FIGURE=strada+SHAPE=CURVILINEAR+CHANGE_VECTOR +DIRECTION=LEFT>
[...] aggirati alcuni valloni secondari [...]	<ME+SHAPE=CIRCULAR+GROUND=alcuni valloni secondari>

Figure 16: Samples of extracted shape structures

5 Evaluation of the system

In order to evaluate our system we have collected a corpus of about 300 texts describing hiking tours in Western Alps. Texts are extracted from hiker's fan websites (our main source was the site *http://www.inalto.org*).

These descriptions, from the point of view of language variation determined by the medium of communication, share characteristics both of written and spoken language. This is due to the distinctive traits of Web-Mediated communication where the language, although written, shows features of spoken language and also to the reduced perceived distance between addresser and addressee. Route descriptions posted in a blog brings similar characteristics: in this way we can easily have a corpus positioned "half-way" along the *diamesic* dimension (Mioni, 1983).

A hiking tour description, also, contains motion events where all three space dimensions are involved while describing paths. These can run up and down, going along grounds elements with directions that can be expressed lexically through both absolute or relative frames of references. All these features make hiking descriptions a well suitable test corpus for the system.

The dimension of our corpus is around 100kwords with a type/token ratio of 8%. In Table 2 we show the score of the system tested on the evaluation corpus at the current stage of development.

Precision	Recall	F1 score
70,5%	80,4%	75,1%

Table 2: System's scores

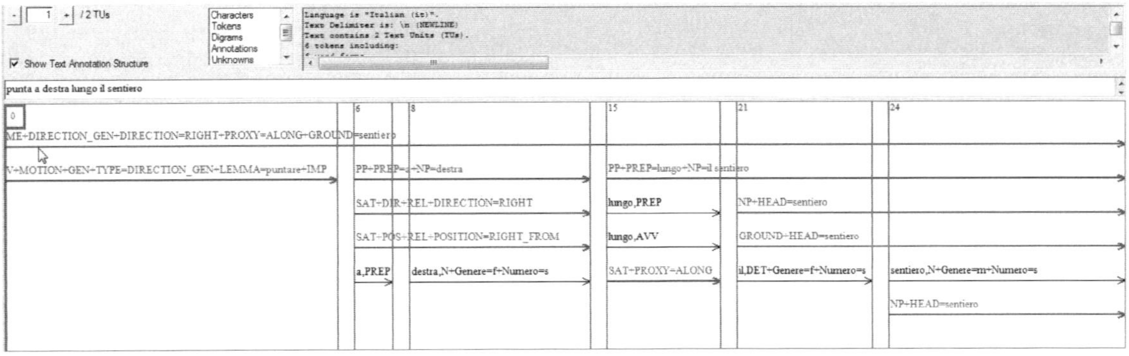

Figure 17: Annotation structure of a sample sentence

The evaluation is conducted on recognized sentences not taking into account the annotation structure. We show in Figure 17 a sample of the annotation structure of a sample sentence.

The proposed system can be used to extract motion structures with complex combines of features. Here we extract events involving a changing vector to left (see Figure 18):

`<ME+CHANGE_VECTOR+DIRECTION=LEFT>`

Text	Before	Seq.
ESC_1_060.not		imboccare sulla sinistra la Via S
ESC_1_139.not		si imbocca a sinistra un più largo
ESC_1_192.not		Il sentiero volge a sinistra
ESC_1_360.not		si svolta a sinistra iniziando
ESC_1_403.not		si imbocca a sinistra una pista ombrosa
ESC_1_417.not		prendere a sinistra un sentiero fra i prati
ESC_1_498.not		la strada vira a sinistra

Figure 18: Samples of extracted motion structures

Our system can also make queries using lower annotation layers as in:

`<V+SD_CONT> <PCM+PREP=su> <GROUND>`

where the system extracts all motion events in which the FIGURE continues along a PATH expressed by a GROUND and introduced by the preposition *su* (on) used here as a case-marker. Results are shown in Figure 19.

6 Conclusions and future work

We have described here a system that recognizes sentences expressing motion events and annotates them extracting the information about the type of performed motion. This information is gathered from the meaning of the verb and explicitly lexicalized by verb's satellites expressing motion features such as position, direction or shape. Elements participating in motion process are annotated according to concepts borrowed from psychological theory of Gestalt as used in Talmy's theory of motion events. It would be possible to expand the scope of our system making it able to recognize more complex and longer patterns of expressions. We could also make use of lexico-syntactic constraints in order to filter out relevant sentences and thus improve precision. Thanks to the integration capability of NooJ our system is designed to be also part of more complex applications in a NLP pipeline. As an example, it is possible to use the information extracted and reported on annotation layers to populate an ontology in the domain of space or motion (Salza, 2013). Moreover, the described system can be extended to recognize a large variety of lexical structures; among these, the vocabulary related to manner of motion lacks a deeper theoretical analysis and requires further work.

Text	Before	Seq.
ESC_1_050.not		prosegue sulla pista asfaltata
ESC_1_084.not		prosegue sulla traccia di una mulattiera
ESC_1_119.not		prosegue sul largo crinale sempre più roccioso
ESC_1_121.not		Proseguendo sul filo della cresta sommitale
ESC_1_124.not		prosegue sul panoramicissimo crinale prativo
ESC_1_128.not		prosegue sul filo della cresta
ESC_1_129.not		procede sul versante bergamasco
ESC_1_146.not		prosegue sulla strada forestale interdetta
ESC_1_160.not		prosegue sulla pista
ESC_1_209.not		prosegue sulla traccia
ESC_1_209.not		prosegue sul fondo del vallone
ESC_1_212.not		continuando sulla traccia
ESC_1_304.not		prosegue sul crinale in piano
ESC_1_329.not		prosegue sui poco inclinati pendii erbosi
ESC_1_396.not		Proseguendo su traccia più deteriorata
ESC_1_445.not		proseguire sulla destra col sentiero
ESC_1_475.not		prosegue sulla pista sterrata fin quasi
ESC_1_497.not		procede sulla pista di servizio

Figure 19: Samples of extraction of lower annotation layers

References

Steven Abney. 1996 Partial parsing via finite-state cascades. *Natural Language Engineering*, 1996.

Annibale Elia and Simonetta Vietri. 2002 *L'analisi automatica dei testi e i dizionari elettronici, in E. Burattini, R. Cordeschi, (eds.), Manuale di Intelligenza Artificiale per le Scienze Umane*. Carocci, Roma, 2002.

Peter Exner and Pierre Nugues 2011 Using semantic role labeling to extract events from Wikipedia. *In Proceedings of the Workshop on Detection, Representation, and Exploitation of Events in the Semantic Web (DeRiVE 2011). Workshop in conjunction with the 10th International Semantic Web Conference 2011 (ISWC 2011)* Bonn, October 23–24 2011

Daniel Gildea and Daniel Jurafsky 2002 Automatic labeling of semantic roles. In *Proceedings of the 38th Annual Conference of the Association for Computational Linguistics (ACL-00)*, pages 512–520, Hong Kong, October 2000.

Maurice Gross. 1993 Local grammars and their representation by finite automata. In *M. Hoey - Data, Description, Discourse. Harper Collins, London*, pages 26–38, 1993.

Zellig S. Harris. 1991 A theory of language and information: a mathematical approach. Clarendon Press, Oxford

Mark L. Johnson 1987. *The Body in the Mind: The Bodily Basis of Meaning, Imagination, and Reason*. University of Chicago Press, 1987.

George Lakoff and Mark L. Johnson 1980. *Metaphors we live by*. University of Chicago Press, Chicago, 1980.

Stephen C. Levinson 2003. *Space in language and cognition*. Cambridge, Cambridge University Press, 1977.

John Lyons 1977. *Semantics*. Cambridge, Cambridge University Press, 1977.

Monica Mosca 2007. *Spatial language in spoken Italian dialogues. A cognitive linguistics perspective*. Ph.D. Thesis, Pisa, Università di Pisa

Monica Mosca 2010. *Eventi di moto in italiano tra sintassi e semantica. Uno studio cognitivo empirico*. Edizioni Plus - Pisa University Press

Monica Mosca 2012. *Italian motion constructions - Different functions of particles*. In: Filipović, Luna and Kasia M. Jaszczolt (eds.), Space and Time in Languages and Cultures: Linguistic diversity . 2012. xv, 492 pp. (pp. 373394) John Benjamins John Benjamins

Marvin Minsky 1975. A Framework for Representing Knowledge. In The Psychology of Computer Vision, ed. P. H. Winston, 211 277. New York: McGraw-Hill.

Alberto M. Mioni 1983 Italiano tendenziale: osservazioni su alcuni aspetti della standardizzazione, in Scritti liguistici in onore di Giovan Battista Pellegrini, Pacini, Pisa 495-517.

R. G. Piotrowski and I. V. Palibina 1973. Automatic pattern recognition applied to semantic problems. In *Proceedings of the 5th conference on Computational linguistics - Volume 2*, COLING '73, pages 104–106 Stroudsburg, PA, USA, 1973. Association for Computational Linguistics.

Edoardo Salza 2013. Using NooJ as a system for (shallow) ontology population from Italian texts. Unpublished conference proceedings, NooJ International Conference. June 3–5 2013, Saarbrücken University.

Max Silberztein 2004. NooJ : an Object-Oriented Approach. In INTEX pour la Linguistique et le Traitement Automatique des Langues, C. Muller, J. Royauté, M. Silberztein Eds, Cahiers de la MSH Ledoux. Presses Universitaires de Franche-Comté, pp. 359-369.

Mihai Surdeanu and Sanda Harabagiu and John Williams and Paul Aarseth. 2003. Using predicate-argument structures for information extraction. In *Proceedings of the 41st Annual Meeting on Association for Computational Linguistics-Volume 1*, pages 8–15. Association for Computational Linguistics, 2003.

Henry S. Thompson and Anne Anderson and Ellen Gurman Bard and Gwyneth Doherty-Sneddon and Alison Newlands and Cathy Sotillo 1993. The hcrc map task corpus: natural dialogue for speech recognition. In *Proceedings of the workshop on Human Language Technology*, HLT '93, pages 25–30, Stroudsburg, PA, USA, 1993. Association for Computational Linguistics.

Mark B. Turner and Gilles Fauconnier 1995. Conceptual Integration and Formal Expression (July 28, 1995). Metaphor and Symbolic Activity, Vol. 10, No. 3, pp. 183-203, 1995. Available at SSRN: http://ssrn.com/abstract=1650417

Leonard Talmy 1985. Lexicalization Patterns:Semantic Structure in Lexical Forms, in T.Shopen, *Language Typology and Syntactc Dess-cription. Vol. III Gramamtical Categories and Lexicon*. Cambridge, Cambridge University Press:57-149

Leonard Talmy 2000. *Toward a Cognitive Semantics: Vol.I Concept Structuring Systems*. Cambridge(MA), MIT Press

Miriam Voghera. 2004 Polirematiche. In *Grossmann M., Rainer F., (a cura di) La formazione delle parole in italiano.Tbingen, Niemeyer*, pages 56–69, 2004.

Franz Wüllner 1827. *Die Bedeutung der sprachlichen Casus und Modi*. Münster, Theissigsche Buchhandlung

Multi-threaded composition of finite-state automata

Bryan Jurish
Berlin-Brandenburg Academy of Sciences
Jägerstr 22/23 · 10117 Berlin · Germany
jurish@bbaw.de

Kay-Michael Würzner
University of Potsdam · Psychology Dept.
Karl-Liebknecht-Str. 24-25 · 14476 Potsdam · Germany
wuerzner@uni-potsdam.de

Abstract

We investigate the composition of finite-state automata in a multiprocessor environment, presenting a parallel variant of a widely-used composition algorithm. We provide an approximate upper bound for composition speedup of the parallel variant with respect to serial execution, and empirically evaluate the performance of our implementation with respect to this bound.

1 Introduction

Finite-state automata[1] allow for efficient implementations in terms of directed graphs with designated initial and final states, as well as labeled edges facilitating efficient storage and lookup. Complex systems based on (weighted) finite-state automata have been successfully used in language processing (Mohri et al., 2007), image compression (Culik II and Kari, 1993), computational biology (Krogh et al., 1994), and many other applications. Composition is a binary operation on finite-state transducers (FSTs) which creates transitions for matching output- and input-labels of the outgoing transitions of two operand states. It is an important operation in both compile-time construction (where it may be employed e.g. to combine different levels of representation) and – since lookup may be considered a special case of composition – run-time querying of the aforementioned systems.

Despite the increasing trend towards multiprocessor systems and the resulting demand for efficient parallel implementations for common operations (Sutter, 2005), no generic parallel algorithm for the composition of FSTs has yet been established, although many efforts have been made to improve composition performance in special cases. In Holub and Štekr (2009), a parallel implementation for the case of string lookup in a deterministic finite-state acceptor (FSA) is presented. A generalization to n operands which prevents the construction of large intermediate results is given in Allauzen and Mohri (2009). A good deal of work has focussed on *dynamic*, *on-the-fly*, or *lazy* implementations (Hori et al., 2004; Cheng et al., 2007; Mohri et al., 2007), in which the composition of FSTs is only partly computed, new states and transitions being added to the result only when necessary.

In this article, we present a parallel variant of a widely-used composition algorithm (Hanneforth, 2004; Allauzen et al., 2007, etc.) which can make use of multiprocessor architectures by employing multiple concurrent threads of execution. We provide an approximate upper bound for composition speedup using a state-wise parallel algorithm with respect to serial execution, and empirically evaluate the performance of our implementation with respect to this bound.

2 Preliminaries

2.1 Definitions

Definition 1 (FST). *A* finite-state transducer[2] *is a 6-tuple* $\mathcal{T} = \langle \Sigma, \Gamma, Q, q_0, F, E \rangle$ *with* Σ *a finite input alphabet,* Γ *a finite output alphabet,* Q *a finite set of automaton states,* $q_0 \in Q$ *the designated initial state,* $F \subseteq Q$ *a set of final states, and* $E \subseteq Q \times Q \times (\Sigma \cup \{\varepsilon\}) \times (\Gamma \cup \{\varepsilon\})$ *a set of transitions.*

For a transition $e = (q_1, q_2, a, b) \in E$, we denote by $\mathrm{p}[e]$ its source state q_1, by $\mathrm{n}[e]$ its destination state q_2, by $\mathrm{i}[e]$ its input label a, and by $\mathrm{o}[e]$

[1] Where appropriate, we use the term *automata* as a generic subsuming both *acceptors* and *transducers*.

[2] Here and in the sequel, we restrict our attention to *unweighted* automata. The algorithms described here trivially extend to the weighted case. In fact, the implementations used in the current experiments (Sec. 4) operate on weighted automata.

its output label b. A finite-state acceptor (FSA) can be regarded as an FST with $\Sigma = \Gamma$ and $\mathrm{i}[e] = \mathrm{o}[e]$ for all $e \in E$.

A *path* π is a sequence $e_1 \ldots e_n$ of n transitions such that $\mathrm{n}[e_i] = \mathrm{p}[e_{i+1}]$ for $1 \le i < n$. We denote by $|\pi|$ the length of π: $|e_1 \ldots e_n| = n$. Extending the notation for transitions, we define the source and destination states of a path as $\mathrm{p}[\pi] = \mathrm{p}[e_1]$ and $\mathrm{n}[\pi] = \mathrm{n}[e_n]$, respectively. The input label string $\mathrm{i}[\pi]$ yielded by a path π is the concatenation of the input labels of its transitions: $\mathrm{i}[\pi] = \mathrm{i}[e_1]\mathrm{i}[e_2] \ldots \mathrm{i}[e_n]$; the output label string $\mathrm{o}[\pi]$ is defined analogously.

For $q \in Q$, $x \in \Sigma^*$, $y \in \Gamma^*$, and $R \subseteq Q$, $\Pi(q, x, y, R)$ denotes the set of paths from q to some $r \in R$ with input string x and output string y, and $\Pi(q, R) = \bigcup_{x \in \Sigma^*, y \in \Gamma^*} \Pi(q, x, y, R)$ denotes the set of paths originating at q and ending at some $r \in R$. A state $r \in Q$ is said to be *accessible from* a state $q \in Q$ if there exists a path π with $\mathrm{p}[\pi] = q$ and $\mathrm{n}[\pi] = r$; r is *accessible* if it is accessible from q_0. $[\![\mathcal{T}]\!] \subseteq \Sigma^* \times \Gamma^*$ denotes the string relation associated with $\mathcal{T}$, and is defined as the set of input- and output-string pairs labelling successful paths in $\mathcal{T}$: $[\![\mathcal{T}]\!] = \{(\mathrm{i}[\pi], \mathrm{o}[\pi]) : \pi \in \Pi(q_0, F)\}$

Definition 2 (Depth). *For any accessible $q \in Q$, $\mathrm{depth}(q)$ denotes the depth of q, defined as the length of the shortest path from the initial state to q:*

$$\mathrm{depth}(q) = \begin{cases} 0 & \text{if } q = q_0 \\ \min_{\pi \in \Pi(q_0, \{q\})} |\pi| & \text{otherwise} \end{cases}$$

The depth of a transducer $\mathcal{T}$ is defined as the maximum depth over all its accessible states: $\mathrm{depth}(\mathcal{T}) = \max_{q \in Q : \Pi(q_0, \{q\}) \neq \emptyset} \mathrm{depth}(q)$.

2.2 Composition

Composition is a binary operation on FSTs $\mathcal{T}_1$ and $\mathcal{T}_2$ which share an "inner" alphabet. Informally, the composition operation matches transitions from $\mathcal{T}_1$ to transitions from $\mathcal{T}_2$ if the corresponding output and input labels coincide. Formally:

Definition 3 (Composition of FSTs). *Given two FSTs $\mathcal{T}_1 = \langle \Sigma, \Gamma, Q_1, q_{0_1}, F_1, E_1 \rangle$ and $\mathcal{T}_2 = \langle \Gamma, \Delta, Q_2, q_{0_2}, F_2, E_2 \rangle$, the composition of $\mathcal{T}_1$ and $\mathcal{T}_2$ is denoted by $\mathcal{T}_1 \circ \mathcal{T}_2$, and is itself an FST whose string relation is the composition of the string relations of $\mathcal{T}_1$ and $\mathcal{T}_2$, $[\![\mathcal{T}_1 \circ \mathcal{T}_2]\!] = [\![\mathcal{T}_1]\!] \circ [\![\mathcal{T}_2]\!]$, i.e. for all $x \in \Sigma^*$, $y \in \Delta^*$, $(x, y) \in [\![\mathcal{T}_1 \circ \mathcal{T}_2]\!]$ if and only if there exists some $z \in \Gamma^*$ such that $(x, z) \in [\![\mathcal{T}_1]\!]$ and $(z, y) \in [\![\mathcal{T}_2]\!]$. Further, $\mathcal{C} = \langle \Sigma, \Delta, (Q_1 \times Q_2), E, (q_{0_1}, q_{0_2}), (F_1 \times F_2) \rangle$ is such an FST, $[\![\mathcal{C}]\!] = [\![\mathcal{T}_1 \circ \mathcal{T}_2]\!]$, where:*

$$E = \bigcup_{\substack{(q,r,a,b) \in E_1 \\ (s,t,b,c) \in E_2}} \{((q, s), (r, t), a, c)\} \tag{1}$$

The construction above is only correct if $\mathcal{T}_1$ and $\mathcal{T}_2$ are ε-free on their output and input tapes, respectively. The generalization to ε-transitions has been discussed e.g. by Mohri (2009). Since the generalization can be reduced to the above construction applied to ε-free WFSTs, we ignore it here in the interest of clarity.

The most common serial algorithm (Mohri, 2009) for computing the composition of two WFSTs is presented here as Algorithm 1, and can be considered a variant of the standard intersection algorithm for unweighted FSAs as described by Hopcroft and Ullman (1979). Unlike the "brute force" construction of Definition 3, the algorithm generates only those states and transitions of the output automaton which are accessible from the initial state. In this manner, the algorithm manages to avoid the combinatorial explosion of states and transitions implicit in Definition 3 in the overwhelming majority of cases.

2.3 Amdahl's Law

Amdahl's law (Amdahl, 1967) describes the theoretical bound on speeding up a program in terms of improvements made to specific parts of that program. In particular, it can be used to predict the maximum speedup resulting from executing specific parts of a program in parallel on a multiprocessor architecture.

$$S_N = \frac{1}{(1 - P) + \frac{P}{N}} \tag{2}$$

Equation (2) states that the maximum speedup S_N of a parallel program is the inverse sum of the serial proportion of that program (those parts which cannot be executed in parallel, $1 - P$) and the parallel proportion P divided by the number of processors N. As the number of available processors increases, $\frac{P}{N}$ approaches zero and S_N approaches $\frac{1}{1-P}$.

3 State-wise parallelization

Using a first-in-first-out protocol for the visitation queue V, Algorithm 1 effectively performs a

Algorithm 1: COMPOSE: serial composition of ε-free FSTs

Input: $\mathcal{T}_1 = \langle \Sigma, \Gamma, Q_1, q_{0_1}, F_1, E_1 \rangle$ an FST
Input: $\mathcal{T}_2 = \langle \Gamma, \Delta, Q_2, q_{0_2}, F_2, E_2 \rangle$ an FST

1 **function** COMPOSE($\mathcal{T}_1, \mathcal{T}_2$)
2    $Q, F, E \leftarrow \emptyset$ /* initialize */
3    $V \leftarrow \{(q_{0_1}, q_{0_2})\}$ /* visitation queue */
4   **while** $V \neq \emptyset$ **do**
5      $(q_1, q_2) \leftarrow \texttt{pop}(V)$ /* visit state */
6      $Q \leftarrow Q \cup \{(q_1, q_2)\}$
7   **if** $(q_1, q_2) \in F_1 \times F_2$ **then** /* final state */
8        $F \leftarrow F \cup \{(q_1, q_2)\}$
9   **for** $(e_1, e_2) \in E[q_1] \times E[q_2]$ **with** $\mathrm{o}[e_1] = \mathrm{i}[e_2]$ **do** /* align transitions */
10        $E \leftarrow E \cup \{((q_1, q_2), (\mathrm{n}[e_1], \mathrm{n}[e_2]), \mathrm{i}[e_1], \mathrm{o}[e_2])\}$
11   **if** $(\mathrm{n}[e_1], \mathrm{n}[e_2]) \notin Q$ **then**
12          $\texttt{push}(V, (\mathrm{n}[e_1], \mathrm{n}[e_2]))$ /* enqueue for visitation */
13   **return** $\mathcal{C} = \langle \Sigma, \Delta, Q, (q_{0_1}, q_{0_2}), F, E \rangle$

breadth-first traversal of the output automaton $\mathcal{C}$. Pairs of destination states for aligned transitions are enqueued only if they have not yet been visited. Our parallelization scheme is based on concurrent processing of multiple result states – multiple concurrent executions of the while loop at lines 4-12. Such state-wise parallelization is a common approach for breadth-first traversals of graphs in a multiprocessor environment (Roosta, 2000).

3.1 An approximate upper bound for state-wise parallel speedup

In this section, we investigate the potential speedup resulting from a state-wise parallelization of Algorithm 1 as described above. We assume that Algorithm 1 constructs an automaton $\mathcal{C} = \langle \Sigma, \Gamma, Q, q_0, F, E \rangle$, and show that the maximum speedup of a state-wise parallel composition algorithm depends on the topological properties of $\mathcal{C}$, specifically on its state-to-depth ratio.

We call a single evaluation of lines 4-12 a *visitation* of the state $q = (q_1, q_2) \in Q$, and we call a state *discovered* when it has been pushed to the visitation queue during the visitation of a predecessor at line 12. For each $q \in Q$, let $t_0(q)$ represent the time at which the visitation of q begins, let $t_1(q)$ be the earliest time at which the visitation of q has completed. We assume a strict breadth-first visitation order on states: for all $q, q' \in Q$,

$$\mathrm{depth}(q) < \mathrm{depth}(q') \implies t_1(q) \leq t_0(q') \quad (3)$$

i.e. visitation of all states at depth d must have completed before any state with depth $d' > d$ can itself be visited. In order to approximate a worst-case scenario for state-wise parallelization, we assume that the duration of a visitation $t_{\text{visit}}(q)$ is independent of the state q being visited, defining this constant as our elementary time unit:

$$\forall q \in Q, (t_1(q) - t_0(q)) = t_{\text{visit}}(q) = 1 \quad (4)$$

We restrict our attention to the execution of the visitation loop of lines 4-12, ignoring the constant administrative overhead of lines 2-3 and 13, and assume the convention that visitation of the initial state begins at $t_0(q_0) = 0$.

Lemma 1 (Serial composition running time). *Let $\mathcal{C} = \langle \Sigma, \Gamma, Q, q_0, F, E \rangle$ be an FST constructed by Algorithm 1. Serial execution of the algorithm requires exactly $t_{\text{serial}} = |Q|$ time units.*

Proof. Since each state is visited exactly once and no two states can be visited concurrently, the algorithm terminates after exactly $|Q|$ visitations. No code is executed between visitations, so $t_{\text{serial}} = \sum_{q \in Q} t_{\text{visit}}(q) = |Q|$ by Equation 4. □

Lemma 2 (Parallel state visitation bound). *Let $\mathcal{C} = \langle \Sigma, \Gamma, Q, q_0, F, E \rangle$ be an FST constructed by Algorithm 1 executed in state-wise parallel fashion using an unbounded number of processors $N \geq |Q|$. The completion time of any given state's visitation is determined by that state's depth:*

$$\forall q \in Q, t_1(q) = \mathrm{depth}(q) + 1$$

Proof. We proceed by induction over $\mathrm{depth}(q)$. For $\mathrm{depth}(q) = 0$, it must be that $q = q_0$ and

$t_0(q) = t_0(q_0) = 0$ by convention. Since visitation time is constant, $t_1(q) = t_0(q) + t_{\text{visit}}(q) = 1 = \text{depth}(q) + 1$, so the lemma holds.

For the inductive step, consider an arbitrary $q \in Q$ with $\text{depth}(q) = d$ and assume that the lemma holds for all $q' \in Q$ with $\text{depth}(q') < d$. Since $\text{depth}(q) = d$, there exist $p \in Q$ and $e \in E$ with $\text{p}[e] = p$, $\text{n}[e] = q$, and $\text{depth}(p) = d - 1$ by Definition 2. By inductive hypothesis, $t_1(p) = \text{depth}(p) + 1 = d$. Since we have $N \geq Q$ processors available and at most $|Q|$ visitations to perform, we can begin processing q as soon as it is discovered during the visitation of p: $t_0(p) < t_0(q) \leq t_1(p)$, but the strict breadth-first visitation constraint of Equation (3) dictates that visitation of q cannot begin until all states of lesser depth have been visited, so $t_0(q) = t_1(p) = d$ and $t_1(q) = t_0(q) + t_{\text{visit}}(q) = d + 1$ by Equation (4). □

Lemma 3 (State-wise parallel composition running time)**.** *Let $\mathcal{C} = \langle \Sigma, \Gamma, Q, q_0, F, E \rangle$ be an FST constructed by Algorithm 1. State-wise parallel execution of the algorithm with $N \geq Q$ available processors requires exactly $t_{\text{parallel}:N} = 1 + \text{depth}(\mathcal{C})$ time units.*

Proof. The algorithm terminates when all states have been visited at time $t_1(\mathcal{C}) = \max_{q \in Q} t_1(q)$. By Lemma 2, all states in each depth-slice $\text{depth}^{-1}(d) \subseteq Q$ are visited concurrently, completing at time $d + 1$. Since $\text{depth}(\mathcal{C}) = \max_{q \in Q} \text{depth}(Q)$ by Definition 2, $t_{\text{parallel}:N} = t_1(\mathcal{C}) = 1 + \text{depth}(\mathcal{C})$. □

Having derived approximate running times of both serial and parallel executions, we can now compute the maximum speedup of a state-wise parallel execution.

Theorem 1 (Maximum speedup of state-wise parallelization)**.** *The maximum speedup $S_{\max}$ of a state-wise parallel execution of Algorithm 1 constructing an output FST $\mathcal{C} = \langle \Sigma, \Gamma, Q, q_0, F, E \rangle$ with respect to serial execution is approximated for $N \geq |Q|$ by:*

$$S_{\max} = \frac{t_{\text{serial}}(\mathcal{C})}{t_{\text{parallel}:N}(\mathcal{C})} = \frac{|Q|}{1 + \text{depth}(\mathcal{C})}$$

Proof. Follows from Lemmas 1 and 3. □

Corollary 1 (Composition parallelizability)**.** *$P_{\max}$ is an approximate upper bound on the proportion of the total execution time of Algorithm 1 which can be effectively run in parallel:*

$$P_{\max} = 1 - \frac{1}{S_{\max}}$$

Proof. Follows from Theorem 1 and Amdahl's law (Eq. 2). □

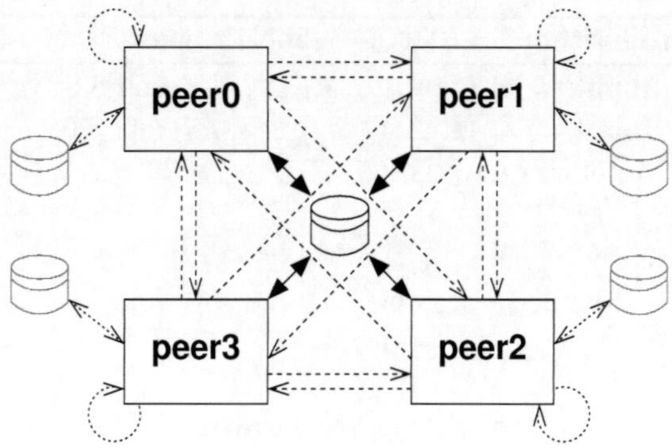

Figure 1: Data-flow diagram for the peer-to-peer parallel composition algorithm using 4 peers. Lock-free data access is displayed with dotted lines, data channels shared by exactly two peers appear as dashed lines, and globally shared data channels which can be locked by any peer are solid black.

3.2 Algorithm

Apart from the bounds implied by automaton topology, practical issues such as shared data structures and the necessarily associated synchronization between otherwise independent threads must be considered in the development of any parallel algorithm. Access to shared data is typically controlled by mutual exclusion locks (*mutexes*): when altering a shared data structure s, a thread t must first lock that structure. Other threads must then wait for t to unlock s before they can access it themselves. Competition for mutex locks therefore has a strong impact on the overall performance of multi-threaded implementations, since lock acquisition is an inherently synchronous operation, and thus decreases the proportion of the program which can actually be executed in parallel.

Our approach is presented as pseudo-code in Algorithm 2 and schematically depicted in Figure 1. We make use of a set of $N > 1$ "peer" threads $p_{i \in N}$, each of which simulates the execution of lines 4-12 from Algorithm 1. To minimize competition over shared data structures, each peer allocates and maintains its own local partition of

Algorithm 2: PPCOMPOSE: peer-to-peer parallel composition

Input: $\mathcal{T}_1 = \langle \Sigma, \Gamma, Q_1, q_{0_1}, F_1, E_1 \rangle$ an FST
Input: $\mathcal{T}_2 = \langle \Gamma, \Delta, Q_2, q_{0_2}, F_2, E_2 \rangle$ an FST
Input: $N \in \mathbb{N}$, number of peer threads to spawn

1 **function** PPCOMPOSE$(\mathcal{T}_1, \mathcal{T}_2, N)$
2   **for** $0 \leq i, j < N$ **do** $V_{i,j} \leftarrow \emptyset$ */* initialize queue matrix */*
3     $V_{0,r(q_{0_1}, q_{0_2})} = \{(q_{0_1}, q_{0_2})\}$
4     $n_{\text{up}} = 1$ */* shared queue-size counter */*
5   **for** $0 \leq i < N$ **do spawn** PEER(i) */* spawn peer threads */*
6   `wait_on_all_peers()`
7   **return** $\mathcal{C} = \langle \Sigma, \Delta, \bigcup_{i \in N} Q'_i, (q_{0_1}, q_{0_2}), \bigcup_{i \in N} F'_i, \bigcup_{i \in N} E'_i \rangle$

8 **procedure** PEER(i)
9     $Q'_i, F'_i, E'_i \leftarrow \emptyset$ */* initialize peer-local data */*
10   **while** `true` **do**
11   **find** j **with** $0 \leq j < N$ **and** $V_{j,i} \neq \emptyset$
12         $v \leftarrow \texttt{pop}(V_{j,i})$
13   **if** $v = \texttt{eof}$ **then return**   */* terminate thread */*
14   **if** $v \notin Q'_i$ **then** VISIT(i, v) */* visit state */*
15   **if** $n_{\text{up}} = 1$ **then**
16   **for** $0 \leq j < N$ **do** $\texttt{push}(V_{i,j}, \texttt{eof})$ */* terminate peers */*
17         $n_{\text{up}} \leftarrow n_{\text{up}} - 1$ */* update shared counter */*

18 **procedure** VISIT$(i, (q_1, q_2))$
19     $Q'_i \leftarrow Q'_i \cup \{(q_1, q_2)\}$
20   **if** $(q_1, q_2) \in F_1 \times F_2$ **then**   */* final state */*
21         $F'_i \leftarrow F'_i \cup \{(q_1, q_2)\}$
22   **for** $(e_1, e_2) \in E[q_1] \times E[q_2]$ **with** $\text{o}[e_1] = \text{i}[e_2]$ **do**   */* align transitions */*
23         $E'_i \leftarrow E'_i \cup \{((q_1, q_2), (\text{n}[e_1], \text{n}[e_2]), \text{i}[e_1], \text{o}[e_2])\}$
24         $n_{\text{up}} \leftarrow n_{\text{up}} + 1$ */* update shared counter */*
25         $\texttt{push}(V_{i,r(\text{n}[e_1],\text{n}[e_2])}, (\text{n}[e_1], \text{n}[e_2]))$ */* enqueue for visitation */*

the output automaton structure (Q'_i, F'_i, E'_i), and the visitation queue V is replaced by an $(N \times N)$ matrix of peer-to-peer local message queues: $V_{i,j}$ contains messages originating at peer p_i and destined for peer p_j.

This technique relies for its correctness on the prior specification of a partitioning function $r : Q_1 \times Q_2 \to N$ over states of the result automaton, used to determine which peer is responsible for visiting any such state. For the experiments described in section 4, our input automata provided injective functions $[\![\cdot]\!]_1 : Q_1 \to \mathbb{N}$ and $[\![\cdot]\!]_2 : Q_2 \to \mathbb{N}$, and we used the partitioning function given in Equation (5).

$$r(q_1, q_2) = \left\lfloor \frac{[\![q_1]\!]_1 + [\![q_2]\!]_2}{2} \right\rfloor \mod N \qquad (5)$$

Since the visitation queue V is no longer a shared atomic structure, an additional shared global counter n_{up} is required to keep track of the number of visitation requests currently enqueued in any $V_{i,j}$. Only when the last such request has been processed does the algorithm terminate by sending a designated message $\texttt{eof} \notin Q_1 \times Q_2$ to all peers at line 16.

Also worth noting is that due to the peer-wise partitioning of result data – in particular that of Q into $Q'_{i \in N}$ – a new visitation request must be enqueued at line 25 for every aligned transition, and the decision of whether or not a visit is actually required deferred to the responsible peer at line 14. This can be expected to result in larger queues, correspondingly increased memory requirements, and an additional $\mathcal{O}(E - Q)$ copy operations compared to Algorithm 1. Any additional computational load – in particular the inclusion of an implicit epsilon-filter such as described by Mohri

(2009) – associated only with a single state visitation will remain confined to a single peer, and can thus only serve to improve the performance of the parallel algorithm with respect to its serial counterpart.

Our parallelization strategy does not alter the worst-case complexity of the composition algorithm, since the partitioning function may fail for certain pathological configurations. More precisely, whenever there is an $i \in \mathbb{N}$ such that $r(q_1, q_2) = i$ for all accessible $(q_1, q_2) \in Q$, then the unique peer-thread p_i will be responsible for visiting all of the states of the output transducer. In this case, Algorithm 2 essentially reduces to Algorithm 1 with the worst-case complexity $\mathcal{O}(|Q_1 \times Q_2| + |E_1 \times E_2|)$, which is dominated by $\mathcal{O}(|E_1 \times E_2|)$.

Many other operations on finite-state transducers have traditional implementations in terms of a state-processing queue, exhibiting the same high-level structure as Algorithm 1. The parallelization strategy used here may also be employed in such cases, whenever a suitable state-partitioning function (analogous to r) can be defined. Consider for example the case of unweighted acceptor determinization as presented by Hopcroft and Ullman (1979): output automaton states are identified by sets of prefix-equivalent states of the input automaton. A generic partitioning function for mapping state sets to peers would suffice to extend our parallelization strategy to this algorithm.

4 Experiment

To investigate the practical utility of our multi-threaded composition algorithm, we compared running times of Algorithms 1 and 2.

4.1 Materials

We began by generating a sample set of random input FSTs $\mathcal{T}_{i \in I}$. Each input $\mathcal{T}_i$ was built from a deterministic trie "skeleton" of a given size $|Q_i|$ with maximum depth 32. The trie skeleton was then augmented by adding random edges between existing states, and finally randomizing all edge labels. The target size parameters $|Q_i|$ were piecewise-uniformly distributed within exponentially sized bins such that $2^5 \leq |Q_i| \leq 2^{21}$, i.e. input automata had between 32 and 2,097,152 states. The number e_i of randomly added edges was dependent on the number of states, $e_i = c_i \times |Q_i|$, where the coefficients c_i were uniformly distributed over the interval $[0, 16]$. In- and output-alphabets were identical for each $\mathcal{T}_i$ with alphabet sizes uniformly distributed over the discrete set $\bigcup_{i=0}^{10}\{2^i\}$, i.e. between 2 and 1024. For each input automaton $\mathcal{T}_i$ so generated, we measured the running time $t_{\text{serial},i}$ of the serial composition algorithm $\textsc{compose}(\mathcal{T}_i^{-1}, \mathcal{T}_i)$, and retained only those samples $\mathcal{T}_i$ for which $\frac{1}{64}$ sec $\leq t_{\text{serial},i} \leq 8$ sec.

We implemented Algorithms 1 and 2 in C++, using the GNU C compiler (`g++` version 4.4.5), the C++ standard template library, as well as the auxiliary libraries `boost` (Schäling, 2011) and `TBB` (Reinders, 2007) for common data structures and programming idioms. Automata were represented using adjacency vectors, and the edge alignments of Algorithm 1 line 9 (respectively Alg. 2 line 22) were implemented using an optimized routine[3] for sorted edge-vectors in order to minimize running times for both conditions. The implementations were tested on a dedicated 64-bit machine with 16 logical processors running debian linux.

4.2 Method

For each of the 2,266 random input automata $\mathcal{T}_i$, we measured the time required[4] to compute the composition $\mathcal{C}_i = (\mathcal{T}_i^{-1} \circ \mathcal{T}_i)$ using the serial algorithm ($t_{\text{serial},i}$) as well as the parallel algorithm ($t_{\text{pp}:N,i}$), varying the number of peer-threads employed by the latter, $N \in \{2, 4, 8, 16\}$.[5] Each of these 11,330 invocations was iterated 8 times in order to ameliorate cache effects. Raw and mean running times were stored for each invocation, together with various structural properties of the input and result automata.

4.3 Results & Discussion

Inspection of the generated sample set revealed that all of the tested compositions exhibited an "embarrassingly parallel" topology: applying Corollary 1 yielded $P_{\max} > 99\%$ for all $\mathcal{C}_i$ ($\mu =$

[3]Specifically, we used a modified version of the edge alignment code from the GFSM (Jurish, 2009) library function `gfsm_automaton_compose_visit_()` to implement a generic function template shared by both serial and parallel implementations.

[4]Neither I/O nor serialization of the result transducer were included in our measurements of the running time.

[5]While not necessarily representative of FST compositions in general, restricting our attention to compositions of the form $(\mathcal{T}^{-1} \circ \mathcal{T})$ ensures that the output automaton $\mathcal{C}$ is at least as large as $\mathcal{T}$ itself, since the main diagonal of the output state-set $\mathrm{Id}(Q_{\mathcal{T}})$ will be accessible whenever $\mathcal{T}$ contains no non-accessible states.

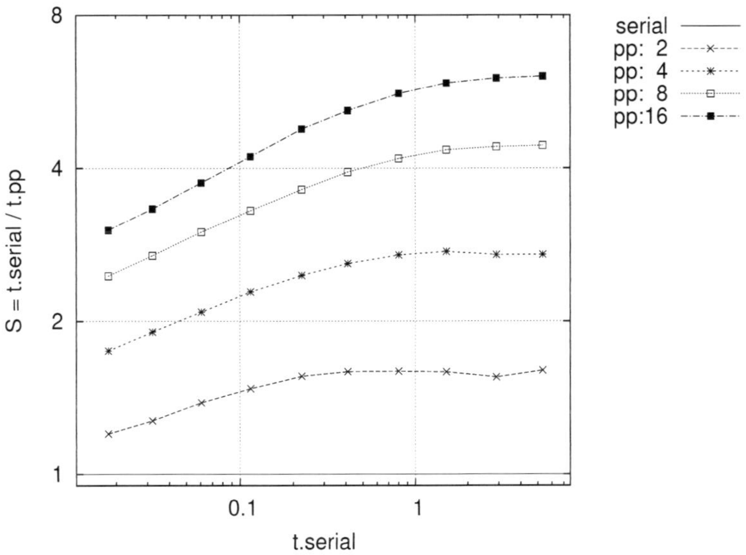

Figure 2: Observed speedup for peer-to-peer parallel composition with respect to serial running time for randomly generated automata (log-scaled).

$.9998, \sigma = 2.949 \times 10^{-4}$). Although it is certainly the case that not all FST compositions possess such characteristics (as follows from Theorem 1), the uniformly large state-to-depth ratio exhibited by our sample set makes it a particularly good testing ground for state-wise parallel processing techniques such as Algorithm 2.

Results of the runtime measurements are depicted in Figure 2, expressed as the measured speedup for the parallel implementation with respect to the serial one. The samples i were sorted into 10 exponentially sized bins by serial running time $t_{\text{serial},i}$, and the speedup data $S_{N,i} = t_{\text{serial},i}/t_{\text{pp:}N,i}$ are plotted on logarithmic scales for each $n \in N$ as a piecewise linear fit over bin-wise averages.[6]

Immediately apparent from the data in Figure 2 is a typical pattern of diminishing returns for increasing values of N, reflecting an empirical value of $P \ll 1$. Solving Equation (2) for P and applying it to the measured speedup values yields the data in Table 1, corresponding to an estimated $P = .749$ ($\sigma = .154$) over all tested parallel compositions. Interestingly, the empirically estimated values for P increase monotonically with N, which indicates that the use of a distributed

N	μ_S	σ_S	μ_P	σ_P
2	1.474	0.209	0.615	0.207
4	2.372	0.423	0.751	0.116
8	3.585	0.788	0.806	0.083
16	4.701	1.156	0.824	0.066

Table 1: Global mean (μ) and standard deviation (σ) of observed speedup (S) and associated degree of parallelization (P) for peer-to-peer parallel composition using N concurrent threads.

message queue did in fact reduce the competition over shared resources between peer-threads, thereby effectively reducing the serial portion of the program itself.

Despite this tendency, the data from Table 1 clearly indicate that the measured performance of our implementation remained well below the upper bound given by Theorem 1 for our sample set. This discrepancy can be attributed in part to constant overhead associated with thread allocation and maintenance (cf. Section 3.2), whose effects can also be observed in the tendency of speedup to improve with increasing serial running time as seen in Figure 2. Restricting our attention to the 598 samples with $t_{\text{serial},i} \geq 1$ second, we computed an average empirical estimate of $P = .8867$ for $N = 16$ ($\sigma = .01676$). The remaining discrepancy between the empirical estimates and the "embarrassingly parallel" theoreti-

[6] Since $P_{\max} \approx 1$ for all of our test automata, we ignore the contribution of automaton topology to actual observed speedup here. For a more heterogeneous test set, it would make more sense to measure speedup relative to the respective automaton-dependent maxima, i.e. $S_{N,i}/S_{\max,N,i}$.

cal upper bounds must be attributed to the necessarily serial aspects of inter-thread communication and synchronization.

5 Conclusion

We have presented a generic state-wise parallel algorithm for computing the composition of ε-free finite-state transducers which minimizes competition for global locks by employing distributed data structures and localized communication channels. This algorithm relies on the prior specification of a partitioning function which effectively maps each state of the result automaton to the execution thread responsible for processing that state.

An approximate upper bound for composition speedup using a state-wise parallel algorithm such as that presented here was proposed and defined in terms of the state-to-depth ratio of the result automaton. Empirical investigation of the actual speedup achieved by our algorithm on a test set of "embarrassingly parallel" compositions showed that although the use of distributed data structures and communication channels was successful in reducing the serial proportion of the code when more processors were used, constant overhead and the remaining synchronizations led to the pattern of diminishing returns associated with an actual parallel execution of about 89% of the program.

We are interested in evaluating the performance of our approach in other scenarios, including string lookup in (weighted) FSTs, n-way or "cascaded" composition, and "lazy" online constructions. We believe that the peer-to-peer parallelization strategy can also be employed to improve the performance of other common finite-state algebraic operations in a multiprocessor context.

Acknowledgements

Research was supported by the *Deutsche Forschungsgemeinschaft* grants KL 337/12-2 and KL 955/19-1. Additionally, we would like to thank this article's anonymous reviewers for their helpful comments.

References

Cyril Allauzen and Mehryar Mohri. 2009. N-way composition of weighted finite-state transducers. *International Journal of Foundations of Computer Science*, 20(4):613–627.

Cyril Allauzen, Michael Riley, Johan Schalkwyk, Wojciech Skut, and Mehryar Mohri. 2007. OpenFst: A General and Efficient Weighted Finite-State Transducer Library. In Jan Holub and Jan Žďárek, editors, *Implementation and Application of Automata*, volume 4783 of *Lecture Notes in Computer Science*, pages 11–23. Springer, Berlin/Heidelberg.

Gene M. Amdahl. 1967. Validity of the single processor approach to achieving large scale computing capabilities. In *Proceedings of the AFIPS spring joint computer conference*, pages 483–485, New York, NY. ACM.

Octavian Cheng, John Dines, and Mathew Magimai Doss. 2007. A Generalized Dynamic Composition Algorithm of Weighted Finite State Transducers for Large Vocabulary Speech Recognition. In *IEEE International Conference on Acoustics, Speech and Signal Processing (ICASSP 2007)*, volume 4, pages 345–348. IEEE.

Karel Culik II and Jarkko Kari. 1993. Image compression using weighted finite automata. *Computers & Graphics*, 17(3):305–313.

Thomas Hanneforth. 2004. FSM<2.0> – C++ library for manipulating (weighted) finite automata. http://www.fsmlib.org.

Jan Holub and Stanislav Štekr. 2009. On parallel implementations of deterministic finite automata. In Sebastian Maneth, editor, *Implementation and Application of Automata*, volume 5642 of *Lecture Notes in Computer Science*, pages 54–64, Berlin/Heidelberg. Springer.

John E. Hopcroft and Jeffrey D. Ullman. 1979. *Introduction to Automata Theory, Languages, and Computation*. Addison Wesley, Reading, MA.

Takaaki Hori, Chiori Hori, and Yasuhiro Minami. 2004. Fast On-The-Fly Composition for Weighted Finite-State Transducers in 1.8 Million-Word Vocabulary Continuous Speech Recognition. *INTERSPEECH*, pages 289–292.

Bryan Jurish. 2009. libgfsm C library, version 0.0.10. `http://kaskade.dwds.de/~moocow/projects/gfsm/`.

Anders Krogh, Michael Brown, I. Saira Mian, Kimmen Sjölander, and David Haussler. 1994. Hidden Markov models in computational biology : applications to protein modeling. *Journal of Molecular Biology*, 235(5):1501–1531.

Mehryar Mohri, Fernando Carlos Pereira, and Michael Dennis Riley. 2007. Speech Recognition with Weighted Finite-State Transducers. In Larry Rabiner and Fred Juang, editors, *Handbook on Speech Processing and Speech Communication, Part E: Speech recognition*, pages 1–31. Springer, Berlin/Heidelberg.

Mehryar Mohri. 2009. Weighted automata algorithms. In Manfred Droste, Werner Kuich, and

Heiko Vogler, editors, *Handbook of Weighted Automata*, Monographs in Theoretical Computer Science, chapter Concepts of Weighted Recognizability, pages 213–254. Springer, Berlin/Heidelberg.

James Reinders. 2007. *Intel Threading Building Blocks*. O'Reilly, Sebastopol, CA.

Seyed H. Roosta. 2000. *Parallel Processing and Parallel Algorithms: Theory and Computation*. Springer, Berlin/Heidelberg.

Boris Schäling. 2011. *The Boost C++ Libraries*. XML Press.

Herb Sutter. 2005. The free lunch is over – a fundamental turn toward concurrency in software. *Dr. Dobb's Journal*, 30(3).

On Finite-State Tonology with Autosegmental Representations

Anssi Yli-Jyrä
University of Helsinki, Department of Modern Languages
PO Box 24, 00014 University of Helsinki
anssi.yli-jyra@helsinki.fi

Abstract

Building finite-state transducers from written autosegmental grammars of tonal languages involves compiling the rules into a notation provided by the finite-state tools. This work tests a simple, human readable approach to compile and debug autosegmental rules using a simple string encoding for autosegmental representations. The proposal is based on brackets that mark the edges of the tone autosegments. The bracket encoding of the autosegments is compact and directly human readable. The paper also presents a usual finite-state transducer for transforming a concatenated string of lexemes where each lexeme (such as "babaa|HH") consists of a segmental substring and a tonal substring into a chronological master string ("b[a]b[aa]") where the tone autosegments are associated with their segmental spans.

1 Introduction

In Bantu linguistics, *Autosegmental (AS) Phonology* (Goldsmith, 1976) is a standard theory in phonological description of tone. The widely available finite-state compilers are, however, not directly applicable in this context because autosegmental phonology uses a two-tier representation for the phonological content. The aim of this paper is to address this obvious shortcoming in finite-state technology. I will, therefore, pursue a practical approach that facilitates conversion of an existing multi-tiered lexicon and an autosegmental rule system into a lexical transducer.

In the past, various finite-state approaches to autosegmental phonology have been proposed. Kay's (1987) early proposal about processing multilinear structures with an extended finite-state transducer model has inspired further research on multi-tape automata (Wiebe, 1992) and linear codes (Kornai, 1995) that encode events when an autosegmental representation is scanned from left to right. Kornai (1995) has qualified the proposed codes with a set of desiderata. All these desiderata cannot be, however, fully satisfied by any of the linear codes (Wiebe, 1992). An alternative to these multi-tape approaches is proposed by Bird and Ellison (1994) who posit that all tiers are partical descriptions of the common synchronized structure and they can, therefore, be combined via intersection. This constraint-based approach is very natural and it has nice formal properties such as declarativeness and connection to logic. However, the resulting one-level phonology (Bird and Ellison, 1994) is also somewhat incompatible with the autosegmental theory. For example, it does not posit floating tones that are a crucial formal device in many existing accounts of Bantu tone.

The key idea in this paper is to represent the tone units, i.e., autosegments, as time spans that have a start and an end marked with brackets in the timing tier. The key idea is complemented with a finite-state technique for producing tone associations from the lexical forms and a new, tailored finite-state formalism for autosegmental alternation rules. The implementation of each alternation rule is based on declarative, constraint-based techniques.

The resulting formalism can be seen as a reimplementation of the classical two-level formalism (Koskenniemi, 1983). The new formalism allows the user to specify even complex parallel changes to the autosegmental representation in a compact way. The reimplementation is based on generalizations that support parallel compilation of rules (Yli-Jyrä and Koskenniemi, 2006; Yli-Jyrä, 2008a) and the new, lenient semantics of obligatory rules (Yli-Jyrä, 2008b). The bracketing that I use to represent tone is reminiscent of foot bracketing (Karttunen, 2006), syllable bracketing (Idsardi, 2009) and the bracketing of tone domains (Leben, 2006), all representing Optimality Theoretical (Prince and Smolensky, 2004) approaches to phonology.

2 Theories of Tone

Tone in phonology relates to such a pitch contrast that distinguishes the meanings of two word forms. There are level tones such as: High (H), Low (L) and Mid (M), and contour tones such as: Rising (LH), Falling (HL), and Rising-falling (LHL), Mid-hig (MH), Mid-low-high (MLH). A segment (a mora or syllable) having the tone feature is called a *tone bearing unit (TBU)*.[1]

Williams (1976) and Leben (1973) distinguish and compare three different theories that claim to describe the nature of tone:

- the *segmental theory*,
- the *syllabic theory*, and
- the *morphemic theory*.

This taxonomy gives use a good starting point for explaining how suprasegmental and autosegmental phonology differs from the segmental phonology. It is important to note that the newer theories are improved generalizations inspired by the former theories rather than completely opposed to them.

2.1 Segmental and Syllabic Theories

Features and Natural Classes It would be the simplest theoretical solution to process sounds as segments having tonal features. Then the treatment of tone would not differ from any other features such as nasality or openness. Sounds and their classes would be viewed as a Boolean algebra and the feature geometry would define what sound classes or their changes are natural and what are not. In finite-state phonology, the natural classes, such as "V [+ High]" can generally be implemented as character lists, but Bird (1994; 1995) and Heinz and Koirala (2010) go much further in capturing the notions of feature geometry by computational means.

The segment-based representation of tone gives a clumsy treatment to *floating tones* that are not carried by any segmental units. The same weakness is true for syllabic theory: there are floating tones that are not linked to any syllable (Leben, 1973).

Subsegmental Diacritics as Segments A slightly more modular solution would treat tone as a diacritic character that affects the adjacent character. This is how UNICODE or the IPA standard handle tone at the character level. Likewise, some computational morphologies use segments such as H or L to represent the tone in the morphophonological representation. Muhirwe (2010) uses this in his finite-state description of Kinyarwuanda:

(1) *baHzaHaHriHriimba<ba-zaHa-riHriimba*
REL.FUTURE
'they might sing'

2.2 Morphemic Theories

In a morphemic theory of tone, the tone of underlying morphemes is indicated separated from rather than pre-assigned to the phonemic sequence. This separation is indicated in the lexicons of some descriptive grammars, such as (Halme, 2004):

(2) **elifikameno** *n LHHHL 5* independence.
elifiyepo *n LHLH 5* contest.
elifo *n LH 5* likeness.

Suprasegmental Phonology According to Williams (1976) and Leben (1973), tones are suprasegmental. They are not marked underlyingly to the segments, but they constitute units in their own right. To merge the phonemic and tonemic sequences of morpheme, Williams proposes a Tone Mapping Rule (3).

(3)
Tonemic sequence ⇘ Phonemic sequence ⇙
Tone Mapping Rule
⇓
Master phonemic sequence

A shortcoming of the original formulation of the Time Mapping Rule is that its output representation is purely linear, which complicates the description of further phonological processes. Therefore, Goldsmith (1973) argues that Leben's theory does not adequately describe some effects of floating tone.

[1]For simplicity, this paper assumes that each vowel is the tone bearing unit.

Multi-Tiered Representation The Autosegmental Phonology (AST) (Goldsmith, 1976) claims that what we see in the segmental representations of the language is an image of a richer multi-tiered representation that involves simultaneously pronounced sequences (Goldsmith, 1973). One tier represents the tone patterns via H/L tonemes, called *autosegments*, while another tier represents the usual C/V segments in the pronunciation. These two underlying tiers are integrated through the timing tier that consists of a sequence of ×'s:

(4) 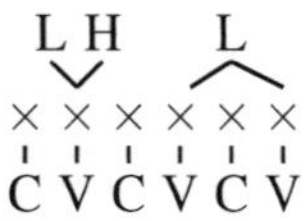

Tones are not necessarily in a one-to-one relationship with the segments. Instead, the nature of tone can be suprasegmental or subsegmental and therefore it cannot be incorporated to or ordered among the segments.

A two-tiered morphemic representation avoids the loss of tonemic structure. The tone associations (links) simplify the rules considerably and let the AST posit a simple, elegant theory of operations: add/delete a tone/link. This elegancy is perhaps the most attractive aspect of AST.

2.3 Autosegmental Derivation

Goldsmith (1976) defines the autosegmental derivation as follows:

Step 1: Initialization The phonological and tonological sequences are set out as parallel strings and the tone boundaries[2] are associated with each other.

(5) 

Step 2: Association Rule (AR) The ASSOCIATION RULE associates the first toneme with the first tone bearing unit and proceeds rightward as long as the segments match one another.

(6) 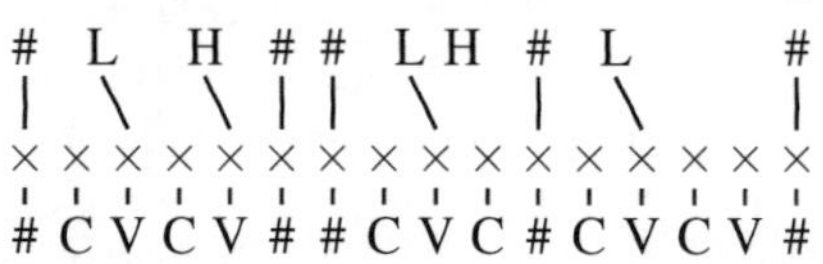

[2]In this paper, we will naively assume that all morpheme boundaries are also tone boundaries.

Step 3: Well-Formedness Condition The well-formedness condition makes sure (i) that every toneme has a corresponding segment, (ii) that every phoneme segment is linked to a tone, and (iii) that the links do not cross one another. The changes required to enforce the well-formedness condition are unambiguous after the AR. At this point, only the rightmost member of a tier can be associated with more than one member of another tier of the word.[3]

(7) 

Step 4: Mutations The phonological derivation with autosegmental rules now starts.

3 The Bracket Encoding of Associations

The encoding of autosegmental representations proposed in this paper is based on brackets that indicate the span of each tone autosegment in the segmental string. Instead of marking the tones separately, we only mark their links – in fact the first and the last link only – to the segmental tier. This means that the general bracketing approach familiar from e.g. Leben (2006) and Idsardi (2009) is now developed further and applied to non-OT representations of tone.

3.1 Common Timing Elements of All Tiers

The timing tier synchronizes the segmental and tonal tiers using morphological boundary symbols.

- the prefix/suffix boundaries (–/+)
- named affix boundaries (such as `AUG`–).
- the clitic boundary (=)
- the infix boundaries (<`IFX` and `IFX`>)
- the reduplication boundary (˜)
- the word boundary (#)
- morphological categories (such as `N5`).

These boundaries are shared both by the segmental and tonal tiers. Thus there is no need to *add* separate inter-tier associations for the morpheme boundaries.

[3]On different assumptions on tone association rule and tonal boundary markers, see Leben (1978).

3.2 Segmental Tier

Segmental tier consists of segmental phonemes – vowels (V) and consonants (C). The segmental tier may also contain the syllable boundary (.).[4]

The foot structure can be marked with additional types of syllable boundaries .(. , .). and .)(. that are considered as multi-character symbols, in contrast to Karttunen (2006).

3.3 Tone Associations

There is usually only a small number of underlying tone level distinctions such as: Toneless (∅), Low (L), and High (H). As to the surface tones, the international phonetic alphabet lists, for example, five level tones and suggests many more contour tones. However, it is now not necessary to go through all the theoretically possible surface tones that might occur in the languages of the world.

The key proposal of this paper is to indicate the association of tone autosegments by showing the span of the tone via brackets.

```
     ∅            L          H
     |            |          |
(8)  ×↔×↔a        ×↔(a)      ×↔[a]
     |   |        |          |
     a   a        a          a
```

In the lexical representation, an unspecified tone can be marked with X. When the lexical tones undergo changes, the tonal tier can also contain additional tones such as Middle (M) and Downstepped High (!H):

```
     X            M            !H
     |            |            |
(9)  ×↔[XaX]      ×↔[MaM]      ×↔![a]
     |            |            |
     a            a            a
```

The basic contour tones, such as ĤL and L̂H, are notated by mixing the brackets of two different tones. To facilitate notating more complex contour tones, we can introduce labeled brackets for simpler contour tones:

```
      H L                    L H
      \/                     \/
(10)  ×↔[a)↔[HLa)            ×↔(a]↔(LHa]
      |                      |
      a                      a
```

Contour tones with three underlying tones are represented using simpler contour tone brackets as needed:

```
      L H L
      \|/
(11)  ×  ↔ (LHa)
      |
      a
```

Floating tones do not contain any vowels in their spans. If a floating tone emerges due to the well-formedness condition after the association rule, it will be placed immediately before the next tone (i.e., morpheme) boundary. In all other cases, the place of the floating tone in the segmental tier is specified by its derivation history.[5]

```
           L    H L H
           |    |
(12)  a. × × × × ×    ↔b(a)b[a]n()[]
         | | | | |
         b a b a n
```

We posit a convention according to which the brackets of a linked tone will be inserted immediately around the linked segments, without any intervening boundary symbols, syllable boundaries and stress markers. If more than one segment are linked to one tone, the brackets span all the linked segments:

```
        L       H   L
       / \      |   |
(13)  × × × × × × × ↔ (oku)t[e]m(a)
      | | | | | | |
      o k u t e m a
```

4 Derivation of the Input for the Rules

In oder to use the bracketed representation, we need to implement the first three steps of the autosegmental derivation.

4.1 Specifying the Task

The first derivation step takes the lexical form as its input and produces a string where the tones are associated with the segments. The underlying lexical form contains at least the tonal string, the phonemic string and morphological boundaries. In practice, it is convenient to have also some information on the morphological categories and the glosses in the morpheme lexicon. For example, CL5 and N5 in the glossed underlying string (14) are morphological category labels and 'likeness' is the semantic gloss of the stem.

[4]Syllable stress markers such as ′ could be added near the syllable boundaries, but we try to avoid going into the stress structure in too much detail in this work.

[5]We will need to experiment more before we know if there is a need to normalize the floating tones. Meanwhile, it would seem natural to migrate the brackets of floating tones as little as possible.

Table 1: The *foma* Syntax and Basic Definitions

<table>
<tr><td>0</td><td>empty string</td></tr>
<tr><td>"|"</td><td>protected special symbol</td></tr>
<tr><td>{abc}</td><td>a string of letters</td></tr>
<tr><td>?</td><td>all (identity pairs of) symbols</td></tr>
<tr><td>A B</td><td>concatenation</td></tr>
<tr><td>A|B</td><td>union</td></tr>
<tr><td>[A]</td><td>grouping</td></tr>
<tr><td>(A)</td><td>optionality</td></tr>
<tr><td>A*, A+</td><td>Kleene star, Kleene plus</td></tr>
<tr><td>A&B</td><td>intersection of 0-padded relations</td></tr>
<tr><td>A-B</td><td>difference of 0-padded relations</td></tr>
<tr><td>A:B</td><td>left-aligned cross product</td></tr>
<tr><td>A.x.B</td><td>left-aligned cross product</td></tr>
<tr><td>A.o.B</td><td>composition</td></tr>
<tr><td>A.i</td><td>inverse relation</td></tr>
<tr><td>A.1, A.2</td><td>input projection, output projection</td></tr>
<tr><td>A/B</td><td>free insertion of symbol pairs B</td></tr>
<tr><td>def A B;</td><td>definition of a constant expression</td></tr>
<tr><td>def A(X) X X;</td><td>definition of a regex macro</td></tr>
</table>

```
Phonemic (Segmental) Tier
def V      a | e | i | o | u ;
def C      b | d | ... | y ;
def S      "." | ".(." | ".)." | ".)(." ;
def M      "-" | "AUG-" | "+" | "#" | "::";
```

```
Tonemic (Autosegmental) Tier
def L      "(" | "[" | "![" | "[LH" | "[HL" ;
def R      ")" | "]" ;
def T      L | R ;
def X      L:L | R:R | T:0 | 0:T;
```

(14) **elifo** *n LH 5* likeness. (Halme, 2004)

 # e- lifo|LH *#*

In a finite-state implementation, the underlying form (14) can be written as string (15) where `::`, `CL5`, `N5` and `'likeness'` are multi-character symbols. In this string, the double colon `::` indicates the glossing relation.

(15) `#e :: CL5 - l i f o | L H :: N5 'likeness'#`

The task of the first three steps of the autosegmental derivation is to implement the mapping (16a) or just to produce the output of the mapping (16b). The output will then be the autosegmental representation fed to the autosegmental alternation rules.

(16) a.
```
#e::CL5-l i f o |LH::N5'likeness'#
#e::CL5-l(i)f[o]    ::N5'likeness'#
```

b.
```
#e::CL5-l i f o |LH::N5'likeness'#
#e     -l(i)f[o]                  #
```

4.2 The Implementation Formalism

We will use the regular expressions of the freely available *foma* tool (Hulden, 2009) when implementing all the rules. This flavour of regular expressions has been originally developed at Xerox. The relevant syntax of the formalism is summarized in Table 1.

Using the regexp syntax, we first define frequently used constant expressions for the rules. These expressions define symbol sets used in Phonemic and Tonemic tiers in Table 1.

Table 2: The Definition of the Association Rule

```
def Tones            "L" | "H" ;
def Mapper(TBUs) [ "L"  .x. "(" TBUs ")" ] |
                 [ "0"  .x.     TBUs     ] |
                 [ "H"  .x. "[" TBUs "]" ] ;
def Asso(Pat,TBUs) [ [?-T] | 0:T ]* .o.
          [ Pat .o. [0:C | Mapper(TBUs)]* ].2 ;
def Single    V | Beyond ;
def TheRest   V [[C|S]* V]* | Beyond ;
def Map(Pat)  Asso([Pat .o. ?* ?:0 ].2, Single  )
              Asso([Pat .o. ?:0* ? ].2, TheRest )
               "|":0  Pat:0 ;
def Maps      Map({LH}) | Map({LLH}) | Map({LHL}) |
              Map({0H}) | Map({00H}) | Map({0H0}) ;
def AR    [ [ ? - Beyond] | 0:Beyond* "|" ]* .o.
          [ ?* M |          Maps M ]* .o.
          [ [ ? - Tones - Beyond ] | Beyond:0 ]*;
```

4.3 Implementing the Association Rule

A crucial assumption in this paper is that the tone patterns can be stored into a finite-state memory. For each tonemic sequence `Pat`, I construct a transducer `Map(Pat)` that assings the sequence of tones to all the tone bearing segments of a morpheme and then removes the lexical tone pattern from the end of the morpheme. If there are fewer tones than TBUs, the last one will be spread over the rest. More concretely, the expression `Map({H})` is compiled into the transducer (17). A finite union of such transducers is stored under the name `Maps`.

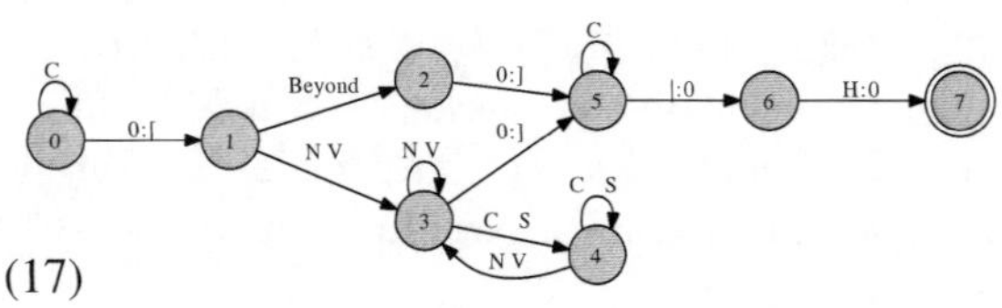

(17)

The expression `AR` is a transducer that applies the `Maps` transducer to every morpheme in the input. In its definition, a hidden symbol, `Beyond` is used as a temporary TBU for tones that are left over. This implementation of the AR synthesizes the first three steps of the autosegmental derivation into one transducer.

After the appropriate language-specific changes to the tier definitions and the `Maps` transducer have been made, we can use the *foma* command line interface to see how some example strings are processed by the AR rule:

(18)
```
: regex {#olu|LL-vala|HH#}.o.AR;
: print lower-words
#(o)l(u)-v[a]l[a]#
```

5 The Tone Alternations

The autosegmental rule formalism is based on rewriting rules. However, the input and the output are not just strings but linked pairs of strings. Most rules are notated using a shorthand convention according to which the input and output representations of the rule are combined into one representation where the tone delinking, deletions, insertions, replacements, and linking are indicated.

In this section, every rule will be written in two ways: with the original autosegmental notation and with regular expressions.

5.1 The New Rule Formalism

The rules will be expressed as regular expressions that describe the changes and the context conditions under which the changes can take place. The currently available definitions of the formalism are listed in Table 3.

Table 3: Formalism for bracketed rules

<table>
<tr><th>notation = foma expr.</th><th>meaning</th></tr>
<tr><td>L,R,T</td><td>sets of tone brackets</td></tr>
<tr><td>S,M</td><td>sets of syll., morph. boundary</td></tr>
<tr><td>V,C</td><td>sets of vowels and consonants</td></tr>
<tr><td>A=?-"<>"</td><td>any symbol</td></tr>
<tr><td>α_U=α</td><td>protected constant tone bracket α</td></tr>
<tr><td>($_U$</td><td>example: constant tone bracket (</td></tr>
<tr><td>α_I=X&[α|α:T|α:0]</td><td>tone bracket α in input</td></tr>
<tr><td>α_O=X&[α|T:α|0:α]</td><td>tone bracket α in output</td></tr>
<tr><td>α_X=α_I|α_O</td><td>mutable tone bracket α</td></tr>
<tr><td>α_C=[X& T:α]-T</td><td>changed tone bracket α</td></tr>
<tr><td>Q=[C|S]*</td><td>consonants and syll. boundaries</td></tr>
<tr><td>N=[C|S|M]*</td><td>anything constant but T and V</td></tr>
<tr><td>P=[C|S|M|V]*</td><td>anything constant but T</td></tr>
<tr><td>Z=[A|T$_X$]*</td><td>anything, including the mutable</td></tr>
<tr><td>α_D="<>"* α:0</td><td>delete bracket α</td></tr>
<tr><td>α_A="<>"* 0:α</td><td>add bracket α</td></tr>
<tr><td>α_F="<>"* α_O</td><td>enforce output bracket α</td></tr>
<tr><td>α_M="<>"* α_C</td><td>mutate bracket α</td></tr>
<tr><td>α:0</td><td>test for deleted α</td></tr>
<tr><td>$\overline{\alpha}$=Z-α</td><td>negates the expression α</td></tr>
<tr><td>α*</td><td>iterate α zero or more times</td></tr>
<tr><td>α+</td><td>iterate α one or more times</td></tr>
<tr><td>(α)</td><td>make α optional</td></tr>
<tr><td>[α]</td><td>grouping</td></tr>
<tr><td>α|β</td><td>α and β are alternatives</td></tr>
</table>

5.2 Example Rules

Anyanwu (2008) classifies some universally accepted tonal rules. Given such a classification, we consider some example rules from Kwanyama (Halme, 2004) and Ikoma (Aunio, 2010) and extend the classification where needed. By compiling different kinds of rules into the new notation, we get an estimate on out how the bracket-based formalism applies to the practical needs in general.

5.2.1 Spreading

The TONE SPREADING rules affect the following tone (e.g. LHH → LLH). If the spreading effect is partial, this results into a contour tone as in (e.g. LH → L$\widehat{\text{L}}$H) (Anyanwu, 2008).

AUGMENT HIGH SPREAD (AHS) of Kwanyama (Halme, 2004) causes the underlying High of the augment prefix to spread onto the following Low-toned mora (dotted line) whose tone is delinked (cut line).

(19) a. 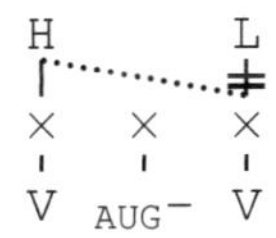

b. Z]$_D$ N AUG- N ($_D$ V]$_A$ ($_A$)$_U$ Z

5.2.2 Assimilation

The TONE ASSIMILATION rules can be either regressive (HL → ML) or progressive (LH → LM) (Anyanwu, 2008).

HIGH LOWERING (HL) of Ikoma (Halme, 2004) causes a floating Low tone to link (dotted line) to the following mora whose High tone is delinked (cut line) and deleted (parentheses):

(20) a. 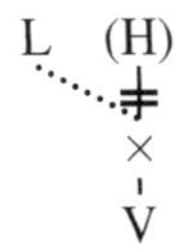

b. Z ($_D$)$_D$ N ($_M$ V)$_M$ Z |
Z ($_D$)$_D$ N ($_M$ V)$_A$ N [$_A$ V Z

5.2.3 Simplifications

The TONE ABSORPTION rules (e.g. $\widehat{\text{L}}$HH → LH) simplify two adjacent identical tones (Anyanwu, 2008). This rule is motivated by the OBLIGATORY CONTOUR PRINCIPLE (OCP) (Leben, 1973) that bans two consecutive features in the underlying representation.

FLOATING LOW DELETION (FLD) of Kwanyama (Halme, 2004) occurs when a floating

Low occurs next to a linked Low:

(21) a. 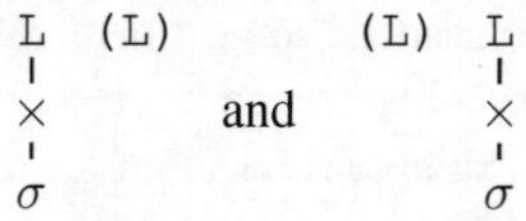

b. Z V $)_U$ N $(_D$ $)_D$ Z |
Z $(_D$ $)_D$ N $(_U$ V Z

In contrast to the TONE ABSORPTION rules, the CONTOUR LEVELING rules make two adjacent tones similar by simplifying a contour tone. (e.g. HL͡H → HH) (Anyanwu, 2008).

PLATEAUING in Ikoma (Aunio, 2010) is a variant of this kind of simplification:

(22) a. 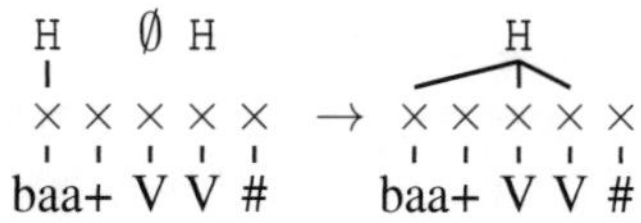

b. Z $]_D$ "-" N V N $[_D$ V $]_U$ N "#" Z

5.2.4 Dissimilation

DISSIMILATION (HH → HL) and TONAL POLARIZATION (HX → HL) are rules that are motivated by the OCP because they differentiate adjacent tones.

MEEUSSEN'S RULE in Ikoma (Aunio, 2010) lowers the last H in a sequence of two HH's:

(23) a. 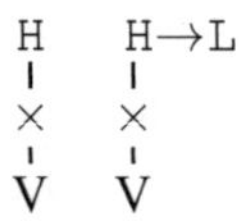

b. Z $]_U$ N $(_M$ V P $)_M$ Z

5.2.5 Tone Shift

TONE SHIFT (TS) in Kwanyama (Halme, 2004) moves all tones one mora (TBU) to the right (HLHL → ∅HLH). The correct interpretation of the rule assumes that there is no floating tones. [6].

(24) a. 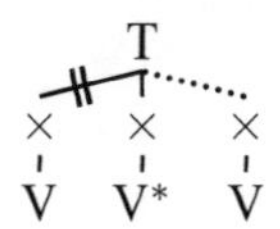

b.
Z $(_I$ V (R_X) N $(_F$ V Z |
Z $[_I$ V (R_X) N $[_F$ V Z |
Z L_I V (R_X) N L_D V Z |
Z L_O (P|T:0)⋆ R_D Z |
Z R_I N (L_X) V R_D P (L_X) V Z |
Z $)_I$ N (L_X) V $)_F$ (L_X) P Z |
Z $]_I$ N (L_X) V $]_F$ (L_X) P Z

[6] The last shifted tone could land to a final position, but the current formulation does not support this. The floating tones can be shifted and produced using temporary tone bearers during the rule application as we did in the TONE ASSOCIATION RULE

5.3 The Rule Compiler

My *foma* code for the rule compiler is given in Table 4. This compiler consists of two parts:

- The macro `CR(Rule)` produces a transducer that contains the final rule transducer as its subset.
- The second macro, `COERCE(Rule)`, produces the final rule transducer by restricting `CR(Rule)` in such a way, that it performs, in a sense, as many individual changes as it can.

The first macro, `CR(Rule)`, works as follows. The basic compilation of the regular expression corresponding to an autosegmental rule notation (such as 23b) yields a 0-padded transducer, `Rule`, where an optional, freely iterated marker `"<>"` has been added at the positions where the input string is expected to change.[7] Another transducer, `W`, contains all possible string pairs `Z` into which we have added the marker for an arbitrary change concerning a tone bracket. The purpose of this transducer is to tell that the marked change requires a permission from rule to be acceptable. When these two 0-padded transducers are differentiated, the resulting transducer contains all those string pairs that have an unwanted change. The complement of this 0-padded transducer with respect to `Z` is then exactly the transducer whose string pairs contains only such changes that are specified by the rule. For MEEUSSEN'S RULE, this transducer is (25).

(25) 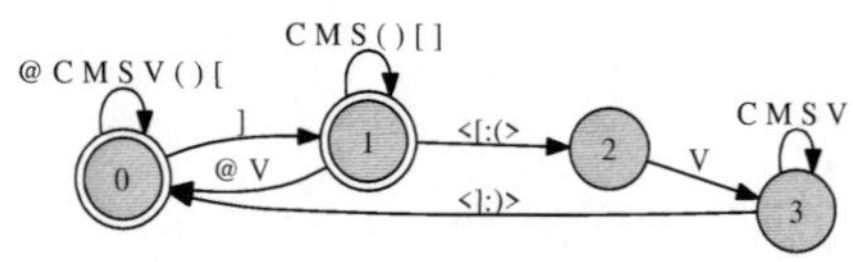

The second macro, `COERCE(Rule)`, refines the transducer computed by the first macro. This macro marks, in each 0-padded string pair, all those positions where a bracket changes. The markup is done, again, using the same marker symbol, `"<>"`, as before. The input projection of this transducer gives a regular language without the zeros that were used in the transducer. An auxiliary macro, `TooFew(X)`, is now used to find out in this projection such marked input strings that are like some other string in the projection but contain markers only in a subset of the positions marked in the second string. This gives us the set

[7] I have tried to stick to a convention that a diamond ◇ has been used as such a marker.

Table 4: Definitions of the Rule Compiler

```
Compiler for Optional Rules
def Chg          A:A  - A | A:0 | 0:A ;
def W            Z "<>" Chg Z ;
def Intro        [ A | 0:"<>" ]* ;
def Hide(X)      Intro  .o. X .o. Intro .i ;
def CR(Rule)     Z - Hide(W - Rule) ;
```

```
Compiler for Obligatory Rules
def Chg            A:A - A | A:0 | 0:A ;
def MarkChg(X)     X/"<>" & [A | "<>" Chg ]* ;
def FewerT         ?* [ 0:"<>" ?* ]+ ;
def TooFew(X)      [ MarkChg(CR(X)).1 .o. FewerT .o.
                     MarkChg(CR(X)).1 ].1 ;
def COERCE(Rule) Hide( [ ?* - TooFew(Rule) ]
                         .o. MarkChg(CR(Rule)) ) ;
```

of marked strings that indicate which paths in the first resulting transducer fail applying the rules as often as possible. When these paths are removed from `CR(Rule)`, we obtain a transducer where the rule's application is obligatory whenever there is a choice. For (23b), this transducer is (26).

(26)

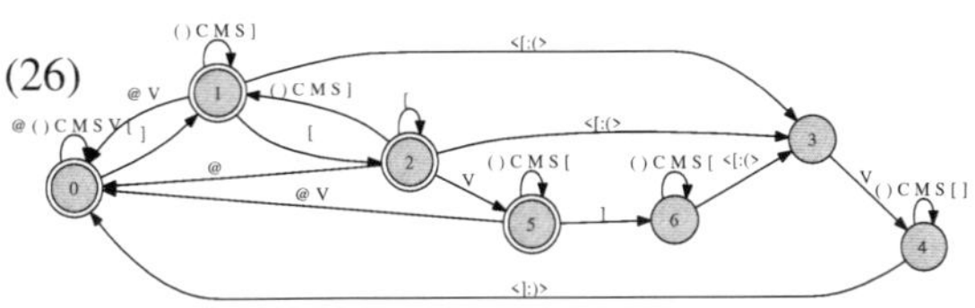

6 Evaluation

All linear encodings for autosegmental structure have some limitations. While the strength of the proposed notation is the easiness to link multiple segments to a single autosegment and multiple tones to single segment, it is not perfect concerning the treatment of floating tone. In terms of Kornai's (1995) criteria, it seems to be compositional, computable, and iconic, but not fully invertible because there are such bracketed strings that have no interpretation as a graphical autosegmental representation.

The purpose of the current proposal has been to present just the core ideas of the new representation, not to make universal claims. For example, tones do not always realize (Leben, 2006). The current proposal can be criticized also for other simplifying assumptions about TBUs and tone assignment boundaries.

The original two-level formalism (Koskenniemi, 1983) is difficult to use because it is based on implications and because the rule system may be overconstrained. The new rule formalism seems to address both of these problems, making

Table 5: # of states in compiled rules

name	Rule	CR	COERCE
AHS	25	7	11
High Lowering	27	7	12
FLD	21	7	13
Plateauing	21	7	16
Meeussen	13	4	7
Tone Shift	235	96	117

the rule semantics very much like replace rules in the state-of-the-art finite-state toolkits.

Simultaneous compilation of multiple two-level rules has been proposed in (Yli-Jyrä and Koskenniemi, 2006; Yli-Jyrä, 2008a), but this has not been put into practice in full scale, except in one special case (Yli-Jyrä, 2009). The current compilation method compiles, however, all the subrules of the TONE SHIFT simultaneously.

The compilation method is easy to implement and easy to use. In addition, the formalism is flexible because simultaneous, interlinked changes can be described. The only really complex exception discovered so far is the TONE SHIFT rule. Excepting TONE SHIFT, the sizes of rule transducers (Table 5) are quite small.

My resources did not allow me to rewrite a complete tonal description such as (Halme, 2004). I hope, however, that the presented ideas and (really open source) formalism are useful for later efforts.

It would be possible to define rule templates to be used routinely in experimental descriptive efforts. Tentative accounts of various phenomena could then be iteratively tested and debugged with finite-state tools, giving valuable feedback to a descriptive linguist, a resource builder or a theoretic phonologist working on tonal languages. The experimental verification would finally contribute towards the quality and wide applicability of descriptive grammars. The simultaneously applicable rule templates could also facilitate the development of machine learning methods for tonology.

References

Rose-Juliet Anyanwu. 2008. *Fundamentals of Phonetics, Phonology and Tonology*. Number 15 in Schriften zur Afrikanistik - Research in African Studies. Peter Lang.

Lotta Aunio. 2010. Ikoma nominal tone. *Africana Linguistica*, 16:3–30.

Steven Bird and T. Mark Ellison. 1994. One-level phonology: autosegmental representations and rules as finite automata. *Computational Linguistics*, 20(1).

Steven Bird and Ewan Klein. 1994. Phonological analysis in typed feature systems. *Computational Linguistics*, 20(3):455–491.

Steven Bird. 1995. *Computational Phonology. A constraint-based approach*. Studies in Natural Language Processing. Cambridge University Press.

John Goldsmith. 1973. Tonemic structure. Manuscript, downloaded from `http://hum.uchicago.edu/jagoldsm/Webpage/Courses/HistoryOfPhonology/` in June 2013.

John Goldsmith. 1976. *Autosegmental Phonology*. Ph.D. thesis, MIT.

Riikka Halme. 2004. *A tonal grammar of Kwanyama*. Rüdiger Köppe Verlag, Köln.

Jeffrey Heinz and Cesar Koirala. 2010. Maximum likelihood estimation of feature-based distributions. In *Proceedings of the 11th Meeting of the ACL-SIGMORPHON, ACL 2010*, pages 28–37, Uppsala, Sweden, 15 July.

Mans Hulden. 2009. Foma: a finite-state compiler and library. In *Proceedings of the 12th EACL: Demonstrations Session*, pages 29–32. Association for Computational Linguistics.

William J. Idsardi. 2009. Calculating metrical structure. In Charles Cairns and Eric Raimy, editors, *Contemporary Views on Architecture and Representations in Phonological Theory*, pages 191–211. MIT Press, Cambridge.

Lauri Karttunen. 2006. A finite-state approximation of Optimality Theory: The case of Finnish prosody. In T. Salakoski et al., editor, *FinTAL 2006*, volume 4139 of *LNAI*, pages 4–15, Berlin Heidelberg. Springer-Verla.

Martin Kay. 1987. Nonconcatenative finite-state morphology. In *Proceedings, Third Meeting of the European Chapterof the Associationfor Computational Linguistics*, pages 2–10.

András Kornai. 1995. *Formal Phonology*. Garland Publishing, New York.

Kimmo Koskenniemi. 1983. *Two-Level Morphology: A General Computational Model for Word-Form Recognition and Production*. Ph.D. thesis, University of Helsinki.

William Leben. 1973. *Suprasegmental phonology*. Ph.D. thesis, MIT.

William R. Leben. 1978. The representation of tone. In Victoria A. Fromkin, editor, *Tone: A Linguistic Survey*. Academic Press, New York.

William R. Leben. 2006. Rethinking autosegmental phonology. In John Mugane et al., editor, *Selected Proceedings of the 35th Annual Conference on African Linguistics*, pages 1–9, Somerville, MA. Cascadilla Proceedings Project.

Jackson Muhirwe. 2010. Morphological analysis of tone marked kinyarwanda text. In Anssi Yli-Jyr, Andrs Kornai, Jacques Sakarovitch, and Bruce Watson, editors, *Finite-State Methods and Natural Language Processing*, volume 6062 of *Lecture Notes in Computer Science*, pages 48–55. Springer Berlin Heidelberg.

Alan Prince and Paul Smolensky. 2004. *Optimality Theory: Constraint Interaction in Generative Grammar*. Blackwell Publishing.

Bruce Wiebe. 1992. Modelling autosegmental phonology with multitape finite state transducers. Master's thesis, Simon Fraser University.

Edwin S. Williams. 1976. Underlying tone in Margi and Igbo. *Linguistic Inquiry*, 7:463–484.

Anssi Yli-Jyrä and Kimmo Koskenniemi. 2006. Compiling generalized two-level rules and grammars. In Tapio Salakoski, Filip Ginter, Sampo Pyysalo, and Tapio Pahikkala, editors, *Advances in Natural Language Processing*, volume 4139 of *Lecture Notes in Computer Science*, pages 174–185. Springer Berlin Heidelberg.

Anssi Yli-Jyrä. 2008a. Applications of diamonded double negation. In T. Hanneforth and K-M. Würzner, editors, *Finite-State Methods and Natural Language Processing, 6th International Workshop, FSMNL-2007, Potsdam, Germany, September 14–16, Revised Papers*, pages 6–30. Potsdam University Press, Potsdam.

Anssi Yli-Jyrä. 2008b. Transducers from parallel replacement rules and modes with generalized lenient composition. In T. Hanneforth and K-M. Würzner, editors, *Finite-State Methods and Natural Language Processing, 6th International Workshop, FSMNL-2007, Potsdam, Germany, September 14–16, Revised Papers*, pages 197–212, Potsdam. Potsdam University Press.

Anssi Yli-Jyrä. 2009. An efficient double complementation algorithm for superposition-based finite-state morphology. In *Proceedings of NODALIDA 2009*, pages 206–213.

A Finite-State Approach to Translate SNOMED CT Terms into Basque Using Medical Prefixes and Suffixes

Olatz Perez-de-Viñaspre, Maite Oronoz, Manex Agirrezabal and Mikel Lersundi
IXA NLP Group
University of the Basque Country UPV/EHU
operezdevina001@ikasle.ehu.es

Abstract

This paper presents a system that generates Basque equivalents to terms that describe disorders in SNOMED CT. This task has been performed using Finite-State transducers and a medical prefixes and suffixes lexicon. This lexicon is composed of English-Basque translation pairs, and it is used both for the identification of the affixes of the English term and for the translation of them into Basque. The translated affixes are composed using morphotactic rules. We evaluated the system with a Gold Standard obtaining promising results (0.93 of precision). This system is part of a more general system which aim is the translation of SNOMED CT into Basque.

1 Introduction

SNOMED Clinical Terms (SNOMED CT) (College of American Pathologists, 1993) is considered the most comprehensive, multilingual clinical healthcare terminology in the world. It does not exist in Basque language, and we think that the semi-automatic translation of SNOMED CT terms into Basque will help to fill the gap of this type of medical terminology in our language. By its translation we have a double objective: i) to offer a medical lexicon in Basque to the bio-medical personnel to try to enforce its use in the bio-sanitary area, and ii) to access multilingual medical resources as the UMLS (***U****nified* ***M****edical* ***L****anguage* ***S****ystem*) (Bodenreider, 2004) in our language.

Basque is a minority language in its standardization process and persists between two powerful languages, Spanish and French. Although today Basque holds co-official language status in the Basque Autonomy Community, during centuries it was out of educational and sanitary systems, media, and industry.

We have defined a general algorithm (see section 2) based on Natural Language Processing (NLP) resources that tries to achieve the translation with an incremental approach. The first step of the algorithm is based on the mapping of some lexical resources and has been already developed. Considering the huge size of SNOMED CT (296,000 active concepts and around 1,000,000 descriptions in the English version dated 31-01-2012) the contribution of the specialized dictionaries has been limited. In the second step that is specified in this paper, we have used Finite State Machines (FSM) in the form of transducers to generate one-word-terms in Basque taking as a basis terms from the English release of SNOMED CT mentioned before. The generation is based on the translation by means of medical suffixes (i.e. *-dipsia*, *-megaly*) and prefixes (i.e. *episio-*, *aesthesi-*) and in their correct composition, considering morphotactic rules. (Lovis et al., 1995) stated that a big group of medical terms can be created by neologisms, that is, concatenations of existing morphosemantic units understood by anybody. This units usually have Greek and Latin origins and their meaning is known by the specialists. (Banay, 1948) specified that about three-fourths of the medical terminology is of Greek origin.

In this work we take advantage of these features to try to translate terms from the *Disorder* sub-hierarchy of SNOMED CT. This corresponds to one of the 19 top level hierarchies of SNOMED CT, to the one called *Clinical Finding/Disorder*. In our general approach, we prioritized the translation of the most populated hierarchies: *Clinical Finding/Disorder* (139,643 concepts), *Procedure* (75,078 concepts) and *Body Structure* (26,960 concepts). Using lexical resources, we obtained the equivalents in Basque of the 19.32 % of the disorders. In this work we will try to obtain the one-word-terms that are not found in dictionaries.

There are several general-purpose libraries for

the creation of transducers as XFST (Karttunen et al., 1997), Nooj[1] or AT&T's FSM (Mohri et al., 2006). We have used Foma, a free software tool to specify finite-state automata and transducers (Hulden, 2009).

In the rest of the paper the translation algorithm is briefly described in section 2. The use of finite state machines in order to obtain Basque equivalents is explained in section 3. Finally, some conclusions and future work are listed in section 4.

2 Translation of SNOMED CT

The general algorithm (see figure 1) is language-independent. It could be used to translate any term if the linguistic resources for the input and output languages are available.

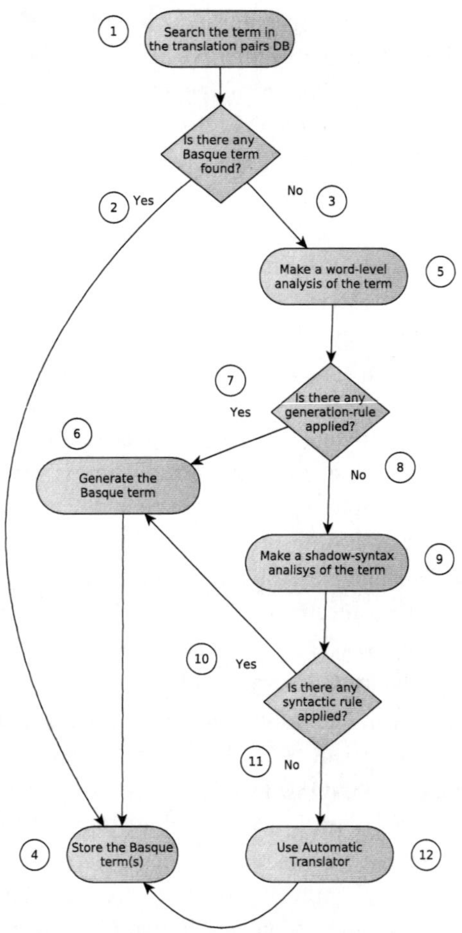

Figure 1: Schema of the Algorithm.

In the first step of the algorithm (see numbers 1-2-4 in Figure 1), some specialized dictionaries and the English, Spanish and Basque versions of the *International Statistical* **C***lassification of* **D***iseases and Related Health in its 10th version* (ICD-10) are used. For example for the input term "abortus" all its Basque equivalents *"abortu"*, *"abortatze"* and *"hilaurtze"* are obtained.

[1]http://www.nooj4nlp.net/NooJManual.pdf

The second phase of the algorithm is described in this paper in section 3. When a term is not found in the dictionaries (number 3 in Figure 1) generation-rules are used to create the translation.

In the case that an output is not obtained in the previous phases (number 8 in the algorithm), chunk-level generation rules are used. Our hypothesis is that some chunks of the term will be already translated. The application should generate the entire term using the translated components.

In the last step, we want to adapt a rule-based automatic translation system called *Matxin* (Mayor et al., 2011) to the medical domain.

We want to remark that all the processes finish in the 4th step. That is, we store the generated translations with the intention of using them to translate new terms.

3 Finite-State Models and Translation

This section exposes the system that obtains Basque equivalent terms from English one-word-terms based on FSMs.

3.1 Translation process

The generation of Basque equivalents is performed in two phases: the identification of the affixes first, and the translation and composition of the affixes secondly. All the linguistic information is stored in lexica and 31 rules are written for the process (1 for identification, 1 for translation and 28 for morphotactics).

Figure 2 shows the Finite State Transducer for the identification of the affixes. The lexica of the affixes is loaded (1-6) and then any prefix (the "*" symbol indicates 0 or more times) followed by one unique suffix is identified. The letter "o" may be also identified as it is used to join medical affixes. The "+" symbol is used for splitting the term.

```
1 read lexc prefixes.lex
2 define PREFALL
3 define PREF PREFALL.u ;
4 read lexc suffixes.lex
5 define SUFALL
6 define SUFF SUFALL.u ;
7 regex [[[PREF 0:%+] (o 0:%+)]* SUFF] ;
```

Figure 2: Rules for the affix identification.

The combination of the finite state transducers

for the translation and for the composition using morphotactics is shown in Figure 3. First, the lexica for the translation task is loaded (1-4), then 28 rules for the morphotactics are defined (simplified in the rule numbered 5). The translation rule (shown in rule number 6) is composed of the word-start mark (the ^ symbol), the prefix followed by the optional linking "o" letter zero or more times, and a single compulsory suffix; finally the transducer combines the translation and the morphotactic finite state transducers (7).

```
1 read lexc prefixes.lex
2 define TRANSPRE
3 read lexc suffixes.lex
4 define TRANSSUF
5 define MORPHO ...
6 define TRANS (%^ ) [[[TRANSPRE %+] (o:o %+)]*
TRANSSUF] ;
7 regex TRANS .o.  MORPH ;
```

Figure 3: Rules for the affix translation.

Figure 4 shows the whole process with an example. First, we identify the prefixes and suffixes of the English input term by means of the transducer that marks those affixes (schiz+encephal+y). Then, we obtain the corresponding Basque equivalent for each part and we form the term (eskiz+entzefal+ia).

Input term: schizencephaly
Identified affixes: schiz+encephal+y
Translated affixes: *eskiz+entzefal+ia*
Output. Basque term: *eskizentzefalia*

Figure 4: Basque term generation.

As we said before, in order to obtain a well formed Basque term, we apply different morphotactic rules. For example, in Basque, words starting with the "r" letter are not allowed, and an "e" is needed at the beginning. Figure 5 shows an example where the translated prefix *"radio"* needs of the mentioned rule, obtaining *"erradio"*.

Input term: radionecrosis
Identified affixes: radio+necr+osis
Translated affixes: *radio+nekr+osi*
Basque term: *erradionekrosi*

Figure 5: Morphotactic rule application.

3.2 Resources

In order to identify the English medical suffixes and prefixes we have joined two lists: the "Medical Prefixes, Suffixes, and Combining Forms" from Stedman's Medical Dictionary (Stedman's, 2005) and the "List of medical roots, suffixes and prefixes" from Wikipedia (Wikipedia, 2013). We obtained a list of 826 prefixes and 143 suffixes.

For the translation task, we have manually checked the Basque equivalents of the previously mentioned medical suffixes and prefixes list in specialized dictionaries such as *Zientzia eta Teknologiaren Hiztegi Entziklopedikoa* (Dictionary of Science and Technology) (Elhuyar, 2009), Euskalterm (UZEI, 2004) and *Erizaintzako Hiztegia* (Nursing Dictionary) (EHUko Euskara Zerbitzua and Donostiako Erizaintza Eskola, 2005).

By means of checking the behavior of the prefixes and suffixes in the English and Basque terms we have manually deduced the appropriate Basque equivalent. Table 1 shows an example of obtaining the equivalent of the "encephal" prefix, deducing that *"entzefal"* is the most appropriate equivalent.

English terms	Basque terms
echo**encephal**ogram	*eko**entzefal**ograma*
encephalitis	***entzefal**itis*
encephalomyelitis	***entzefal**omielitis*
leuko**encephal**itis	*leuko**entzefal**itis*
...	...

Table 1: The translation of the "encephal" prefix.

From all the prefixes and suffixes listed, we are able to deduce 812 prefixes and 139 suffixes for Basque. Those are currently being supervised by an expert to give them the highest confidence possible. This technique allows the inferring of new medical terms not appearing in dictionaries.

3.3 Results

We selected the one-word-terms of the *Disorder* sub-hierarchy of SNOMED CT. This sub-hierarchy with terms representing disorders or diseases is formed by 107,448 descriptions, being 3,979 one-word-terms. Even this last quantity is low considering the whole sub-hierarchy, we must take into account that the influence of those one-word-terms is very high, appearing around 79,000 times among all the descriptions.

The total one-word-term set has been split into two sets, one for defining and developing the system and another one for evaluating it. The evaluation set is composed of the 885 one-word-terms that have been previously translated in the first step of the algorithm (see section 2). That is we have the correct English-Basque pairs as Gold Standard. For the development set we have selected the remaining 3,094 one-word-terms.

As mentioned before, in this paper we show the results obtained from the translation of the medical prefixes and suffixes forming the terms. That is, we have only translated the terms that have been completely identified with the medical prefixes and suffixes. For example, terms with the suffix "thorax" have not been translated as it does not appear in the prefixes and suffixes list. That is, the "hydropneumothorax" term has not been translated even though the "hydro" and "pneumo" prefixes have been identified.

In Table 2 we show the quantities and percentages of the terms that have been completely identified in both sets. Our set of the one-word-terms has not been cleaned up to remove the words without any medical affix. Thus, the percentages from the table will never reach 100 per cent.

	Total	Identified	Percent
Development	3,094	834	26.96%
Evaluation	885	309	34.92%

Table 2: Quantities of completely identified terms.

From the 885 terms in the evaluation set, 728 terms contain at least one medical prefix or suffix, being 309 completely identified. The results obtained in this fist approach are shown in Table 3 by means of True Positives (TP), False Negatives (FN), False Positives (FP), Precision (Prec.), Recall (Rec.) and F-measure (F-M). A recall of 0.41 is obtained (287 correctly identified from 706 TP and FN) and a precision of 0.93 (287 out of 309). The recall will be increased in the future, including not completely identified terms in the system. Thus, we can conclude that the results obtained are very good concerning precision.

Total	TP	FN	FP	Prec.	Rec.	F-M
728	287	419	22	0.93	0.41	0.56

Table 3: Precision and recall of the evaluating set.

Moreover, the quality of the results obtained is also very good. We have been able to give correct equivalents to complex terms such as "hyperprolactinemia", that has five medical prefixes and suffixes ("hyper+pro+lact+in+emia").

We have also analyzed the incorrect results in order to be able to improve the system. For example, the prefix "myc" has been translated as "miz", but we realized that whenever the prefix is followed by an "o", it should be "mik" in order to generate a correct Basque term. Many of the mistakes are easily rectifiable for the final purpose of translating SNOMED CT.

4 Conclusions and future work

We implemented an application that generates Basque terms for diseases in English, by means of finite-state transducers. This application is one of the phases in the way to translate SNOMED CT into Basque. In order to translate the medical prefixes and suffixes, we have manually generated the translation pairs for 951 prefixes and suffixes, obtaining a very useful resource for Basque.

The FSTs exposed in this paper could be easily applicably to other languages whether an affix lexicon with its translation is defined and the morphotactic rules adapted to the target language.

As we have seen in section 3.3, most of the English terms have not been identified completely and that prevented the translation of them. To cope with this problem we have two developing paths: the deduction of new suffixes and prefixes from specialized dictionaries (Hulden et al., 2011); and the implementation of transliteration transformations to those parts (Alegria et al., 2006).

We have only applied the transducers to the *Disorder* sub-hierarchy, and we will have to check the results we can obtain applying it to the *Finding* sub-hierarchy and to the *Procedure* and *Body Structure* hierarchies. We found terms such as "electroencephalography" or "oligomenorrhea" in those hierarchies, formed with medical prefixes and suffixes identified for this task.

The promising results obtained will contribute to the translation of the whole SNOMED CT, but also to the normalization of Basque in the biosanitary domain, as new terms are generated.

References

I. Alegria, N. Ezeiza, and I. Fernandez. 2006. Named Entities Translation Based on Comparable Corpora. In *Multi-Word-Expressions in a Multilingual Context Workshop on EACL06*, pages 1–8.

G. Banay. 1948. An introduction to medical terminology, Greek and Latin derivations. *Bulletin of the Medical Library Association*, 36(1):1–27, Jan.

O. Bodenreider. 2004. The Unified Medical Language System (UMLS): integrating biomedical terminology. *Nucleic Acids Research*, 32:267–270.

College of American Pathologists. 1993. The Systematized Nomenclature of Human and Veterinary Medicine: SNOMED International.

EHUko Euskara Zerbitzua and Donostiako Erizaintza Eskola. 2005. *Erizaintzako Hiztegia*. EHU. Argitalpen Zerbitzua.

Elhuyar. 2009. *Elhuyar Zientzia eta Teknologiaren Hiztegi Entziklopedikoa*. Elhuyar Edizioak & Euskal Herriko Unibertsitatea.

M. Hulden, I. Alegria, I. Etxeberria, and M. Maritxalar. 2011. Learning word-level dialectal variation as phonological replacement rules using a limited parallel corpus. In *EMLP 2011: Dialects2011*, pages 39–48.

M. Hulden. 2009. Foma: a Finite-State Compiler and Library. In *Proceedings of EACL 2009*, pages 29–32, Stroudsburg, PA, USA.

L. Karttunen, T. Gaál, and A. Kempe. 1997. *Xerox Finite State Tool*.

C. Lovis, Pa. Michel, R. Baud, and Jr. Scherrer. 1995. Word Segmentation Processing: A Way To Exponentially Extend Medical Dictionaries. *MEDINFO*, 8:28–32.

A. Mayor, I. Alegria, A. Díaz de Ilarraza, G. Labaka, M. Lersundi, and K. Sarasola. 2011. Matxin, an Open-source Rule-based Machine Translation System for Basque. *Machine Translation*, 25:53–82.

M. Mohri, F. Pereira, M. Riley, and C. Allauzen. 2006. AT & T FSM Library Finite-State Machine Library. Technical report, AT&T Labs-Research, NJ, USA.

Stedman's, 2005. *Stedman's Medical Dictionary*, chapter Medical Prefixes, Suffixes, and Combining Forms. Lippincott Williams & Wilkins, twenty-eighth edition edition.

UZEI. 2004. Euskalterm Terminologia Banku Publikoa. `http://www.euskadi.net/euskalterm`.

Wikipedia. 2013. List of medical roots, suffixes and prefixes – Wikipedia, The Free Encyclopedia. `http://en.wikipedia.org/w/index.php?title=List_of_medical_roots,_suffixes_and_prefixeso`.

Syncretism and How to Deal with it in a Morphological Analyzer: a German Example

Katina Bontcheva
Heinrich-Heine-University Düsseldorf
bontcheva@phil.uni-duesseldorf.de

Abstract

Syncretism is the area of the morphology-syntax interface where morphology fails the syntax. Inadequate treatment in the design of a morphological analyzer can lead to unbalanced performance of the analyzer either at generation, or at analysis. Furthermore, adequate and consistent treatment of syncretism is needed if the analyzer is to be used for language modeling, especially modeling of the syncretism. In this paper I will show that it is possible to create a morphological analyzer that can be tailored to various intended uses with minimal effort.

1 Introduction

Syncretism may seem to be a minor morphological phenomenon, but this is the place in the morphology-syntax interface where morphology fails syntax. Inadequate treatment in the design stage of a morphological analyzer can lead to undesirable ambiguities in generation or analysis.

A morphological analyzer can have different applications. It can be used in a pipeline with a POS tagger, a shallow or deep-syntactic parser, a semantic parser, for generation or language modeling, among other things.

Depending on the intended use, one might wish to avoid the ambiguity in analysis caused by multiple possible readings of syncretic forms if they are morphosyntactically fully specified. On the other hand, underspecification at the lexical level will lead to multiple output strings at generation.

In this paper I will show that it is possible to create a morphological analyzer that can be tailored with minimal effort to various intended uses.

In section 2 I will briefly discuss syncretism, what types of syncretism exist, and how one can model syncretism using or not using rules of referral. The prototypical finite-state morphological analyzer for German that I am currently working on will be described in section 3, while in section 4 I will present the paradigms of adjectival agreement in standard German that are heavily affected by syncretism. In section 5 I will explain on the basis of the German example and examples from other languages how with minimal changes one can tune the prototypical morphological analyzer to perform the different tasks outlined earlier in this section.

In section 6 I will draw some conclusions, and in the Appendix I will show a code excerpt.

2 Syncretism

Syncretism is the identity of two or more inflected forms of the same lexeme. The identity of two forms that belong to different lexemes should be treated as accidental homonymy. Thus the form *books* is not syncretic since *book-N.PL* and *book-V.PRES.3SG* belong to different lexemes. However, the form *book* is syncretic within the paradigm of the verb *book* since it is associated with a set of morphosyntactically distinct feature values, e.g., *book-V.PRES.1SG*, *book-V.PRES.2SG*. *book-V.PRES.1PL*. *book-V.PRES.2PL*, etc.

One of the characteristics of syncretism is *directionality*. "Directionality concerns the possible morphological affiliation of the syncretic form to one of its component values" (Baerman, Brown and Corbett 2005, p. 24).

Since syncretism involves a set of morphosyntactic values that are associated with a single form, the question is how exactly they are associated. There are two options (cf. Baerman, Brown and Corbett 2005, p. 133): a) the form is related to the set as a whole or b) the form is related to one of the values and the other morphosyntactic values "borrow" the form. Stump (2001) calls the former *symmetric rules* and the latter *directional rules*. Symmetric rules simply map a form/string to a set of values in one step, whereas directional rules entail more than one step. In the first step there is a mapping of a form/string to a particular value of the set, and in the consecutive step(s) this value is associated with the rest of the set. We call such directional rules *rules of referral* (cf. Zwicky 1985).

Lack of directionality is often caused by uninflectedness, loss of inflection, or the merger of the reflexes of two or more phonemes. Examples of directional and non-directional syncretism are presented in section 5.

Syncretism can be caused phonologically, i.e., it can be the result solely of a phonological rule, lexically, i.e., within a single lexical item, or morphologically, i.e., spanning over at least one inflectional class.

3 The Prototypical Morphological Analyzer for German

The prototypical morphological analyzer for German consists of a lexc lexicon that describes the morphotactics of the language, and of phonological and orthographical alternations and realizational rules, and possibly also rules of referral, that are handled elsewhere by finite-state replace rules.

The bases for the regular inflectional classes are stored separately in text files. Bases of words that are subject to morphographemic alternations (e.g. *Umlaut*) have abstract representations at the surface level and lemmata on the lexical level. There are no semantic features in the current version of the lexicon.

The tagset that is used in this version of the analyzer is compatible with the MULTEXT-East morphosyntactic specifications (cf. MULTEXT-East morphosyntactic specifications, Version 4, 2010). It was chosen in preference to the Stuttgart-Tübingen tagset (STTS) (Telljohann et al., 2009) because it implements atomic values and is compatible with the tagsets for other (European) languages.

Here is an excerpt from a text file that contains qualitative-adjective bases with *Umlaut*:

```
{alt}:{1lt}
```

On the left is the lemma (*alt* 'old') that will appear in the analysis output and on the right is the abstract form that contains the abstract symbol *1* for a lowercase *a* which is subject to *Umlaut* alternations under certain conditions.

And here is an excerpt from the lexc lexicon:

```
LEXICON Adjectives
LxAQUAL             Adj ;
LxAQUAL             AdjCmpSpl ;

LEXICON Adj
<"+A" 0:"+Uninfl"> # ;
<"+A" 0:"+Pos">  AStrong;
<"+A" 0:"+Pos">  AWeakMixed;

LEXICON AdjCmpSpl
<"+A" 0:"+Cmp" 0:"+Uninfl"> #;
<"+A" 0:"+Cmp">  AStrong;
<"+A" 0:"+Spl">  AStrong;
<"+A" 0:"+Cmp">  AWeakMixed;
<"+A" 0:"+Spl">  AWeakMixed;

LEXICON AStrong
...
```

This excerpt partially illustrates the morphotactics of the adjectives. The rest - inflection for gender/number/case - will not be presented because of space limitations. The excerpt shows that at the surface level the forms are morphosyntactically fully specified, while at the lexical level the morphological tags are suppressed and only the POS information is available.

The analyzer has parallel implementations in xfst (cf. Beesley and Karttunen 2003) and foma (cf. Hulden 2009a and 2009b).

An example derivation and a detailed excerpt from the analyzer are provided in the Appendix.

4 The Paradigms of Adjective Agreement in Standard German

German adjectives are inflected for 3 genders (masculine, feminine, and neuter), 2 numbers (singular and plural) and 4 cases (nominative, accusative, dative, and genitive). There are no gender differences in the plural.

There are three adjective agreement paradigms in Standard German: a) the strong declension (SD); b) the weak declension (WD); c) the mixed declension (MD). Additionally, there is a single uninflected[1] form that is used predicatively and is chosen as the lemma.

Below are the positive strong inflected forms of *schnell* 'fast':

	Masc	Neut	Femn	Plur
Nom	*schneller*	*schnelles*	*schnelle*	*schnelle*
Acc	*schnellen*	*schnelles*	*schnelle*	*schnelle*
Dat	*schnellem*	*schnellem*	*schneller*	*schnellen*
Gen	*schnellen*	*schnellen*	*schneller*	*schneller*

[1] This form is uninflected for gender/number/case but can be inflected for degree of comparison if the adjective is qualitative.

Five inflected forms (*schneller, schnelles, schnelle, schnellen, schnellem,*) are associated with 5 syncretic sets of fully specified morphosyntactic feature values of the positive degree of a German adjective. These sets are disjunctive and their union represents the 48 possible feature values of the positive degree of an adjective in German. The same applies to the comparative and superlative degree. To make things even more complicated, the uninflected comparative form (e.g., *schneller*) is identical with some of the inflected forms for the positive degree.

5 Fine-Tuning of the Prototypical Analyzer for Different Uses

Now let us consider what can be done so that the analyzer performs optimally in all the cases of intended uses that were listed in section 1.

5.1 Intended Use in a Pipeline with a POS Tagger

The code excerpt from the lexicon in section 3 illustrates how the use of underspecification at the lexical level can reduce ambiguities in the analysis when only lemmata and POS tags are needed by the next application in the pipeline. Thus the output for *schneller* will be:

```
schnell   +A
```

and not:

```
schnell +A+Cmp+Uninfl
schnell +A+Pos+SD+Masc+Sg+Nom
schnell +A+Pos+SD+Femn+Sg+Dat
schnell +A+Pos+SD+Femn+Sg+Gen
schnell +A+Pos+SD+Pl
schnell +A+Pos+MD+Masc+Sg+Nom
```

5.2 Intended Use in a Pipeline with a Deep-Syntactic or Semantic Parser, or for Generation

On the other hand, deep-syntactic and semantic parsers will benefit from the ambiguous output listed in the previous subsection. To achieve this we need to modify the lexical level accordingly:

```
LEXICON Adj
<"+A" "+Uninfl"> # ;
<"+A" "+Pos">  AStrong;
<"+A" "+Pos">  AWeakMixed;

LEXICON AdjCmpSpl
<"+A" "+Cmp" "+Uninfl"> #;
<"+A" "+Cmp">  AStrong;
<"+A" "+Spl">  AStrong;
<"+A" "+Cmp">  AWeakMixed;
<"+A" "+Spl">  AWeakMixed;

LEXICON AStrong
...
```

Now the lexicon and the surface level are identical. The rest – inflection for gender/number/case – is modified in the same way but will not be presented due to space limitations.

This version of the lexicon can also be used for generation.

5.3 Intended Use: Modeling of Syncretism.

In this case it is not essential if the lexical level is underspecified or fully specified. It is important for the surface level to be fully specified.

The modeling of syncretism is performed in the xfst/foma file that contains the phonological and orthographical alternations and realizational rules, and possibly also rules of referral.

As we have seen in section 2, there are different types of syncretism, e.g., phonologically, lexically or morphologically determined syncretism, and different rules, e.g., symmetric or directional.

An example of phonologically determined syncretism is the collapse of the full forms of the personal pronouns for accusative and dative in the 2nd person singular in Bulgarian. The reason for this is the merger of the reflexes of the *jat*-sound (the ending for dative) and the *e*-sound (the ending for accusative). Thus *tebě* 'you-2SG.DAT' and *tebe* 'you-2SG.ACC' collapsed into *tebe*. In this case a realizational rule is more appropriate than the use of a rule of referral:

```
+Acc|+Dat -> e ||
        +PronP +2P +Sg _ ;
```

On the other hand, the syncretism involving the forms for genitive, dative, and locative singular of 3rd-declension-class (D3) Russian nouns, e.g., *kosti* from *kost'* 'bone' (cf. Baerman, Brown and Corbett 2005, p. 208) is better modeled using a cascade of rules of referral, followed by a realizational rule, since this is a directional syncretism. The syncretism of dative and locative singular is well established throughout the Russian nominal declension, with locative providing the form. In this case, however, genitive provides the form for all three feature values:

```
+Dat -> +Loc ||
        +N +D2|+D3 +Sg _ ;
```

```
+Loc -> +Gen ||
        +N +D3 +Sg _ ;

+Gen -> i ||
        +N +D3 +Sg _ ;
```

For more examples of directional rules of referral, cf. Kilbury (2011) among others.

6 Conclusions

In this paper I have shown that it is possible to create a morphological analyzer that can be tailored to various intended uses with minimal effort. The most important properties of such an analyzer are: a) the surface level in the lexicon consists of tags that represent the (language specific) values of fully specified morphosyntactic features; b) the realizations are described outside the lexicon.

The fine-tuning is achieved by modifying the lexical level to the desired degree of (under)specificity and by restructuring the realizational rules, and possibly by adding rules of referral.

Acknowledgments

I am grateful to Nicolas Kimm, Natalia Mamerow, and particularly to James Kilbury for our discussions on different approaches to language modeling.

While working on this paper, I received funding from the German Research Foundation (DFG, Deutsche Forschungsgemeinschaft) in CRC 991 (SFB 991) "The Structure of Representations in Language, Cognition, and Science".

References

Matthew Baerman, Dunstan Brown, and Greville G. Corbett. 2005. *The Syntax-Morphology Interface. A Study of Syncretism.* Cambridge University Press, Cambridge, UK.

Kenneth R. Beesley and Lauri Karttunen. 2003. *Finite State Morphology.* Palo Alto, CA: CSLI Publications.

Mans Hulden. 2009a. *Finite-State Machine Construction Methods and Algorithms for Phonology and Morphology.* PhD Thesis, University of Arizona.

Mans Hulden. 2009b. Foma: a Finite-State Compiler and Library. In: *Proceedings of the EACL 2009 Demonstrations Session*, 29-32.

James Kilbury, 2011. *Implementing Comparative Reconstruction with Finite-State Methods.* Paper presented at the University of Düsseldorf. (Accessed on 10.04.2012, at http://user.phil-fak.uni-duesseldorf.de/~kilbury/publ.htm)

MULTEXT-East morphosyntactic specifications, Version 4, 2010. *MULTEXT-East Morphosyntactic Specifications, Version 4, 2. Common MULTEXT Specifications.* (Accessed on 10.04.2012, at http://nl.ijs.si/ME/V4/msd/html/msd.common.html

Gregory Stump. 2001. *Inflectional morphology.* Cambridge: Cambridge University Press.

Heike Telljohann, Erhard W. Hinrichs, Sandra Kübler, Heike Zinsmeister, and Kathrin Beck. 2009. *Stylebook for the Tübingen Treebank of Written German (TüBa-D/Z)*

Arnold Zwicky. 1985. How to describe inflection. In *Proceedings of the eleventh annual meeting of the Berkeley Linguistics Society*, 372-386

Appendix. Derivations of *fettarm* 'low-fat'.

Below are the upper and the lower side of the adjective *fettarm* that has been through several continuation lexicons of the lexc-lexicon. The desired analysis output is on the upper side, while the morphotactics is on the lower side. The realizational rules operate only on the lower side.

Upper:	fett#arm	0	+A	0	0	0	0	0
Lower:	fett1rm	+Uml	+A	+Pos	+SD	+Msc	+Sg	+Nom

Rule (1) below defines the realization of *1* as *ä*:

```
(1) define UML  [1 -> ä || _ $["+Uml" "+A" ["+Cmp"|"+Spl"] ] ;
```

Since the conditions are not met, the lower-side string remains unchanged. The next rule (2) defines the realization of the adjectival suffix *-er*:

```
(2) define AEr  [ [ [ "+SD" | "+MD" ] "+Masc" "+Sg" "+Nom" |
                 "+SD" "+Femn" "+Sg" [ "+Dat" | "+Gen" ] |
          "+SD" ["+Masc" | "+Femn" | "+Neut"] "+Pl" "+Gen" ]
                 -> %+ e r || _ .#.] ;
```

The string is now: fett1rm+Uml+A+Pos+er. Rule (3) defines the realization of the comparative *–er* suffix:

```
(3) define ACmp   [ "+Cmp" -> %+ e r || _ [%+|"+Uninfl"] ] ;
```

Since the conditions are not met, the surface string remains unchanged. The next rule (4) defines the realization of *1* as *a*:

```
(4) define UMLT     [1 -> a, 2 -> o, 3 -> u, 4 -> A] ;
```

The lower-side string is: fettarm+Uml+A+Pos+er. The last rule (5) deletes the + and the remaining tags that were not used in the realization:

```
(5) define TagDel     [RestTag -> 0 ] ;
```

The lower-side string is now: fettarmer.

A lower-side string fett1rm+Uml+A+Cmp+Uninfl will render fettärm+Uml+A+Cmp+Uninfl after the application of rule (1), fettärm+Uml+A+er+Uninfl after rule (3), and fettärmer after rule (5).

Finite State Approach to the Kazakh Nominal Paradigm

Bakyt M. Kairakbay
K.I.Satpayev Kazakh National Technical University, National Open Research Laboratory of Information and Space Technologies / Satpayev str., 22, Almaty 050000, Republic of Kazakhstan
bkairakbay@gmail.com, b.kairakbay@norlist.kz

David L. Zaurbekov
K.I.Satpayev Kazakh National Technical University, National Open Research Laboratory of Information and Space Technologies / Satpayev str., 22, Almaty 050000, Republic of Kazakhstan
d.zaurbekov@norlist.kz

Abstract

This work presents the finite state approach to the Kazakh nominal paradigm. The development and implementation of a finite-state transducer for the nominal paradigm of the Kazakh language belonging to agglutinative languages were undertaken. The morphophonemic constraints that are imposed by the Kazakh language synharmonism (vowels and consonants harmony) on the combinations of letters under affix joining as well as morphotactics are considered. Developed Kazakh finite state transducer realizes some morphological analysis/generation functions. A preliminary testing on the use of the morphological analyzer after OCR preprocessing for correcting errors in the Kazakh texts was made.

1 Introduction

Morphological transformations of words of a natural language are relevant to many application areas relating to information processing. Finite state methodology is sufficiently mature and well-developed for use in a number of areas of natural language processing (NLP). This paper presents the development and implementation of a finite-state transducer for a nominal paradigm of the Kazakh language. The morphophonemic constraints that are imposed by the Kazakh language synharmonism (vowels and consonants harmony) on the combinations of letters under affix joining as well as morphotactics are considered. Then on the basis of the nominal paradigm formalization it is possible to build a computer implementation of morphological analysis/synthesis of word forms (morphological module) with using of two-level morphology (Koskenniemi, 1983) and finite state morphology (Beesley and Karttunen, 2003). Our morphological module, in turn, is the part of larger Web 2.0 service-oriented system of the Kazakh text recognition involving the Kazakh OCR-module (Kairakbay et al, 2012).

The finite state and two-level morphology approach has been used successfully in a broad number of NLP applications including agglutinative languages. Among them one can be noted the Basque language (Alegria et al, 1996, 2002) belonging to ergative-absolutive languages with agglutinative features, nonconcatenative Arabic language (Beesley, 2001; Attia et al, 2011), pure agglutinative languages as Turkish (Oflazer, 1994, 1996; Eryiğit and Adalı, 2004; Çöltekin, 2010), Turkmen language (Tantuğ et al, 2006), Crimean Tatar language (Altintas and Cicekli, 2001), Uygur language (Orhun et al, 2009; Wumaier et al, 2009), Kyrgyz language (Washington et al, 2012), Kazakh language (Altenbek and Wang, 2010), and many others. Last cited paper studies the Kazakh as minority language in Xinjiang of China where obsolete alphabet based on Arabic notations is used, so that is just indirectly related to our research.

The Kazakh language (Baskakov et al, 1966; Krippes, 1996; Mussayev, 2008) belongs to Ural-Altaic family of agglutinating languages (Baskakov, 1981). In such languages the concept of the word is much broader than simply a set of items of vocabulary. As an illustration for the inflectional paradigm of the Kazakh language let's give the following example a Kazakh word (Mussayev, 2008): "*ata +lar +ymyz +da +ġy +lar+dìkì+n*"[1] that is equivalent to English sentence "*that there is at the items belonging to our fathers*".

[1] Further we follow the notations of ISO 9 (1995) for the transliteration of modern Kazakh letters.

Historically a variety of alphabets had been used for the Kazakh language. Arabic alphabet was used from the tenth century until 1929. This alphabet is still prevalent in Xinjiang, China and in some Kazakh Diaspora abroad. From 1929 to 1940 there was the Latin alphabet which was replaced then on the Cyrillic alphabet. Modern Kazakh alphabet based on Cyrillic contains 33 standard Cyrillic characters of Russian and 9 additional characters that reflect specific sounds of the Kazakh language.

2 The Kazakh Nominal Paradigm

Morphophonemics of the Kazakh language can be expressed by the following set of rules.

Vowels harmony

Consonance of syllables

- Vowel is a syllable-forming element;
- The number of syllables in a word is equal to the number of vowels in the word;
- Vowel determines a type of word: original Kazakh words are either only the back or front only;
- If the preceding syllable contains a back (front) vowel the appended affixes should be back (front);
- Exceptions apply to the borrowed words only.

Consonance of sounds

- Consonants *ġ, ķ, h, ḥ* are combined only with back vowels *a, o, u̇, y*;
- Consonants *g, k* are combined only with front vowels *a̋, ô, ù, ì, e*.

Consonants harmony

Progressive assimilation: a subsequent consonant has become like the preceding consonant on the syllable boundary;

Regressive assimilation: the subsequent sound affects to the preceding one.

The order of attachment of inflectional affixes (morphotactics) to the Kazakh stem is as follows:

Stem + plural affix + possessive personal affix + possessive abstract affix + case affix

The choice of concrete surface form of affix formal representation is determined by the phonological rules, i.e. by the vowels and consonants harmony. Then:

- Plural affix is appended directly to the stem. Singular is determined by the absence of plural affix;
- Possession affix is placed after plural affix (if any);
- Plural and possessive affixes can be swapped for collective nouns;
- Case affixes that are located after the plural and possessive affixes are the same for all categories of nouns;
- Possession affix *-Dìkì/(n)ìkì* can append additionally after other possession affixes under predicative substantivation.

Total number of formulated rules for the Kazakh nominal paradigm morphophonemics and morphotactics by now is 46 (ongoing and not final status). According these rules we can generate in the nominal paradigm from one noun root 112 word forms. Full details concerning the Kazakh nominal paradigm can be found in (Kairakbay, 2013).

3 Finite State Transducer for the Kazakh Nominal Paradigm

Creating a morphological analyzer/generator is based on the nominal paradigm of the Kazakh language as applied to the noun. For the formation the finite state transducer we used XFST (Xerox Finite State Tools) (Beesley and Karttunen, 2003).

Properly a process of building up morphological analyzer consists of the following steps:

- Noun morphotactics description;
- Morphophonemics rules description;
- Finite state automata (transducer) network formation.

Let's consider these steps more in details.

3.1 Noun morphotactics description

Morphotactics description is carried out using a special language lexc. lexc is high-level and declarative programming language. The finite state automata formation is done by a special compiler lexc (Lexicon Compiler). Affix morphemes are designated with so-called Multichar Symbols. These symbols need to be described at the beginning of the file after Multichar_Symbols declaration. The following is an example of declaring Multichar Symbols:

```
Multichar_Symbols
+N              ! Noun
+Pl             ! Plural
+Sngl           ! Singular
+Poss12Sngl     ! Possession 1-2:Singular
+Poss12Pl       ! Possession 1-2:Plural
```

After Multichar Symbols declaration lexc program body is described. The body consists of LEXICONs. LEXICON is one of morpheme composing a word. At the beginning LEXICON Root must be declared. It corresponds to the Start State of the resulting Network. There can be declared roots of words if file is formed for one part of speech or we can declare part of speech if network is building up for the whole language. After LEXICON Root all remaining morphemes are described according the morphotactics rules. Next is an example of lexc file body for the Kazakh nouns: *ăke – father* (English), *tôlem – payment* (English).

```
LEXICON Root
        Noun;
LEXICON Noun
        ăke             NounTag;
        tôlem           NounTag;
        LEXICON NounTag
%+N:0                           SingularPlural;
LEXICON SingularPlural
%+Pl:lAr/DAr                    #;
%+Sngl:0                        #;
```

This is the example of description of noun partial morphotactics. In LEXICON Root a part of speech is declared – noun as Noun. Then LEXICON Root which contains word roots (ăke, tôlem, etc.) is necessary to describe, and to point out transition to the next morpheme NounTag. LEXICON NounTag does not contain any morpheme if we point out null in expression %+N:0 but it adds Multichar Symbol +N which allows us to identify the word as noun at morphological analysis. % sign shields the + sign to use it only as a symbol, not lexc-operator because else the compilator will generate an error in given case. Further next morpheme SingularPlural is pointed out in LEXICON NounTag. In LEXICON SingularPlural we add plural morpheme lAr/DAr (formalized denotation lAr/DAr after morphophonemic rules is transformed to one of final endings: lar/ler, dar/der, tar/ter) and respective Multichar Symbol: +Pl. Symbol # indicates end of the word. Recall that this example is only a small part of the whole and does not describe a noun morphotactics for the Kazakh language. As a whole the description of all noun morphotactics is carried in a like manner.

3.2 Morphophonemics rules description

Morphophonemic rules are described in XFST by regular expressions and replace rules. Let's present a general scheme of replacement rule: `upper -> lower || left _ right`, where upper, lower, left, and right are regular expressions designating regular languages.

Example for Kazakh: a -> e || [g | k | ŋ] _ [g | k | ŋ] which can be read in natural language as "character 'a' replaces onto character 'e' if one of the letters [g | k | ŋ] is located before it, and of the letters [g | k | ŋ] is located after it". Here is an example of morphophonemics rules writing for the plural affix.

```
define plural1f [ {lAr/DAr} -> {der} || FrontStem
[LMNN | JZ] _ ];
define plural1b [ {lAr/DAr} -> {dar} || BackStem
[LMNN | JZ] _ ];
```

where plural1f, plural1b, plural2f, plural2b, plural3f, plural3b are declared names of replace rules (name can be any suitable word consisting of Latin letters and numbers); FrontStem, BackStem, LMNN, JZ are the regular expressions.

```
define Consonants [ b | v | g | ġ | d | ž | z | j | k | ķ | l |
m | n | ŋ | p | r | s | t | f | h | ḥ | c | č | š | ŝ | " | ' ]; #
Expression of consonants
define BackVowels [ a | o | u̇ | y | ë | û | â | u | i ]; #
Definition of back vowels
define FrontVowels [ă | ô | ù | ì | e | u | i ]; #
Definition of front vowels
define BackStem [ Consonants* BackVowels+
Consonants* ]; # Definition of back syllable
define FrontStem [ Consonants* FrontVowels+
Consonants* ]; # Definition of front syllable
define JZ [ ž | z ]; # Definition of letters ž or z
define LMNN [ l | m | n | ŋ ]; # Definition of letters l,
m, n, and ŋ
```

Let's analyze one of the rule: [{lAr/DAr} -> {der} || FrontStem [LMNN | JZ] _];

This rule can be interpreted as "Replace {lAr/DAr} onto {der} if preceding front syllable is ending on one of characters [l m n ŋ ž z]". In a like manner we describe all morphophonemic rules including all exceptions.

3.3 Finite state automata (transducer) network formation

Once we have described morphotactics and the necessary rules of morphophonemics we need to compose them into a finite transducer network for the final analysis and generation of word forms. The joining up takes place by using the XFST instruments. After coupling of networks into transducer the following set of word forms is obtained:

Upper side:
ăke+N+Pl ăke+N+Sngl tôlem+N+Sngl tôlem+N+Pl
Lower side:
ăkeler ăke tôlem tôlemder

Simplified finite state representation of the Kazakh nominal paradigm is shown in fig.1.

4 Error correction

For very preliminary testing we chose 5 pages of text containing 1630 words of economic and business lexis. This text beforehand was processed by our OCR-module for the Kazakh language text recognition. Then we used the generated from Bektayev (1996) dictionary word forms by morphological module for the

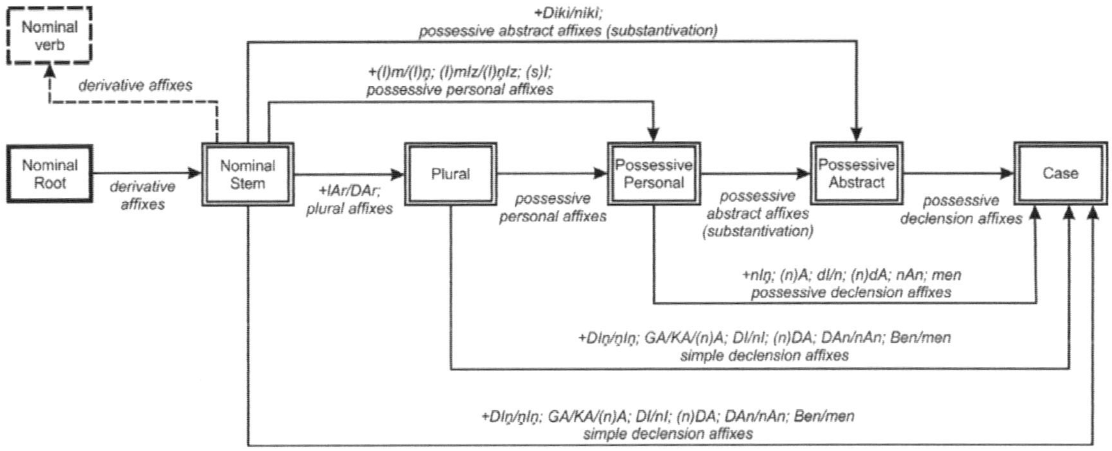

Figure 1. Simplified Finite State Representation of the Kazakh Nominal Paradigm

comparing with the words from OCR-processed text with the aim of search matching (edit distance equals 1). Results are given in the table 1.

As seen using of constructed nominal paradigm allows to improve correction ratio of OCR-module in 1,67 times on average. Introduced errors (in last column of table) are connected with incompleteness of the Kazakh language paradigms formulation for another (than a noun) parts of speech. If we take into account only the number of corrected words which were caused exactly by formulated nominal paradigm then we get average 78%-level of correction. Further improvement can be achieved by the completeness of formulation of the Kazakh language paradigms, addition of specific professional lexicons, editing and cleaning up of dictionary base, and using error-tolerant algorithms of error correction (Oflazer, 1996).

5 Conclusion

We've presented in the paper the finite state approach to the Kazakh nominal paradigm. The main objective is to describe the formalized Kazakh nominal paradigm and to construct its finite state representation with the formation of correspondent finite state transducer that realizes morphological analysis/synthesis functions. We had a very preliminary testing on the use of morphological analyzer after OCR-processing module for correcting errors in the sample Kazakh text. Further the quality would be improved via the completeness of formulation of the Kazakh language paradigms, addition of specific professional lexicons, addition, editing and cleaning up of dictionary's database, and using error-tolerant algorithm of error correction.

File name	The number of words	The number of incorrect words after OCR-processing (% from the number of words)	The number of corrected words (% from number of errors)	The number of introduced errors (% from the number of words)
scan1.tif	315	31(10%)	29(94%)	23(7%)
scan2.tif	295	14(5%)	11(79%)	19(6%)
scan3.tif	293	21(7%)	17(81%)	17(6%)
scan4.tif	352	41(12%)	32(78%)	21(6%)
scan5.tif	375	50(13%)	33(66%)	18(5%)
In total	1630	157(10%)	122(78%)	98(6%)

Table 1. Preliminary Testing of Error Correction in Selected Text (Economic and Business Lexis)

Acknowledgments

We would like to thank the reviewers for valuable comments.

This work was supported by the grant from the Ministry of Education and Science of Republic of Kazakhstan.

References

Iñaki Alegria, Xabier Artola, Kepa Sarasola, and Miriam Urkia. 1996. Automatic morphological analysis of Basque. *Literary and Linguistic Computing*, 11(4):193-203.

Iñaki Alegria, Maxux Aranzabe, Nerea Ezeiza, Aitzol Ezeiza, and Ruben Urizar. 2002. Using Finite State Technology in Natural Language Processing of Basque. *Lecture Notes in Computer Science*, 2494:1-12.

Gulila Altenbek and Xiao-long Wang. 2010. Kazakh Segmentation System of Inflectional Affixes. *Proceedings of CIPS-SIGHAN Joint Conference on Chinese Language Processing* (CLP2010), Beijing, China, p.183–190.

Kemal Altintas and Ilyas Cicekli. 2001. A Morphological Analyser for Crimean Tatar. *Proceedings of the 10th Turkish Symposium on Artificial Intelligence and Neural Networks (TAINN'2001)*, North Cyprus, p.180-189.

Mohammed Attia, Pavel Pecina, Antonio Toral, Lamia Tounsi, and Josef van Genabith. 2011. An Open-Source Finite State Morphological Transducer for Modern Standard Arabic. *Proceedings of the 9th International Workshop on Finite State Methods and Natural Language Processing*, Blois, France, p. 125–133. Association for Computational Linguistics.

N. A. Baskakov. 1981. *Altaic Family of Languages and its Study*. Nauka publishers, Moscow, Russia. (in Russian).

N. A. Baskakov, A.K. Khasenova, V.A. Issengaliyeva, and T.R. Kordabayev (eds.). 1966. *A comparative grammar of the Russian and Kazakh languages. Morphology*. Nauka publishers, Alma-Ata, Kazakhstan. (in Russian).

Kenneth R. Beesley. 2001. Finite-State Morphological Analysis and Generation of Arabic at Xerox Research: Status and Plans in 2001. *Proceedings of the Arabic Language Processing: Status and Prospect--39th Annual Meeting of the Association for Computational Linguistics*, Toulouse, France.

Kenneth R. Beesley and Lauri Karttunen.2003. *Finite State Morphology*. CSLI Publications, Stanford, CA.

Kaldybaj Bektayev. 1996. *Large Kazakh-Russian and Russian-Kazakh dictionary*. Kazakhstanskij proekt publishers, Almaty, Republic of Kazakhstan.

Çağrı Çöltekin. 2010. A Freely Available Morphological Analyzer for Turkish. *Proceedings of the 7th International Conference on Language Resources and Evaluation (LREC'10)*, Valletta, Malta.

Gülşen Eryiğit and Eşref Adalı. 2004. An Affix Stripping Morphological Analyzer for Turkish. *Proceedings of the IASTED International Conference Artificial Intelligence and Applications*, Innsbruck, Austria.

ISO 9: 1995. Information and documentation. Transliteration of Cyrillic characters into Latin characters. Slavic and non-Slavic languages. *International Organization for Standardization*.

Bakyt M. Kairakbay, Ilyas E. Tursunov, and David L. Zaurbekov. 2012. A Design of Computer Recognition System of Kazakh Language Text: OCR, Morphotactics and Morphophonemics. *Proceedings of the 3rd World Conference on Information Technologies (WCIT 2012)/Elsevier Procedia Technology*, Barselona, Spain. (to be published).

Bakyt M. Kairakbay. 2013. A Nominal Paradigm of the Kazakh Language. *1st International Symposium "Morphology and its Interfaces"*, Lille, France. (submitted).

Kimmo Koskenniemi. 1983. *Two-level morphology: A general computational model for word-form recognition and production*. Publication 11, University of Helsinki, Department of General Linguistics, Helsinki, Finland.

Karl A. Krippes. 1996. *Kazakh Grammar with Affix List*. Dunwoody Press, Kensington, MD.

K.M. Mussayev 2008. *The Kazakh Language*. Vostochnaya literatura publishers, Moscow, Russia. (in Russian).

Kemal Oflazer. 1994. Two-level Description of Turkish Morphology. *Literary and Linguistic Computing*, 9(2):137-148.

Kemal Oflazer. 1996. Error-tolerant finite-state recognition with applications to morphological analysis and spelling correction. *Journal of Computational Linguistics*, 22(1):73-89.

Murat Orhun, A.Cüneyd Tantug and Esref Adalı. 2009. Rule Based Analysis of the Uyghur Nouns. *International Journal on Asian Language Processing,* 19 (1): 33-43.

Cüneyd Tantuğ, Eşref Adalı, and Kemal Oflazer. 2006. Computer Analysis of the Turkmen Language Morphology. *Lecture Notes in Computer Science*, 4139:186-193.

Jonathan North Washington, Mirlan Ipasov, and Francis M. Tyers. 2012. A finite-state morphological transducer for Kyrgyz. *Proceedings of the Eight International Conference on Language Resources and Evaluation (LREC'12)*, Istanbul, Turkey.

Aishan Wumaier, Parida Tursun, Zaokere Kadeer, Tuergen Yibulayin. 2009. Uyghur Noun Suffix Finite State Machine for Stemming. *Proceedings of the 2nd IEEE International Conference on Computer Science and Information Technology (ICCSIT 2009)*, Beijing, China, p.161-164.

Author Index

Association for Computational Linguistics
209 N. Eighth Street
Stroudsburg, Pennsylvania 18360

8th Workshop on Innovative Use of NLP for Building Educational Applications 2013

Atlanta, Georgia, USA
13 June 2013

ISBN: 978-1-62993-001-5